Healing From Within
Be Still and Know

Healing From Within
Be Still and Know

◆

Fourth Edition

Robert C. Brooksby, DO

iUniverse, Inc.
New York Lincoln Shanghai

Healing From Within Be Still and Know
Fourth Edition

Copyright © 2005 by Robert C. Brooksby, DO

All rights reserved. No part of this book may be used or reproduced by any means, graphic, electronic, or mechanical, including photocopying, recording, taping or by any information storage retrieval system without the written permission of the publisher except in the case of brief quotations embodied in critical articles and reviews.

iUniverse books may be ordered through booksellers or by contacting:

iUniverse
2021 Pine Lake Road, Suite 100
Lincoln, NE 68512
www.iuniverse.com
1-800-Authors (1-800-288-4677)

ISBN-13: 978-0-595-37693-3 (pbk)
ISBN-13: 978-0-595-67546-3 (cloth)
ISBN-13: 978-0-595-82075-7 (ebk)
ISBN-10: 0-595-37693-2 (pbk)
ISBN-10: 0-595-67546-8 (cloth)
ISBN-10: 0-595-82075-1 (ebk)

Printed in the United States of America

To Jacqui
Once again with love through time

"Our deepest fear is not that we are inadequate,
Our deepest fear is that we are powerful beyond measure.
It is our Light, not our darkness, that most frightens us.
We ask ourselves, who am I to be brilliant, gorgeous, talented, and fabulous?
Actually, who are you not to be?
You are a child of God. Your playing small doesn't serve the world.
There's nothing enlightened about shrinking so that other people won't feel insecure around you.
We were born to make manifest the Glory of God that is within us.
It's not just in some of us; it's in everyone.
And as we let our own light shine,
We unconsciously give other people permission to do the same.
As we are liberated from our own fear, our presence automatically liberates others."

Nelson Mandela
Inaugural Speech 1994
Taken from:
"A Return to Love" Ch. 7, Sec. 3
Marianne Williamson

Contents

Introduction		xi
Chapter 1	Osteopathic Medicine, A Brief History	1
Chapter 2	Osteopathic Medicine	5
Chapter 3	My Introduction to Osteopathic Medicine	9
Chapter 4	My First Course	15
Chapter 5	Miraculous Cures	19
Chapter 6	Treatment Reaction	27
Chapter 7	My Internship	35
Chapter 8	The Dead Guy and Other Spiritual Matters	39
Chapter 9	Balance	50
Chapter 10	The Cranial Rhythmic Impulse	65
Chapter 11	Choosing a Physician	71
Chapter 12	My Practice	74
Chapter 13	The Treatment	79
Chapter 14	Unwinding	93
Chapter 15	The Fascia	103
Chapter 16	The Boundary	107
Chapter 17	Liquid Light	110
Chapter 18	Children	113

Chapter 19	Congenital Disorders	119
Chapter 20	Abuse	125
Chapter 21	Trauma	138
Chapter 22	Fatigue and Fibromyalgia	146
Chapter 23	My Second Basic Course	156
Chapter 24	The Healing Crisis	161
Chapter 25	The Mind/Body Connection	164
Chapter 26	Nutrition and Healing	169
Conclusion		189
Appendix	The Death of Osteopathy	191
About the Author		199

Introduction

When I wrote the first edition of *Healing From Within, Be Still and Know*, I couched my words because I didn't think people were ready for what I wanted to say. Time proved me wrong so I wrote a second edition and said more. When I decided it was time to revise my book "Healing From Within, Be Still and Know, 2nd ed.," I realized that the revisions I wanted to make were fairly bold. My first inclination was to author an entirely new book but opted instead for a third edition but once it was published I realized that I needed to say more and I needed to rewrite several passages.

This is the fourth and final edition of *Healing From Within Be Still and Know*, a work documenting my personal discovery in the field of healing. I have emphasized "Be Still and Know" for that is where the "meat" lies. My original motivation in writing a book was to put down that which I have learned so that it would not be lost should something happen to me. My motivation remains the same and though this book takes another bold step forward, there is more. Not a day goes by that I don't learn something new. I don't have all the answers and this work is not meant to be all inclusive. It is simply what I have discovered as I've traveled this path.

This fourth edition puts the final touches on this work. I've reworded and clarified passages that weren't as succinct as I wanted. I also added chapter nine on "balance." It further clarifies the fact that we are spiritual beings having a physical experience. "Life" is balance. If we dwell on the physical, we are out of balance. Likewise, if we dwell only on the spiritual we also are out of balance.

Additionally, in that chapter, I discuss paradigms.

I've long maintained that we are spiritual/energetic beings having a physical experience but most people find it easier to deal with that reality on Sunday, when they "believe." However, once Monday rolls around belief goes out the window in favor of the physical realities of day-to-day life. As the years have gone by, I have become more and more aware that the spiritual reality is much more powerful than the more tangible physical reality. I've seen things that I'm sure few other people have seen. Some events I've seen only once or twice and others I've encountered so many times that they are now very familiar to me. My understanding of reality has changed to where I now jokingly tell my patients that "I live in the Twilight Zone—not the suburbs but right down town."

With that familiarity, the nature of my practice has changed. Initially, I practiced "traditional" family medicine. That's a long way from what I do today. Most of my patients would never consider what I do to be "traditional." Indeed, a large portion of my practice involves treating those individuals that "traditional" medicine has given up on. The results are amazing.

Through the years, it has become increasingly obvious that there are diseases of the spirit that are treatable. Unfortunately, such disorders are never discussed in medical school. In fact, most of the time when a physician can't figure out what is going on, the physician labels it "supratentorial," i.e., it's in the patient's head. In the third edition, I decided that it was time to discuss demons and other afflictions of the spirit. That continues and is further clarified with this edition. Christ freely taught his disciples that demons can and do affect the health and well-being of people. He taught how to deal with these entities. Unfortunately, except in very rare instances, no one talks about, and even fewer people deal with them. They do, however, still exist.

Remember: We are spiritual beings having a physical experience.

Osteopathic Medicine is knocking at death's door. The principles upon which this profession was founded are no longer its governing principles. I will be surprised if it lasts another ten years. It is now virtually impossible to distinguish most D.O.s (osteopathic physicians) from their M.D. (allopathic) counterparts. We have given up our uniqueness in order to be accepted and to be "compensated" by insurance companies.

Fortunately, an ever increasing amount of people are asking for "alternatives" to traditional medicine. I think there will always be holistic physicians who do embrace the principles upon which the osteopathic profession was founded. There will always be physicians who understand that structure and function are interrelated and that we are designed to heal ourselves but they just won't be D.O.s.

I am an osteopathic physician. Since that doesn't set me apart from most physicians, though it should, I tell people that I specialize in Osteopathic Bioenergetic Medicine but the reality is I'm an osteopathic healer.

Mark Twain said, "To a man with a hammer, everything looks like a nail." Please remember that as you read this book. I love what I do. I think it has great value but it is not a "cure all." But, it does offer a therapeutic process that has proven itself to be very beneficial. **It's important to remember healing is not** totally dependent on my skills as a physician/healer. For the patients discussed in this book and for yourselves, your habits, lifestyle, diet, attitudes, <u>fears</u>, self-image, faith, and <u>emotional status</u> all form parts of their and your healing process.

When I wrote the first two editions of *Healing from Within, Be Still and Know*, I referred to what I do in my practice as "cranial" but the truth is that with the passage of time and the accompanying increase in my skill level, that term now seems woefully inadequate.

During the course of this manuscript, I refer to various cases I have personally dealt with. I didn't make anything up. Generally, the names have been changed and some similar cases have been consolidated to reduce the overall length of this work. What I write is from my own experience. Just as every painter has his or her own style, so does every physician. What I am describing is the "art" of medicine at its purest.

Having said that, I have a "gift" that enables me to do things that many who practice the healing arts cannot do. Frankly, I have the "gift to heal" and as such, in addition to being a physician, I am also a healer. It's a nice combination but I still have a lot to learn. In fact, seldom a day goes by I don't learn something new or see something I've never seen before. I have learned to appreciate the quiet and still things that happen around and within each of us for the immense power contained therein. The challenge has been in learning to pay attention.

For example: Awhile ago, while working on the chest of a patient, "something" didn't feel "right." I told him that he needed to have his heart checked in the near future. He went to his cardiologist and an extensive and very expensive series of tests were run and he even wore a heart monitor for a month. He was given a "clean bill of health." A month later, he had a heart attack. Fortunately, due to collateral circulation that had developed over time, he survived.

A few months later a similar incident occurred with another patient but this time a cardiac MRI revealed a pocket of fluid that was pressing against the patient's heart. I didn't know what was wrong; I just knew that when I sensed the area around his heart, it didn't feel right. I simply told him what I was sensing didn't feel right and I encouraged him to find a cardiologist to see if something was indeed not right.

Learning to "pay attention" has revealed other things to me. An example: Something happened in February 1998 that affected and changed the energy around us. That change stabilized, but in July 1998 another change took place that didn't stabilize. I noticed another big change in early 2000 around the time of the lunar eclipse and then another change about the time of the planetary alignment in May 2000.

Changes continue and at times, it feels like the energies in which we are bathed are experiencing an earthquake. In late October 2000, we shook for four days. Almost every patient during that period related that they were having difficulty sleeping. The same thing happened for the first two weeks of March 2004. I knew full well what they were talking about. It felt like a semi was driving around my house in the wee hours of the morning. The intensity and frequency continues to increase with but a few relatively quiescent periods.

Additionally, something miraculous happened in late spring 2003 and the Earth changed. Then, at about the time of the winter solstice 2003, the energy pattern again changed. It felt like we had walked into another room. Changes continue. I am not sure why this is happening and what it means but I feel we are in for some interesting times ahead.

Gregg Braden, in his books, *Walking Between the Worlds, The Science of Compassion,* and *Awakening to Zero Point,* describes a shift happening that might explain some of the energy waves we have been experiencing. He describes "The Zero Point" or "Shift of the Ages" as a new reality that may well occur around November/December 2012 AD.

I recommend his work to anyone who might be interested in pursuing these concepts further. He has recently written two more books that I highly recommend, *The Isaiah Effect* and *The God Code*.

Robert C. Brooksby, D.O.

1

Osteopathic Medicine, A Brief History

"Combining the thoughts of our mind with the love in our heart, we are able to control the electric currents, we are able to revive the suspended forces which submit to the voluntary and involuntary commands of life and mind by which worlds are driven and beings moved." ("The Law of Mind, Matter, and Motion," Andrew Taylor Still, M.D., the founder of osteopathic medicine.)

Osteopathic medicine started as the dream, and then the reality, of Andrew Taylor Still, M.D. He was a frontier physician possessed with the idea that people should be viewed as a whole, and then treated that way. He knew that the cause, not the symptoms of a disease, should be targeted. He also knew that once mobility, balance, and vitality/energy were restored to the tissues, the body would usually heal itself. I say usually because there are circumstances where the damage can be irreparable. Having said that, I must also say that I firmly believe in "miracles," i.e., when tissues that should not heal do heal or when tissues that should heal do so a lot faster than was expected.

Needless to say, in Dr. Still's time, this was a fairly dramatic departure from the "medicine" being practiced on the frontier, let alone throughout the rest of the world. In the latter 1800's, and even today, this concept is far from what is being practiced by most physicians. Osteopathic Medicine was "holistic medicine."

Andrew Taylor Still, M.D. believed we are born with the ability to heal ourselves and when we don't heal, it is because something is out of balance in our lives or our bodies. <u>Our health depends as much on who we are as it does on what</u>

we eat, how much we exercise, and what stresses we expose ourselves to in our environment. When these stresses are minimized and when those factors, which favor healing, are optimized, we flourish. He started Osteopathic Medicine to signal to the world there was a better way to practice medicine.

Several years later but still in the 1800's, one of his students, William G. Sutherland, D.O., examined a human skull, which had been carefully dissected. He understood the concept that structure and function are closely related in the body. And, as he studied the skull, he noticed that on the superior aspect of the temporal bones, the edges narrowed and became almost like a knife's edge. He also noted there were lines on the lower edges of the parietal bones that closely matched grooves in the temporal bone. It appeared the bones were designed to slide on each other. He was reminded of the gills on a fish and suspected that there must be motion in the bones of the head. And, if there was motion in the head, there might be motion in other parts of the body.

Dr. Still agreed with him and encouraged him to pursue this theory. Almost twenty years passed before Dr. Sutherland started to reveal his findings to a skeptical osteopathic community. What he discovered during this period, and throughout the rest of his life, may be the most important medical discovery of all time—Craniosacral Osteopathic Medicine. This is the forerunner for what I do in my practice.

"Cranial" has been a part of osteopathic medicine since Dr. Sutherland's time, but it wasn't until relatively recently that the osteopathic medical community has openly acknowledged the benefits of cranial treatments. There was even a time when osteopathic medical students who attended courses in cranial osteopathic medicine were invited to leave school and not come back. Fortunately, this is no longer the case. Today, courses in cranial or craniosacral manipulation are given at every osteopathic medical school.

Remember, we are spiritual/energetic beings having a physical experience, not physical beings having an occasional spiritual experience. I will say that a lot throughout this book. It is something that I really did not emphasize enough in the first two editions of *Healing From Within, Be Still and Know*. It is something that I emphasized in the third edition and will further emphasize in this edition.

I recommend Gregg Braden's book and audio tape *The Isaiah Effect*. In them, he suggests that the difference between the angels in heaven and us is that we don't remember. A bold statement, indeed, but it may be one of the great truths that we have yet to learn. With each passing day the fact that we are more powerful than we realize sinks in as I see patients heal themselves.

Braden also discusses a "lost mode of prayer" where thought, feeling, and emotion can literally change the fabric of "reality." I have seen it work and I use it in my practice only I call it "bioenergetic medicine."

Years ago, a woman came into my office to introduce herself. She had just completed her training as a massage therapist and was making the rounds of the various physicians' offices in the area in an attempt to drum up referral business. While talking to her, she said that she would be taking a "cranial" course the next week and seemed excited to share that with me. I don't think she was expecting my response because I wasn't happy to hear it.

I think massage therapists, physicians, dentists, and anyone who works with the body should be trained in how to feel the cranial motion but I do not think they should be advertising that they are "cranial" practitioners nor do I think they should be treating people using cranial techniques unless they are skilled. I started learning "cranial" in 1985 and I was in training for five years before I could put out a shingle and treat patients.

A weekend course simply cannot train someone in cranial to the level attained by those in the medical profession who practice this on a daily basis. Simply put, that is what "cranial" is, i.e., it is practicing medicine. If someone advertises that they are doing "cranial" and if they are not a licensed physician or dentist, they are practicing medicine without a license. It's that simple. Unfortunately, there are very few of us who are so trained.

Having said that, the fact remains that people are being taught abbreviated courses in "cranial" outside the medical profession and they are treating people. This problem is compounded by the fact that most "lay" people think that they are receiving the same level of care from a massage therapist who "does cranial" therapy as they do from a physician specializing in "craniosacral" medicine. As you read this book, you will start to understand why first being a physician is so important if you want to practice "cranial" and then "bioenergetic medicine."

Also, bear in mind I will use principles I learned in my study of "cranial" as the vehicle and common thread to the bioenergetic principles discussed but the important thing to remember and to focus on is healing. Something else to bear in mind is that healing or rather the gift to heal is not unique to the osteopathic community nor to the other medical professionals for seldom do these individuals have or at least manifest that gift. Healers in all shapes and forms walk amongst us. You do not have to know "cranial" to heal people. I have found that cranial has helped me unlock the door to an understanding of many things that go beyond medical principles. Remember, we are spiritual beings having a physical experience not physical beings that have an occasional spiritual experience. I should say it again for emphasis. When the "medical" model breaks down, it's <u>always</u> because the model assumes we are physical beings. As for miracles, Gregg Braden said, "They're only miracles until we learn how we relate to creation."

Regardless of the forces that are brought to bear in each case mentioned in this book, healing was manifest from within each patient. Seldom was I alone responsible for what happened. Healing came from within.

2

Osteopathic Medicine

"Do not follow where the path may lead—go instead where there is no path and leave a trail." (R. W. Emerson)

Describing to you what I do will be difficult. My job is to find the health in someone and then do all that I can to help it blossom. Technically, I am an osteopathic family physician who specializes in osteopathic bioenergetic medicine. The name does not really explain or describe what I do in my medical practice. I am a healer.

Osteopathic physicians receive training in medicine. They learn how to diagnose and treat patients. As part of that training, we receive osteopathic manipulative medical training which we refer to as osteopathic manipulative medicine (O.M.M.) or osteopathic manipulative treatment (O.M.T.). (Note: I did not say "therapy" because we are not therapists.)

Osteopathic manipulative medicine encompasses many treatment modalities. Most people think osteopathic manipulative treatment involves the "popping" of bones and it is often compared to what a chiropractor does, but this is just the tip of the iceberg. That specific modality is called high-velocity low-amplitude. Other modalities include counter strain, muscle energy, myofascial, and craniosacral or "cranial," all of which are very gentle.

The number of people, who are not physicians, who say they are skilled in cranial or craniosacral treatment, amazes me. You may know or even be one of these people. Knowing how to change a gasket does not make you a plumber just the same as rubbing someone's sore muscles or feet or sticking a needle in someone's arm does not make you a masseuse, a reflexologist or an acupuncturist. Likewise knowing how to feel the cranial rhythmic impulse does not mean you know cranial. When I hear of these people, I think of those who learn the tricks of a given trade without learning the trade. You should understand that to "know" cranial, <u>you must be a physician.</u>

Very few physicians practice medicine the way I do. Some physicians practice "medicine by the numbers." They simply chase the "numbers." If a patients' blood pressure is low they do one thing. If it is high, they do another. If the patient's calcium is too low they do one thing and if it is too high they do another. Everyone with a certain disorder is treated the same. Unfortunately, this leads to patients taking many different medicines, some of which are to treat the side-effects of other medicines they are taking.

Some physicians practice medicine as an art form. Unfortunately, there has been and will continue to be an ever increasing amount of legal and professional pressures to make all physicians "paint by the numbers." The "art of medicine" is indeed becoming a "lost art." What I do in the course of practicing medicine is an art. Furthermore, there is no way to impart the knowledge and understanding I have accumulated on someone else. In many ways that which I do is instinctual or intuitive. It is literally a God given gift. From time to time, a young medical student has "shadowed" me for a day or two and occasionally worked with me for a month. I hope that has helped them and that it will therefore help others. It all depends on what they do with what they know.

Nevertheless, at the root, Osteopathic physicians are unique. In comparison to our allopathic (M.D.) counterparts, our training is "general" in nature. As such, osteopathic physicians have received training in internal medicine, pediatrics, obstetrics and gynecology, radiology, emergency medicine, family medicine, orthopedics, and surgery. If we choose to specialize, it is done only after our first year of post doctrinal training which is called an internship (first year of residency). Within that general knowledge and background, training in cranial and bioenergetic medicine can blossom. With that knowledge, a physician can put what he has learned about medicine and various disease states to use in interpreting what is perceived through extremely sensitive palpation and intuition.

Medical school is a horrible experience. In some ways, it is much like pledging a fraternity. With few exceptions, you are not treated as a future physician by other physicians. Nurturing seldom takes place. The hours are horrific and it is not much fun. The medical professions are steeped in tradition and appear loath to discard archaic training procedures and tactics that should be discarded if for no other reason than that they are cruel. I expected better from the osteopathic profession but with few exceptions, I did not find it. Unfortunately, putting up with the grief is also part of the price required, if a person really wants to know osteopathic medicine.

There are no shortcuts. Anything less leaves the practitioner vacant in some area of skill. This is not therapy. It is medicine at a very refined level. It takes years of practice to be skilled in what we call palpation or the art of feeling and sensing tissues. That requires years of touching and sensing patients who are in various states of disease or health. In osteopathic medical school, learning to feel tissues starts from almost the first day as we are taught the fundamental skills in numerous manipulative modalities such as what is called high-velocity, low-amplitude (HVLA) osteopathic manipulative treatment.

Three other forms of treatment are counterstrain, muscle energy, and myofascial release. Counterstrain involves placing tissues in a position of ease from which sensitive neuromuscular fibers can reset themselves. Muscle energy involves using the bodies' own muscles to help bring about a correction from a diseased state to a neutral state. Myofascial release involves moving the superficial tissues in the direction of ease or towards the strain and then waiting until a change occurs in the overall tension of the tissues.

The bottom line is that each of these techniques, developed by an osteopathic physician, teaches the practitioner something about the tissues and affords the practitioner a different way to look at healthy tissues and diseased tissues. Each is effective in its' own realm. Each is a brick in the path toward being able to sense what is going on within and around a patients' body. Each requires years of practice.

I remember being with Jim Jealous, D.O., when a patient came in complaining of a headache. He touched her and almost immediately stopped his examination and told her to go directly to a hospital for an MRI of her head. He felt that she had a subdural hematoma. This proved true. If Dr. Jealous had continued to treat her, without knowing the significance of a subdural hematoma, it could have resulted in her death. It's very important to first understand both anatomy and medicine before using what I will talk about in this book.

Recently, a young man came to me because he was having headaches. I put my hands on his head and the trauma I felt was very significant. I stopped and asked what had happened. He is an athlete. He said that his coach has told him that he really hasn't had a "practice" until he has hit his head. He has been hitting his head more and more frequently.

In a recent game, a fellow team member threw the basketball at his head and it hit him hard. He then ran out of bounds and hit his head against the wall. He said that those who witnessed the event said he did the "funky chicken" on the way down. He doesn't remember.

I sent him for an MRI which showed no damage to his brain, but my hands felt a lot of damage. His pediatric neurologist told him not to play basketball for a year. He then sought out another specialist for a "second opinion." That physician told him there was no way someone could put their hands on his head and feel "damage." As it is, his grades have been faltering.

Is he damaged? Absolutely! If he was my son, he would not play any sports for one year and then only if his tissues felt okay. Are M.D.s trained to diagnose with their hands? Not unless they have been trained by a D.O. to do so, and that seldom, but occasionally does happen.

Physicians know things physical therapists, chiropractors, and others who haven't gone through medical training don't know. This additional training is not just useful, but it is vital for our patients' health and it is vital if the practitioner is to properly treat a patient with craniosacral manipulative medicine or bioenergetic medicine. Cranial is, and always has been, part of osteopathic medicine. It is one of the purest and most powerful medical procedures performed today. What I and some other osteopathic physicians do, however, goes beyond that.

Having said that, please don't ask me for the names of other physicians who do what I do because I have no idea who they are. I can speculate on whom some of those physicians are but I don't really know. (See the appendix at the end of this book on the death of osteopathy.)

3

My Introduction to Osteopathic Medicine

Road Not Taken

Two Roads diverged in a yellow wood,
And sorry I could not travel both
And be one traveler, long I stood.
And looked down one as far as I could
To where it bent in the undergrowth;
Then took the other, just as fair,
And having perhaps the better claim,
Because it was grassy and wanted wear;
…And that has made all the difference.
(Robert Frost)

In 1976, while sitting at the bottom of a hill in my Fiat 131, I was rear-ended by a lady in a 1957 Chevy full of kids. The driver, after losing her brakes, decided I was simply unavoidable. The world stopped in an instant. At first, I didn't even hurt, but within hours every bone and muscle in my body ached. During the following month, I experienced more back and neck pain than I thought possible—and it wouldn't go away.

I was an Air Force pilot at the time. Since it hurt for me to turn my head, which is a relatively important thing for a pilot to be able to do, I was told by the flight surgeon that I wouldn't be allowed to fly.

I was an air crew member in the Strategic Air Command flying KC-135Q aircraft, and if I couldn't fly, then my crew wasn't "mission ready." That meant the Air Force wasn't as capable of defending the country and that made my squadron commander look bad to his boss. Because of that, my squadron commander ordered me to go to sick call each morning until I felt better. Needless to say, I became a semi-permanent fixture at sick call.

During the following weeks, I managed to visit six of the seven flight surgeons assigned to Beale AFB in Northern California. Each took his turn at asking where I hurt and what I was doing to get rid of the pain. Each then wrote me a prescription for a muscle relaxant, a pain medication, or a combination of both. Sometimes the medications worked, but when they wore off, the pain returned.

What I later learned is that an estimated eighty-five percent of all visits to family doctors are for musculoskeletal pain, but most physicians aren't trained to do anything about it other than to prescribe medicines. Most physicians simply aren't trained to feel tissues other than at a very rudimentary level.

Eventually, I was told to see Lieutenant Colonel Jimmy Woolbright. His approach was dramatically different. To start off, he actually touched me. This may seem strange, but none of the other flight surgeons had ever gotten out of their chair and walked around their desk to examine me let alone touch me.

He had me lie down on my back on a treatment table, and proceeded to tell me where I hurt. He pressed a spot on my leg and said, "That hurts, doesn't it?" Not only did it hurt, but it made me wonder why an area of my leg hurt if my neck was what was giving me the most grief? Next, he took hold of my neck and head, twisted it to the side rapidly, and "cracked" it.

Well, I'd never experienced this. I swiftly sat up and asked him if he was a doctor. He just laughed and stated he was an osteopath. I should point out here that the term "osteopath" has since fallen into disfavor, having given way to the more appropriate term "osteopathic physician."

I told him I'd never heard of an osteopath, so he asked if I'd ever heard of a "D.O." I still had no idea what he was talking about. You see, I had lived in California for most of my life. In the 1960s, the allopathic profession (M.D.s) had arranged with the state legislature to pass a law making it illegal to license D.O.s in that state. At the same time, they made arrangements through the University of California at Irvine for the D.O.s in California to become M.D.s. All a D.O. had to do was pay sixty-five dollars and attend a one-day seminar. Once that was done, the University of California at Irvine issued them a M.D. degree. Apparently there was "magic" in that seminar because the D.O.s were now fully qualified M.D.s. Amazing!

That essentially wiped out the osteopathic profession in California. Eventually, the California State Supreme Court said the law was unconstitutional, but by then the harm was done and most D.O.s had already become M.D.s. That makes me think of the saying "A rose by any name would smell as sweet." Indeed, a rose by any name would smell as sweet. Today, however and most unfortunately, most D.O.s practice medicine the same as M.D.s so the "holistic" approach, which used to be practiced by most osteopathic physicians, has long gone by the wayside and it is virtually impossible to distinguish most D.O.s from M.D.s.

Nevertheless, after being treated by Dr. Woolbright, my pain went away and I felt better. This relief lasted for about three days. At the end of that time, I started to hurt again, so I went back. He treated me again and, this time, the pain was gone for almost a week. The relief from the next treatment lasted almost two weeks. After four or five treatments, the pain just went away and never came back.

During those weeks that Lieutenant Colonel Woolbright worked on me, I asked quite a few questions. He told me that although he was not one of them, that some osteopathic physicians could actually feel the tissues and energies in the body move. He also told me that those physicians not only can feel this movement, but they can also change the shape of the head. The practical implications for this are that children who have chronic ear infections, due to poor drainage, can be helped by not only wringing out their eustachian tubes, but a permanent change of the shape of their head could affect the function of the ears for the better. Also, ears that stick out can be brought back closer to the head, buck teeth can gently be guided into a more normal position, and so on. The effects are often far more than aesthetic. Profound healing in other parts of the body can also occur.

All these years later, I realize that the energy aspect was so much more important but I was focused on the physical aspect of healing at that time. I now know that the tissues flow into the mold formed by our energies. If they are bent, then we become bent or don't function well if at all. The effects can be very profound and I will try to explain this as this book unfolds.

My father, a pharmacist by training, had encouraged me to study medicine and become a doctor. The problem I had with this was I didn't like what I'd seen of the medical profession. It was too "scientific" and there was much too little "art."

Imagine a doctor who actually took the time to touch his patient and by doing so helped heal them! A whole new approach to medicine was opened to me and I was determined to become an osteopathic physician. Lt. Col. Jimmy Woolbright not only helped me heal, but planted the seed that started my lifelong quest to learn all that I can about this potent form of treatment and about healing itself.

At that point in my life, it was simply a matter of making the correct choices. As I said, I was an Air Force pilot when my neck was injured in the automobile accident. I loved to fly, but understood that at some point in time, if I stayed in the Air Force, I would end up in a desk job not doing what I loved to do most. I also understood I'd eventually retire from the service. I had seen friends retire and none were flying. Some sold insurance, others sold real estate or cars, but no one was flying. I decided to become trained in something where I'd be allowed to continue to fly.

When I graduated from pilot training, I was assigned to fly KC-135 aircraft. These are the military equivalent of Boeing 707s. It is a big plane and not much fun to maneuver. I really wanted to fly fighters, but once pilots are assigned to a "weapon system," they are stuck with it. That means there was essentially no way for me to fly small aircraft unless I did something very dramatic.

After a few years of flying KC-135s, I was asked to teach pilot training as a T-37 instructor. I was later invited to Randolph AFB near San Antonio, Texas to teach pilots how to be instructor pilots. For a pilot, this was more fun than humans should be allowed to have, but I knew my time was running out. Sooner or later, I'd have to return to the KC-135s.

While at Randolph AFB, I had the opportunity to teach flight surgeons a "mini" flight-training program. One of the physicians I taught went on to be the hospital commander at Edwards AFB. During his first year at Edwards, he flew forty-three different types of aircraft. This was a pilot's dream come true and I wanted in on it.

That quest required me to go back to school and complete all of the requirements for entrance into medical school. My original degree was in Political Science. Since I was an Air Force pilot at that time, the only way to take pre-med courses was to do so in the evening at a local college. For five years, I went to night school five days a week for four to five hours a night. Make no mistake; the price to know what I know about Osteopathic Bioenergetic Medicine is a lot more than the price of a weekend or even a one-week long course in "cranial." I've long since left "cranial" behind but at the time, I thought it was the end of the path.

My plan to be an osteopathic physician included becoming a flight surgeon. Eventually, I would retire from the Air Force and then pursue my studies in osteopathic medicine with an emphasis on "cranial." I knew there was a need for flight surgeons and there was a need for flight surgeons that had been pilots. I was told by the recruiters in the Medical Command that after being accepted to medical school, the Air Force would pay my way as long as I committed myself to continue to serve a certain number of years. What I did not count on was what happened next.

Once accepted to medical school, the "flying" side of the Air Force refused to let me switch over to the "medical" side. It costs a lot more to train a pilot than it does to train a physician. This forced my hand. I left the service, took my wife and seven children, and at the age of thirty-five, moved to Old Orchard Beach, Maine to attend the University Of New England College Of Osteopathic Medicine.

It was all simply a matter of being true to me and to what I wanted as opposed to what the Air Force wanted. I was more than willing to put in my time with them, but I wanted to do it as a rated flight surgeon.

Sometimes when I look back on those days I marvel at the string of events that had to fall into place for me to be where I am at this time. At any step along the way, I could have been thwarted in my quest. Everything had to fall into place. I could have inadvertently gotten off the path and never known it but forces far stronger than I have watched over and guided me throughout my life.

An example is that I really wanted to study with Dr. Viola Frymann at the Pomona College of Osteopathic Medicine so I applied there but wasn't accepted. What I didn't know was that at that period of time, "cranial" had fallen into disfavor at PCOM and Dr. Frymann left the department in favor of private practice.

Another example is that one of the flight surgeons I taught to fly was a D.O. whose father was the dean of another college of Osteopathic Medicine. Internal political squabbling squelched that application.

The real kicker is that at that time, the only college of osteopathic medicine open to "cranial" was the University of New England College of Osteopathic Medicine in Biddeford, Maine and that was due to the efforts of Jim Jealous, D.O., and a team of other physicians who freely donated their time to the students. I thought Maine was just beyond that line on the map that stated "There be dragons there"; the place where you fall off the edge of the world. It was the last place I wanted to go but the first to accept my application.

Mind you, when I decided to go to osteopathic medical school, I had to "burn a lot of bridges" in my Air Force career and that upset many people. I had one squadron commander tell me it would be over his dead body that I go to medical school. Believe me; he was malicious in his attacks on my career and me.

Indeed, I knew there would be no going back. It would take too much time to tell the whole story. Nevertheless, after my tour at Randolph AFB I was reassigned to KC-135s, specifically to Plattsburgh AFB in upstate New York, a mere 5-hour drive to Biddeford, Maine, the home of the University of New England College of Osteopathic Medicine. Furthermore, within a few weeks of applying I was invited to interview for one of the 71 positions in the upcoming class. I later learned that over 1,500 people applied for those positions. The one thing I remember from that interview was that the chairman of the acceptance committee was the godfather to the son of one of the flight surgeons I flew with on a regular basis at Randolph AFB, Texas. That flight surgeon wrote me a letter of recommendation to medical school and the first five minutes of my interview centered on my relationship with that flight surgeon. Coincidence? I do not believe in those anymore.

So, without knowing it, events fell into place that allowed me to be accepted at the only medical school in the country that was teaching that which I had set out to learn in the first place, i.e., "Cranial." It was as though I had jumped into a river and was being swept along. All I had to do was stay centered on my goal and never waiver. God took care of the rest. He has always taken care of the rest. Whenever I have been willing to listen, He has been there to teach me and to take care of me. And so, it has continued to this day. I'm sure this is not the end of my journey but I know I'm supposed to be here in Indiana right now (September 2005). I realized last year that I am practicing medicine exactly like I wanted to all those years ago when I set out on this journey, but I never expected to end up in Indiana.

4

My First Course

"I think a man does what he can, until his destiny is revealed." (Nathan Algren, <u>The Last Samurai</u>")

When I showed up for freshman orientation, I was one of the oldest students in my class. Having spent so many years as an Air Force officer, I was accustomed to asking questions, and it didn't bother me to be aggressive in finding out whatever I wanted to know.

During orientation we were assigned group leaders. Mine was Jack. I remember asking him when we would be taught how to feel the tissues of the body move. Jack looked puzzled for a moment, and then asked, "Do you mean cranial?" I told him I didn't know what it was called, but I'd heard that some osteopathic physicians knew how to feel the tissues and bones move. He confirmed this was indeed "cranial" and that we'd get a "few hours" of instruction on cranial during our sophomore year. I was shocked! I didn't want to wait another year, and I wanted a whole lot more than a few hours of training, and I told him so.

I was beginning to wonder if perhaps I had enrolled in the wrong university, but he then told me there was an osteopathic physician who came to the school one weekend a month and taught cranial. Unfortunately, his classes were only open to sophomores and above. He also said the next course would start on Saturday, which was only three days away.

Saturday morning I was there at 7:00 a.m. I figured I was so old no one would know I was a freshman and, if I stood in the back of the room and kept my mouth shut, my ignorance wouldn't give me away.

The visiting osteopathic physician was Dr. Jim Jealous. After about forty minutes of introductory lecture, he told us to pick a partner and to try to feel the craniosacral impulse, or what is called the "mechanism." I asked the fellow standing next to me, a senior, if he would be my partner. He agreed, so I asked if he would let me try to feel the mechanism first. Again, he agreed so I asked him to lie on the table, face up. I gently cradled his head in my hands and almost immediately felt what Dr. Jealous had been describing as a very subtle expansion/contraction of the head. I looked around the room to see if I should be doing something else, but most of the students were asking questions about what they should be feeling or doing. Figuring I had some time to kill, I went back to observing "the mechanism."

The first thing I noticed was there was not only an expansion/contraction occurring, but that it wasn't symmetrical. This motion feels like you are holding a balloon and someone is slowly putting air into and then taking air out of the balloon. In a balloon, however, it's always symmetrical but the motion I was feeling wasn't.

Additionally, I had an impression or a sense of a current, flow, or stream that ran through his head and then into his body. The second thing I noticed was that almost as soon as I was aware of this second motion/current, my partner rolled onto his right side, brought his knees up toward his chest, and started to roll back and forth as though he had a severe stomach ache.

Now, I may have been only a freshman in medical school, but I could recognize someone in pain. So I did what anyone would have done. I let go of his head. He immediately stopped thrashing around and I asked if he was okay and if he was in pain. He said he was okay and there was no pain. He also said that he had no idea why he was thrashing about. It was as if his body had a mind of its own. Since he hadn't experienced any pain during the procedure we decided to try it again.

Once more, I cradled his head in my hands and, within a few moments, I could feel the "flow" of energies through his head and neck into his body. It's important to say that this was not the cranial rhythmic impulse. It was not an expansion/contraction as if the tissues were breathing, which was the first motion I felt, but rather an energy flow through his tissues much as a stream would flow along a river bed. It felt much the same as it did before so I just followed it and watched it change much like a hose would wiggle when the water is turned on.

Within a minute or two, he was again rocking back and forth as if he had a bad bellyache. I was determined not to let go this time so I just held on and "watched." It was fascinating and scary, all at the same time. He still looked as if he was in pain, but he denied it, even while the intensity of his rocking increased. And, not only did it increase, but he started to groan. Initially, it was a soft muted groan, but it increased to the point where everyone in the room could hear it. And, not only could they hear it, but also the room became very quiet as all eyes focused on us.

Now remember, I wasn't supposed to be there so I was trying to be inconspicuous. To make matters worse, as I looked toward the front of the room, Dr. Jealous was heading toward us. I could not hide so to avoid being seen, I looked down. Soon, Dr. Jealous was standing by my side. He stood there for a moment, and then asked, "Do you know what's going on?"

Still not looking up I answered, "I don't have a clue."

"He's unwinding."

I had no idea what he was talking about and didn't really want to show my ignorance, but after a few seconds, I had to ask the obvious, "Is that good?"

He assured me it was then asked, "Do you need any help?"

Somewhat sarcastically and still not looking up, I replied, "This is my first day?"

"Then, you probably need help," he answered. Dr. Jealous sat down facing me and placed a hand under the student's sacrum (tailbone) and directed me to continue doing what I had been doing. It's hard to be inconspicuous when you are three feet away from someone who is talking to you, so I tried to avoid making eye contact with him by keeping my head turn down as if I was concentrating. After a while, the situation went from bad to worse when he said, "I haven't seen you around here before?"

I told him it was my third day. He said, "Oh, you're a transfer student?" I felt honor bound to set him straight, but I really didn't want to.

He then looked at me and said, "Freshmen aren't supposed to be here."

I hesitated, still not looking up, and then said, "Do you want me to leave?" At this point he said, "Do you see anyone else doing this?"

I glanced around the room and told him, "No." He had his eyes closed and was concentrating on something. Without looking up, he said, "You can stay."

From that moment on, I never looked back. At the end of each day I would go home and treat my entire family. I had a portable treatment table that I would set up in the dining room. I would start with the youngest of my seven children, work my way through them, and finish with my wife. My youngest daughter was only a couple of weeks old when I started medical school and the eldest was 15. It gave me a tremendous view of how the "mechanism" changes as we mature.

From that point on, freshmen were allowed to attend Dr. Jealous' courses. Bear in mind that the "basic" course in "cranial" as taught by the Sutherland Cranial Teaching Foundation is a 40-hour course and is taught over a 5-day period.

You have to be a physician or a 3rd or 4th year medical student to attend. We were receiving 18 days of "basic" cranial instruction in addition to our scheduled osteopathic manipulative medical treatment instruction each year.

On top of that, Dr. Jealous would invite us to his home on the weekends to study with him and other notable osteopathic physicians who visited him in the "Octagon" (what he called his home in the Maine woods). I also spent time working with him and his colleague, Dr. Judy Shedd, in their office. I was immersed in knowledge and absorbed all that I could.

5

Miraculous Cures

"Truly, truly, I say to you, he who believes in me, the works that I do shall he do also; ***and greater works than these shall he do…***" *(John 14:12)*

During osteopathic medical training, the first two and a half years are spent in what is called "didactic" or classroom training. During this period, the future physician is bombarded with science courses and it is usual to carry a study load equivalent to about thirty-four semester hours (compared to the fifteen to eighteen hours a college student normally carries). To make matters worse, science courses are the most difficult type of courses. Classes are held from 8:00 a.m. to 5:00 p.m. daily and cover subjects such as anatomy, physiology, biochemistry, gastroenterology, cardiology, obstetrics and gynecology and all those other "ology" courses. In an osteopathic medical school, we are also given courses in areas such as nutrition, human relations, and osteopathic manipulative medicine.

When the didactic or classroom portion of medical school is over, students are sent out to do "clinical" studies or "rotations" in surgery, internal medicine, family medicine, orthopedics, psychology, pediatrics, obstetrics, gynecology, radiology, emergency medicine, and any "elective" rotations that we want to explore. Contracts to train students in certain medical areas are made with different hospitals. Since not all students can go to the same place at the same time, we rotate. However, not all training is done in a hospital. Some training is done with individual physicians in their offices.

There are a certain number of required rotations and a few elective ones. My first rotation took place in a hospital doing an elective in osteopathic manipulative medicine. The second month was spent in a little town in the middle of Maine working with a family physician in his private practice. It was a great month and I enjoyed being out of the hospital. The one problem I faced, though, was that the physician to whom I was assigned was not enthusiastic about my using osteopathic manipulative medicine. He was a country doctor and only did the basic things country doctors do.

After following him around for a few days so he would feel comfortable with my knowledge and training, he allowed me more latitude in how I worked with his patients. If it was appropriate, after doing those procedures I felt he would have done, I would also treat them with osteopathic manipulative medicine techniques.

By the end of the first week, Bill (the country doctor) came to me and said, "Bob, I've never been really big on osteopathic manipulative medicine, but I've been watching you work with the patients and I'd like to run a test."

I told him that after all of the time I had spent in school, I was "tested out" but he insisted, so I relented. He then said, "Good. Melvin is in the next room waiting for you. Go treat him, but don't talk to him or tell him what you're doing." He also asked me to only use cranial techniques on Melvin.

I entered the exam room. Melvin was lying down, face up, on the treatment table. I should probably stop here and explain a few things. Melvin was about sixty-five years old and a "Maine farmer." These folks seldom complain about anything and are as stoic as the day is long. Life is not easy for them, and they often look years beyond their actual age. Melvin was no exception.

Well, I introduced myself and then began to treat him. Bill wanted to know if cranial really worked, so he only wanted me to treat using cranial techniques. This was purely a test for him to see whether cranial was of any value. He also wanted to make sure any positive results were not due to some sort of hypnotic suggestion, hence the request not to talk during the treatment.

Melvin was a mess, but after about forty-five minutes his tissues were feeling pretty good and I knew it was time to turn him loose, so I told him he could go home. He got up, shook my hand, and thanked me, but I could tell he was far from being a "believer" in what I had done.

Nothing more was said and I went back to work. Bill did not mention Melvin's treatment, but he did arrange for me to treat a few of his other patients.

About a week later, Bill came into the room where I was seeing a patient and said, "Melvin's back. He wants to talk to you." I thought this is great, Melvin speaks! I finished what I was doing and went into the room where he was waiting for me. I smiled and said, "Hi Melvin. What can I do for you?"

In his best "Mainer" accent, he replied, "Well, a week ago, you came in here. You held my head. You held my butt. Thought you were a nice enough fella—kinda strange. What I didn't tell you is that for the past twenty years I've been blind in my left eye. My left arm has been numb and my left foot drug the ground when I walked. On the way home last week, the sight came back into my left eye. About two hours later, my left arm got real warm and tingly and now it's back to normal." Then he said, "Look at this." He walked across the room and his left foot didn't drag the floor. He then came up to me and put his face about a foot from mine. For a second, I thought he was going to kiss me. I was getting ready to say "Whoa, Melvin, I'm not that kinda guy." He stopped and while staring me straight in the eye said, "Don't know what you did, but I figured I ought to get some more."

Almost all "ten-fingered" (the term we use for those who use O.M.T. in their practice) osteopathic physicians who utilize cranial techniques in their practice can tell similar stories. They are true but perhaps more importantly; they defy rational explanation by most allopathic and osteopathic physicians.

It would be nice to be able to claim credit for what happened to Melvin, but I can't. "Healing" came from within Melvin. I merely helped put his tissues and energies into "balance." Once that was done, I then reached in, unlocked, and then released that which his spirit had been unable to release so that his body could heal itself.

A week later, he came back and brought a friend for a treatment. The following day, I returned to medical school and the hospital. I have no idea whatever happened to him.

All these years later, I often look back to that event and the necessity for it to happen at that place and time. Things happen for a reason. I am sure it was important to Melvin but it was perhaps more important to me and the thousands of patients I have treated since that time.

It took a long time before I was comfortable talking about the things I was experiencing and there are still things that I don't talk about. Let's face it, a lot of what you will read in this book will sound pretty far fetched. I was a "non-believer" in the process of becoming a "believer," doing things that I could not explain. I was dealing in a realm that was far from tangible and not reproducible from patient to patient. Some patients were miraculously cured while others were not. Sometimes it felt like I was working with the power of God and at other times, it was a struggle.

When I started writing this book, the hardest part was being willing to lay it all out for you, the reader, to read and then trusting that you will feel my sincerity. In this book, I will write about things that no one has ever written about let alone lectured about in the osteopathic community.

One of my motivations to write this book was the understanding that if something happened to me, others might never know what the possibilities are. It is easier to go where others have trod rather than blaze a new trail. R.W. Emerson penned "Do not follow where the path may lead—go instead where there is no path and leave a trail." That is good advice.

As you read this, you may already be aware of others outside or inside the osteopathic community that have experienced similar phenomena. I have tried to keep myself out of those circles so that I am not influenced by someone else's perception of what is happening. This is the truth as I see it. Having said that, I want to tell you about my niece.

In January of 2000, I received a call from my older brother, Bill, in California. He was distraught. His eldest daughter had fallen asleep at the wheel of her car sometime in the early afternoon and had rolled the vehicle. She had broken her neck in two places and the left side of her body was paralyzed. The prognosis was not good. He wanted to know if I could help. In my entire family, Bill is the only one who has been supportive of what I do even though he has cautioned me from time to time that I may be a lunatic. It took a lot for him to call.

I consulted with some friends who are "seers" who have great faith in my abilities. They encouraged me to send healing energy to her. I've long known that it's not necessary for me to touch a patient to help them heal; I just didn't know how far away I could be.

It isn't talked about in the osteopathic community but those who do "hands on medicine" all know that eventually you start to sense things in our patients before we even touch them. Eventually you can stand across a room and feel "lesions" in a person. Why we don't talk about it, I don't know. It is part of the reason osteopathic medicine is dying. What we see is so powerful that we don't trust what we sense. It's hard to know which is more real. How many times have you said, "I wish I had trusted my instincts?"

Anyway, I called my brother and told him I'd try to send her healing energy. I assumed the posture of deep meditation or prayer and established contact with the force within which we reside. Some will call that the "breath of life," others the "light of Christ," while others will call it "prana." Whatever you want to call it, it is real and very powerful. As I sought out my niece and felt the connection form, I was focused on establishing health in her tissues. After awhile, I felt a sense of peace.

When I was in the initial stages of my training, Dr. Jealous allowed me to be in the treatment room with him and his patient, but he didn't allow me to touch his patients. He would then ask me where the lesions were in the patient. Without touching them, I would have to respond. As I got better at pointing out where the lesions were, he had me stand further away in the treatment room from the patient until I would be standing across the room.

When he finally allowed me to touch the patients and then to treat them, he asked me from where in my body was I treating them. That is an important question. I had not even considered it. I was treating by instinct but he was asking me to look within myself to see where the energy connection was being made.

The "texts" are full of statements stating the need to treat from the "Sutherland Fulcrum," which is a variable balance point in the posterior part of our head. I used to use that spot, but now I treat from the area in the middle of my chest associated with the 4th chakra. That is the area with which I formed a connection with my niece and it is the area I often treat from when treating my patients. Often, during a treatment, the point I treat from changes but treating from the heart chakra seems to predominate.

As for my niece, remember, I had never treated someone from a distance before so it was more an act of desperation rather than faith or knowledge. It was quite simply the only thing I could offer at the time. Perhaps I have more faith than I know. Nevertheless, Bill called the next day and said that much to the surprise of her physicians, she was able to move her left arm and leg to a slight extent. I was stunned and not sure what to do next since she was still unable to feel sensation on the left side and was still unable to move her left hand or foot.

We, my brother and I, decided that in a few weeks I would fly to Southern California on a Friday evening, treat her on Saturday and Sunday, and then fly back to Indiana on Sunday evening. In the mean time, my friends with the seer abilities had told me that something was wrong with her left hip and that it was probably broken.

I called Bill and relayed the necessity to have her left hip checked. He was on his cell phone in the hospital room so he told his wife what I had said. About that time, in walked the physician in charge. My sister-in-law told the physician that her brother-in-law was a D.O. in Indiana and that he had "psychic abilities." He said "Like with a hot-line?" She said "No" but went on to say that I felt there was something wrong with my niece's left hip.

At that point, he asked my niece if her hip hurt and she said "No." He then touched her hip and she let out a yelp in pain. We never did confirm a fracture in that hip and the physician never ordered a bone scan but I concentrated more healing energy on that area and it got better. Within days, she was able to sit up and take a few steps.

She was flown from Las Vegas to an excellent hospital in Southern California so she could be closer to her family. The prognosis was still not good.

When I arrived at her hospital room three weeks later, I could still sense that something was wrong with her left hip. As I entered her room, the neurologist was examining her and had chalked it up to muscle strain on the front of her hip. I reached around her left side and placed my finger on a spot, the one I had been sensing, and she confirmed that it hurt.

When I started to treat her, I had decided to work from her head and then into her body to try to establish an energetic midline so the tissues would have a sense of where they were supposed to be. Nothing was moving. Her tissues were in shock. I worked for two and a half hours and accomplished nothing, I thought.

At that point, we took a three-hour break to watch two of my nephews play basketball in a tournament and to allow me time to rest. I then treated her for another two and a half hours and finally felt a midline form. At that point, I felt it best to let her rest for the night so I went back to my motel room.

The next morning Bill drove me back to the hospital and I treated her left side for about three hours. Now I have to say, I have never treated someone so extensively. It was an experiment and an act of desperation. At the end of that treatment, Bill rushed me to the airport and I flew back to Indiana.

By the time Bill got back to the hospital, my niece had walked around the nurses' station and was moving her fingers and toes. Healing continued at an accelerated pace. She left the hospital weeks earlier than expected and was able to walk about one-half mile within a week of leaving the hospital. The neck brace came off early and she graduated on schedule in April from college and walked down the commencement path without any braces, crutches, or assistance.

A miracle? Sure. How did it happen? I'm not sure. It was undoubtedly a lesson I needed to learn. God did indeed manifest His power and I was fortunate to be allowed to participate. Did Emily do her part? Absolutely. I hesitate to take any credit but one of my seer friends says that I have a gift that enables me to release things from within my patients that they are unable to release themselves and as such heal them. That may occasionally be true.

In October 2000, a woman contacted me whose son had broken his neck in a car accident and was at the Indiana University Medical Center. He is also a quadriplegic. She asked if I would look at him. Unfortunately, the medical center would not allow me to examine and treat him.

"Traditional medicine" still doesn't trust "osteopathic medicine", but several weeks later, after becoming stable, he was moved to another hospital where I was granted temporary hospital privileges to evaluate and treat him. This was a learning experience and the results were very exciting.

He was taken off the ventilator after the first treatment. He then healed to where he could feel when his upper and lower extremities were touched and then developed some gross motion in his arms. All of this happened shortly after I started treating him. Fortunately or unfortunately, he improved to the point where he was transferred to a rehabilitation hospital on the West side of Indianapolis. I say unfortunately because the physician in charge of his care at the new hospital would not allow me to continue to treat this young man because there are no published studies to document that which I do is of value for quadriplegics and there are indeed some idiots in the medical profession.

After four months, and no further progress, he was released from the hospital. At that point I treated him several times but it was apparent that he had given up. Remember, healing comes from within and if the patient gives up, there is little I can do.

This all sounds fascinating and may lead me on another interesting path but is it a miracle? Currently, a study is being performed at Indiana University on animals with spinal cord injuries. An electrical current is passed down the spine and remarkable results have occurred in healing. If each cell in our body, and there are over 100 trillion of them (www.sciencenetlinks.com), has about a .04 volt potential, then the total potential is over 4 trillion volts. Not only is this quite significant but it is available and harmonious with the other energies involved with our bodies.

Quite often, while treating a patient, they will say that they can feel the energy run from my hands, through their head and into their body. Generally, their hands will start to tingle first but eventually their feet will tingle as well. What the researchers at IU are doing at a very crude level is what I did with my niece, and that young man, and what I do to one degree or another with each patient I treat.

I inherited one patient from another physician who moved to another state. She is a delightful woman who has become a close friend and is a blessing to me. Her problem was that she had suffered for over twenty years from a disorder called "Trigeminal Neuralgia" or more commonly, "Tic Douloureux." This is a disorder of the fifth cranial nerve and it can make your face feel like it is on fire. She had been all over the country seeking treatment and had even been to some of the finest holistic and traditional medical clinics in Europe. She had experienced some relief but was still suffering when I first met her.

It took a few treatments to figure out the dynamics of her particular problem but the fire is now gone. For her, there was a specific energy layer that had to be balanced and I had to make sure to only do the minimum needed to balance that one particular layer. If I put too much energy in, the "fix" would not hold. It was fascinating. Every case of trigeminal neuralgia that I have treated has responded favorably and every one was different.

It is also fascinating that the osteopathic profession believes that it is the second branch (V2) of the trigeminal nerve that is involved but I've seen one, two, or three of the branches of the trigeminal nerve involved. It doesn't have to be the second branch.

Generally, we all look pretty much the same. The bottom line is, however, we are very different from one another. If that were not true, everyone would drive the same make and model of car and all the other manufacturers would be out of business. We'd all live in identical houses, etc.

Anatomically we are different. There are some major similarities but the differences far out distance the similarities. If that were not true, we could develop an "owner's manual" for physicians to use. Since it is true, however, physicians have to draw on their knowledge and instinct when caring for their patients. Unfortunately, if knowledge is all they have to draw on, healing can be delayed or simply not happen.

It is easy to point out spectacular miracles but the question is: Are the "small" ones any less spectacular? Is helping a person get rid of a persistent headache, back pain or neck ache any less of a miracle? What about the female patients who have been unable to conceive yet are able to do so after a couple of treatments? The list of what I treat is a long one.

A miracle is a miracle, big or small, it does not matter. I see a lot of them.

6

Treatment Reaction

"Tomorrow, you may feel like you've been run over by a truck."

Today, I was thinking of how I go about treating a patient. There is no set pattern. The examination starts when I walk out into my waiting room and first see the patient. It continues as I watch how the patient gets out of their chair and then observe how they walk to the treatment room. All that time is spent watching and sensing. Once the patient is lying on my treatment table, I will place my hands on their head or some other part of the body and then watch and watch and watch. Sometimes, having done that, I stand back and sense their energies.

I will then place my hands on them and search and search until eventually a flow of energy will manifest and I will follow that until, out of nowhere, the surrounding tissues will start to move. I will then continue with the flow while being mindful of movement within the tissues. Eventually the tissues and energies come into harmony with each other and move in sync.

Not every treatment is a "deep" treatment. Sometimes the patient won't let me go deep into their tissues and energies and will allow me to only work with the superficial tissues. That's okay. As they learn to trust me, I will eventually be allowed to go where I need to go and will be allowed to do what I need to do. Sometimes that means that the patient will need to be treated many times.

Thinking back to my first experience, I was just plain lucky and I had a gift for this work. Sure, all these years later, I am now more mindful of other energy patterns and I can look deeper into the tissues. Sure, I am more intuitive and I accomplish more than I did back then, but that is because I now have gone beyond "wanting to believe" to "knowing."

I have noticed that the amount of time it takes to treat a patient has changed and continues to change. Recently it was taking 40-45 minutes to treat a patient, but then I experienced one of my "quantum leaps" in ability. That change enabled me to accomplish the same amount of work with greater clarity in about 20 minutes. Generally, the time it takes to treat a patient varies between 25-40 minutes but it has been a long time since I have been able to do this in only twenty minutes.

The time to treat a patient will eventually increase again because with each "leap" in ability I eventually develop the ability to sense and to do more and so the time increases as I become aware of different things I am able to do. It's so cool!

In the beginning, as will happen with any new medical student, friends and relatives sought me out for free medical advice. The idea, of course, is that the price is right. The same thing happens when anyone actually becomes a physician, but usually the "friend" is a bit more subtle in their approach. Sometimes patients will hit you up for "freebies" at the end of a treatment by asking you to prescribe medicines for their spouse or asking you to refill prescriptions that were written by another physician.

Sometimes they just want me to "take a quick look" at a child or spouse that came with them to the treatment. Essentially, they want me to take the time I allocate to rest between treatments and use it to treat someone else who wasn't scheduled. If I do that, I have to treat the next patient, without being able to rest and "re-energize".

During my first year of medical school, my wife and I became friends with a young couple in our church. Beth had been experiencing severe back pain for many years, and had been receiving chiropractic treatments three times a week for two years. She was not getting any better. Eventually, Beth's husband got around to asking if I could help her out. I told him I didn't know—I never know until I put my hands on a patient and feel what's going on within them.

I was a bit young at that time and was overcome with the power I was able to feel within the tissues and energies of the body and the energies around our bodies. All these years later, there is perhaps one thing that I've learned very well and that is I never know if someone will be healed unless they do so spontaneously at the time they are treated. At the time a treatment is completed, except in increasingly less infrequent instances, I only know if I was able to get the body to respond to what I did. After I'm done, the body, under the guidance of its spirit and the subtle and not so subtle energies, has to do the actual healing.

As for Beth, I scheduled a time for her to come to my house for a treatment. I put up my portable treatment table, hustled the kids out of the room, and placed my hands on her head.

When I first examine a patient, I try to get a "sense" of what is happening in their tissues and energies. There is an "air" or aura about each one of us that helps to define who and what we are. It's said Dr. Sutherland, the originator of the cranial concept, would just look at his patients for about twenty minutes before he talked to or touched them. If this is true, he certainly understood the importance of the information to be gained by just looking at and "feeling" the aura or subtle energies of a patient.

We've all done that at one time or another. Have you ever been around someone that seemed to suck the air out of the room, someone who just felt evil? On the other hand, have you ever been around someone who seemed to give light and life to the room, someone who made you feel so good being round them that you wanted to just stay forever just sucking in the experience? In a crude way, that is what I'm talking about.

The first thing I noticed in Beth was a lack of motion in the bones of her head. There are about twenty-eight bones in the head (depending on how you count them), all of which are supposed to move. With the possible exception of the six ear ossicles, none were moving. Not only were they not moving, they did not even feel like they wanted to move. Her cranial rhythmic impulse was totally shut down. At times, even though the motion is absent in the head, it may be possible to feel it in the sacrum (tailbone). If it's absent there, perhaps it can be found in the arm, leg, or chest. Everywhere I looked, though, it was shut down.

I find it interesting that the osteopathic profession rates that motion on a scale of 1 to 10. That boggles my mind because how can "no motion" be a 1? It makes no sense since 1 implies some motion. There are a lot of things we teach that are nonsensical. Mind you, there is always motion at some level, unless the person is dead, but when evaluating the individual motions, 0 is entirely possible at many of the levels.

I recently talked to a physician who had been to a course in cranial that was not sponsored by either the Cranial Academy or the Sutherland Cranial Teaching Foundation (S.C.T.F.). She said that they talked energies and such and she felt somewhat skilled in those areas but almost flunked out of another course that taught the basics. She wondered if it was important to know the basic stuff taught by the S.C.T.F. or the Cranial Academy. That is an interesting concept because though the basics of tissue motion are mundane, the tissues have to move if the energies are to be able to manifest themselves. It is important to know the basics.

As for Beth, I noticed something different while treating her. For the first time, I became aware that there was an age to the patterns or lack thereof in her tissues. As I looked into her tissues—and this is perhaps the best way to explain it—I sensed this was an old pattern.

Nature teaches us that older patterns feel different from newer ones. If a branch is cut, it is very pliable the first day, but with each following day, it becomes less and less pliable. Tissues are the same. In addition, old patterns are generally colder. A new injury is often very warm. It is possible, during a treatment, to have a patient lie on the table while I slowly move the palm of my hand over them. At a distance of about twelve inches, I can feel cold or hot areas that correspond to areas of injury, which we call "lesions," in the body.

In Beth, I could sense the injury occurred when she was about twelve, so I asked her what happened at that time in her life. She was shocked, to say the least, and told me she had fallen out of a tree. She'd thought she had broken her back and neck and it was hours before she could move.

In the exuberance of youth; I treated her for about two hours which was the amount of time it took for her mechanism to feel alive and well and indeed, her cranial rhythmic impulse felt wonderful. Everything was moving. I figured she would get up, sing my praises, and thank me for setting her free. Wrong!

When she did get up, she was so lightheaded she almost passed out and had to lie back down. It took about twenty minutes for her to finally sit up. She still felt lightheaded and nauseous. When she at last stood up, she wobbled.

I did not particularly like the feeling I was getting from her husband as he herded their two children toward the door while keeping one arm around his wife to support her. Neither of them said a word as they left.

The next day, he called and told me that Beth said she was dying. I immediately went over to their house. You could have cut the chill with a knife when he met me at the door. We were obviously no longer friends. He showed me to the living room couch where Beth was lying in her bathrobe. She looked terrible! I thought that perhaps she was right. The only thing I could think to do was to feel her pulse, which was strong. I then felt her cranial rhythmic impulse, which was also very strong. I knew she would live and would be okay. I assured both of them of this and left.

Somehow, I don't think they were very confident in my abilities. This was even more evident when he called again the next day and said, "Beth says if she didn't die yesterday, she's sure she will today."

After telling him I'd be right over, I hung up the phone and called Dr. Jealous. I ran the whole scenario past him. He told me I had "over-treated" her and as long as the cranial rhythmic impulse was doing well, she'd be fine. He told me to tell her it takes about seventy-two hours for a treatment to work through the tissues.

Again, my meeting was less than hospitable, but again her pulse and cranial rhythmic impulse were outstanding. Beth said she felt like she'd been run over by a truck. I relayed Dr. Jealous' message and left. I was told later that at almost exactly the seventy-two hour mark, the pain left her for the first time in more than ten years. She felt so good, she went out and played volleyball and then went square dancing.

For those of you who are curious, they never credited what I did as being in any way connected with her restoration to health. We were never close after that incident. They figured it was by the grace of God and their fervent prayers that she was delivered from what I had done. That's okay. It comes with the territory. Tissues that have not moved in a long time don't like to be awakened and told to go back to work. Sometimes they get downright cranky. This is often referred to as a "healing crisis."

As demonstrated in Beth's case, sometimes the patient temporarily feels much worse after being treated. The body is an incredible organism. It knows which organs have a need for increased blood flow with its additional supply of oxygen and nutrients, and it knows which organs and tissues are essentially dormant. Those tissues that are the most active get the most blood while those that are dormant get the least. If a tissue becomes more "active," its need for nutrients and oxygen increases. If this need is not met, the tissues don't just "shut down"; the body has a way of continuing to function even though the need for increased oxygen is not met. Physiologically, this is called a shift from an aerobic metabolism to an anaerobic metabolism. The end product of each is different. We normally experience the latter when we decide to go dancing, play golf or tennis, or do some other activity after being inactive for extended periods of time.

Additionally, tissues that have not moved don't rid themselves of toxins the way they were designed to function. When tissues start to move again, toxins are released in large quantities and it can make you feel very ill. It may take a long time to get rid of the years of accumulated sludge/toxins.

When I was a kid, I remember trying out for the gymnastic team at my high school. I really wanted to prove myself worthy of making the team. The coach was unmerciful and worked us to exhaustion. When I got home from the first practice, I was worn out and laid down on my bed for a nap before dinner. In that short period, my body had a chance to tighten up. Even though I'd been fairly active, my body had never been worked to total exhaustion. Simply put, there was not enough oxygen to go around and an anaerobic metabolism took over. Lactic acid had built up in my tissues and I got sore. I could hardly walk to the dinner table.

When tissues get sore, a person gets light headed, or just feels ill after a treatment, we call that a "treatment reaction." If I were to throw a pebble in a pond, it would take awhile for the ripples to move throughout the pond and then to calm down. The same principle applies whenever the body is worked on. It takes a while for the "insult/treatment" to ripple through the different organ systems in the body.

Fortunately, the body can recognize the build-up of lactic acid and other toxic materials. It responds by dilating blood vessels to flood the injured or overworked tissues with more blood. This not only acts to carry off the waste products, but it also supplies more oxygen and nutrients to the tissues. As I said, when the insult occurs excessively and rapidly, the body responds but when it occurs insidiously, over a period of years, the body may not recognize the need to respond until it is told to do so by someone who knows how to bioenergetically get the tissues to move. That may also require having the person go through a detoxification process, which I will discuss later.

As for Beth, all these years later I wonder what I would have felt if I had examined Beth's cranial rhythmic impulse with the knowledge and skill I've developed at this point in time. Each year, I look back at the previous one and marvel at how much more I have learned. I look forward to a year and even a decade from now, and hope I continue to learn.

Generally, it takes about seventy-two hours for the tissues to calm down from a treatment, but it does not necessarily have to be that way. Many times, it takes much longer for the tissues and energies to calm down. Sometimes but not often, it takes more than a month to do so.

Nowadays, I will tell a patient that has experienced a significant release to fill a bathtub with water that is as hot as they can tolerate without burning themselves. I tell them to put one-half gallon of apple cider vinegar into the water and soak for twenty minutes. At ten minutes they will be sweating and will want to get out. At fifteen minutes, they will really want to get out but they are to stay the full twenty minutes. The person will sweat like crazy but it will help avoid the muscle aches associated with being treated. At the end of twenty minutes, they drain the tub and rinse off in a shower and then immediately go lie down and rest. One word of caution, however, this is not to be used by those with high blood pressure or heart disease.

Sweating is one of the best ways to detoxify your body. The apple cider vinegar helps neutralize the lactic acid. If you just want to sweat and improve your health on a daily basis, the regular use of a far-infrared sauna (www.infraredwellnes.com) is a great idea.

Treatment reaction can also take place while a treatment is going on. As the years go by, I have developed increasingly more "power" to treat. Sometimes I use too much power and it hurts. A good example happened a few years ago. I was treating the young man I mentioned earlier who had broken his neck in an automobile accident and is a quadriplegic.

When I started running energy through his tissues he started to wince. I asked if it hurt and he said it did so I dropped the intensity down by about a factor of 10. That stopped the pain and I was still able to treat. Generally, I try to use as much power as possible when working on patients, including quadriplegics, paraplegics and hemiplegics because I'm working with neurological pathways that have gone into shock and shut down and it seems to help. It is not the rule, however.

When I treat someone, I impart some of my energy on that person. The trick is to use as little of my own energy as possible. Some practitioners say it is imperative not to use your own energy and I have heard this in various courses I have attended. I disagree. Even the Master Healer of all time felt "virtue" leave him. It is part of the process and it is part of what He taught. "*Truly, truly, I say to you, he who believes in me, the works that I do shall he do also; and greater works than these shall he do...*" (John 14:12)

Sometimes I can treat and it is a very balanced process and I come away essentially the same as I started but at other times, it is a very draining process. Sometimes I have trouble standing up after a treatment. It is not just a one-way street. The person doing the treatment is influenced by the energies of the person being treated. We are influenced by anyone with whom we come in close contact and some would say we are influenced by every person, plant, and animal that exists, and as the years go by I tend to agree. The secret is, however, to allow that which is harmful to pass through without causing harm. It takes a lot of concentration. It can be fatiguing. In the martial arts, Aikido and Tai-Chi masters are known for their ability to turn the force and energy of their opponents aside. It is much the same principle.

Occasionally a patient will not return because of the discomfort they feel. With practice, I am getting better at being able to judge just how much energy to use during a treatment. The problem is that it is hard to stop when the tissues really start to move. The desire is to stick it out until the tissues are running smoothly and are in harmony. The important thing to remember is that there is always another day. Listen to the tissues. Be still and know…

7

My Internship

"Faith is believing when there is no rational reason to believe." (Anonymous)

What I most enjoyed about working in a hospital was the variety and severity of various disease processes. During my training, I worked in one hospital that had "in house" osteopathic manipulative treatment available to any patient who had a "standing order" from their physician to receive it.

A standing order from a physician means every patient admitted by that physician will be evaluated and treated, as needed, by a member of the osteopathic manipulative medicine staff. This was a wonderful opportunity as I was able to treat a wide spectrum of people, from newborn infants and their mothers to those who were in the last few moments of their life, feeling the "mechanism" as this final release took place.

Unfortunately, that aspect of osteopathic medicine is rapidly becoming a lost art. Though all osteopathic physicians receive some training in that area, few are proficient. The impression I get from my colleagues is that it is an embarrassment to them. Because they are not proficient at it, they ignore it and act as if it has no worth. As I said earlier, osteopathic medicine has given up that which made it unique in an effort to "fit in."

I was in a seminar recently, sponsored by the Indiana Association of Osteopathic Physicians. One of the presenters went into great detail on how to code for manipulative services when filing for insurance reimbursement. That astounds me. The reason I am astounded is that we have put aside that which defines us as osteopathic physicians. We're not allopathic physicians that just happen to do manipulation. It is an integral part of what we are! There should be no separate codes.

It should be considered the "standard of care" and we should be reimbursed for the extra time it takes to do what we do without jumping through a hoop for some insurance company. That we tolerate this treatment is absurd.

The American Medical Association defines the diagnostic and procedure codes we use. Since they don't view us as being more qualified to practice medicine, which we are, they have devised a series of codes and restrictions that we have to use if we want to show we have actually touched our patients and examined them at the same time. Their view is that we can't do both, which is what osteopathic medicine is all about. The code should simply state "osteopathic examination" and it should mean that we not only did what an M.D. would do but we touched the patient and worked with the tissues of the body in the process.

Trust me, the American Medical Association has a lot of power, and we bow down to them and tolerate what they do just so we can practice medicine and get paid. Even more amazing is that we tolerate it.

Additionally, referrals from other osteopathic physicians for my services are almost non-existent. Allopathic physicians (M.D.s) refer patients to me quite frequently. This is not unique to my situation, however. Whenever I encounter another "ten-fingered" osteopath, I will ask them if they get referrals from other osteopathic physicians and all say it is extremely rare for that to happen yet they all receive referrals from local allopathic physicians. In my case, I receive referrals from allopathic physicians in other states as well. I will be surprised if osteopathic medicine lasts another ten years since D.O.s, in general, don't want to be different.

Of those patients I worked with in the hospital, I will always remember Betty. The first time I met her, I was doing my rounds and noticed a card indicating Betty was a new patient. I walked into her room and said, "Hi. I'm Dr. Brooksby," to which she said, "Do you want to buy a car?" I said, "No, thank you."

Well, she wasn't going to be put off that easily. "It's a good car. It has low mileage. It's blue and if you look out the window, you can see it parked in the lot. Go ahead. Look out the window."

I assured her I wasn't interested in buying a car. At that point, she changed her track. "Well, how about a watch? It's a good watch." To further illustrate this, she pulled back the sleeve of her gown and showed me the watch on her wrist.

I replied that I really didn't want to purchase anything, but my curiosity was definitely aroused. "Okay. You've got my attention," I told her. "Why do you want to sell these things?"

"I hurt so badly," she explained. "Every part of my body hurts and I'm tired of it. I'm going to kill myself." She went on to tell me she didn't want her relatives to fight over her belongings, so she was turning her belongings into cash.

I explained that her physician had asked me to check in on her and wondered if she would mind if I examined and treated her. She said she didn't have anything to lose, but since it hurt to ride in a wheelchair, she'd rather walk to the exam room. It took her about thirty minutes to get out of bed and walk the length of the hospital corridor.

When I examined her, I started with her head. It wasn't moving but there was a tremendous urge to move. It felt like someone was on the other side of a door trying to push it open. I gently lifted her head and cradled it in my hands. I placed my thumbs so that I could rock the temporal bones backwards. All of a sudden, I heard two pops as if someone had cracked their knuckles—only it came from the sutures (joints) in her head.

First of all, I did not think it was possible for these joints to "pop." Generally, the motion is so small that many "anatomists" think they do not move at all. However, I can feel them move and so can others trained in cranial techniques. Studies have been done with cats which demonstrate cranial motion. Even at that, I didn't think there was enough motion to "pop," but I definitely heard them pop. In the many years since that happened, I've encountered fewer than twenty patients where I've experienced a similar phenomenon.

Second, not only did the sutures pop, but she also flushed pink immediately thereafter and started to giggle. I asked what was the matter. She said, "Nothing. The pain is gone." Betty went home from the hospital later that same day.

I have since learned when there is restriction of the sutures in the occipitomastoid region (the back of the head in the area behind the ears) the patient will often experience pain, depression, and/or headaches. When motion is restored, these symptoms will often subside. I have also found when there are restrictions of the upper left cervical region, abdominal complaints often exist. The following story illustrates this point even further.

I was on my hospital rounds one day and stopped in to see how Suzie, who was about ten-years-old, was doing. "Not too good," was her reply. "I have to have an operation because my appendix hurts." She showed me her abdomen and indicated a spot on her right side and said, "Feel that."

It was hard to the touch and she flinched when I touched it. She was obviously in some pain. Because I knew that sometimes lesions in the upper left side of the neck could affect the bowels, I examined her there. I found lesions that could have been the cause of her grief so I went to work. I had just treated the area when her surgeon walked in the door. He asked what I was doing, and I explained that I was giving an osteopathic manipulative medical treatment, as was requested by her family physician.

He groaned and said, "Well, okay," and then turned his attention to the little girl. I guess he hoped I'd go away. To her, he asked, "What are you here for?" She told him she had a bad appendix and had a hard spot on her stomach that hurt to touch. He placed his hands over her abdomen but this time, she did not withdraw. In fact, she indicated that it didn't hurt anymore and reached down to find the spot for him. She was unable to locate it. She, too, went home later that day. (I will also say that during my surgical training, I was taught that the "rule of thumb" is that unless a surgeon finds that about ten percent of the appendices that he removes are "healthy," he is probably missing some bad ones. Go figure! That number has improved to about five percent but I feel that's still too high.)

Virtually any patient can benefit from osteopathic manipulative treatment. Seldom do I find a patient to be "perfect." I can usually find something to treat and I have several patients who come to me on a regular basis just to maintain their health. It's a great concept. The body is designed to heal itself, and if allowed to do so, amazing things can happen.

One of my patients sent me an e-mail a few years ago that said "…If you weren't so casual and unsurprised by the results of what you do, I would say a miracle's been taking place…" Little does she know, it has taken a long time for me to become comfortable with what I do as a physician. How can I explain what I do to someone who does not even know what an osteopathic physician is? How can I explain what I do and the forces I work with to someone who does? How can I explain this to another osteopathic physician? As far as I know, I am the first to write about many of the phenomena written about in this book. The reason for this is that many physicians who do this work are embarrassed by what they can do. That is probably because others, who can't accomplish such feats, point their fingers and call us "witch doctors" or "quacks." Unfortunately, some of this criticism comes from within our own profession.

Essentially, the main problem <u>is that we do not believe</u>. Physicians are not trained to be "believers." We are trained to quote "facts" if they are reproducible in "double blind" studies. If results are not quantifiable by a machine and reproducible in every instance, they do not exist and are of no value. It's an absurdity.

What I am describing in this book is not presently measurable and definitely not reproducible on every patient. The only semi-constant in the whole equation is me and even I vary from day to day.

8

The Dead Guy and Other Spiritual Matters

"An appeal to arms and the God of hosts is all that is left us. But we shall not fight our battle alone. **<u>There is a just God that presides over the destinies of nations</u>**. *The battle, sir, is not to the strong alone. Is life so dear or peace so sweet as to be purchased at the price of chains and slavery? Forbid it Almighty God. I know not what course others may take, but as for me, give me liberty, or give me death."* (Patrick Henry)

Our "founding fathers" firmly believed in God. They believed in things "spiritual." The problem we have today is that we don't believe. We put more faith in that which we can touch than that which we "feel." The "rule of thumb" is: "Pick your physician; pick your disease." In other words, physicians look for diseases within their specialty. The problem is that almost none are trained to look for diseases that are "spiritual" in nature.

Part of my medical training required me to spend a month working at the state mental hospital in Augusta, Maine. It was not fun. To help determine the mental health of those we examined, one of the questions we routinely asked was, "Do you see or hear things that other people don't see or hear?" If they said "Yes," then we assumed that the patient had some mental disease/disorder. The problem is that many, many, totally "sane" people see and hear things that others don't. Furthermore, they have learned not to talk about it. It's not socially acceptable to see spirits or entities that exist in the spiritual realm.

Many of us, physicians included, attend church on Sunday. We read and discuss the Bible and the teachings contained therein. We have heard of Moses and the miraculous things that he did in the name of God yet how many people really believe that what he did actually occurred? Many say that the teachings are "metaphorical." Many people say they believe that Moses did indeed do such things but we can't do such things today because God doesn't work that way anymore, i.e., God has changed! I, however, believe that God has not changed. I believe that the only reason we don't see such miraculous events today is that we don't have sufficient faith. Remember what Christ said in John 14:12: "Verily, verily, I say unto you, He that believeth on me, *the works that I do shall he do also; and greater works than these shall he do…*"

Part of my medical training included the dubious distinction of being "house officer." At the hospital where I interned, we rotated through tours of duty in this position. Hospitals exist to make money. To make money, they must have physicians who have tied themselves to the hospital by becoming staff members. Once a physician has received "staff privileges," they are allowed to admit patients and to take care of those who are already hospitalized.

The problem with being on staff is that if I put a patient in the hospital, they are usually very sick. Sick patients need a lot of care, and sometimes that happens when I am not in the hospital. Sometimes they need attention during the middle of the night, on weekends, or when I am some place where I cannot or do not want to be reached.

When you are a patient in a hospital, your doctor controls your life. At the time of admission, he/she writes orders that tell the nursing staff what's wrong with you, what you can eat, if you're allowed out of your room, and what medicines you can have. If you develop a headache, and your physician has neglected to write an order saying you can have Tylenol, the nurses have to call your doctor to get his/her permission to administer it to you. The problem is that doctors need sleep just like everyone else. If you wake them too many times, they get cranky and if they get too cranky, they stop admitting patients and the hospital loses business. This is where the house officer comes into play.

House officers get to do all the "scut" that staff physicians do not like to do. They do admitting physicals and can even write orders for Tylenol if the attending physician has neglected to do so. They put tubes through patient's noses and into their stomachs, and used to stay in the hospital for thirty-six hours at a time. Sometimes they get to sleep during that time, but if they are busy or if a patient is very ill, there is no sleep. Fortunately, this practice has halted and limits have been placed on the amount of time these young physicians can work. I think it's now limited to 80 hours a week. For this privilege, house officers receive no extra pay so the hospital saves a ton of money and their staff physicians are kept happy.

Another aspect of this position is that the house officer is assigned the task of pronouncing people dead.

One day, when it was my turn as house officer, I received a page from the nurse on one of the units saying that Dr. Smith had "passed away" and "Would you please come and pronounce him dead?" Dr. Smith was well known and highly regarded by the staff. He had been suffering with cancer and his death was expected. I finished what I was doing and went to his room to examine him and to make the official pronouncement.

When I entered the room, there were three physicians and several nurses in attendance. The mood was somber. All of the nurses and some of the physicians were crying. They were mourning Dr. Smith's death and obviously recognized me as the final event in his passing. I was there to test him to see if he was, indeed, dead.

For those of you who have not seen someone who is newly "dead," dead people "look" dead. Dr. Smith looked dead. His skin was lifeless and he was not moving. He appeared dead and he acted dead—the first of the criteria for determining if someone is actually dead. He passed with flying colors.

The rest of the tests aren't as subjective. It was for this purpose that I was in Dr. Smith's room, so I went to work examining him. I listened to his heart and there was no audible sound. I pointed a light at his eyes and they didn't react by constricting the pupils. I pinched him to see if he would flinch. I felt for a pulse and there was none. He sure did appear to be dead. So, I decided to check to see if he had a cranial rhythmic impulse. He did.

When I was in the early stages of my training, I had the opportunity to examine the cranial rhythmic impulse as people slipped from this realm of existence. I learned that at one level, it continues for about two minutes after all other signs of life have stopped. I also learned that the various qualities of the cranial rhythmic impulse change during this period. I don't know how long the energy patterns continue. Some say it can take three days or more as the spirit disengages from the body. There are no "hard and set" rules.

I was now in a very difficult situation. If I only used the traditional methods of determining if someone is alive, he was quite dead. The physicians in the room, even though they were osteopathic physicians, had little concept of the cranial rhythmic impulse and they all thought he was dead. If I told them his cranial rhythmic impulse was still present, i.e., his spirit was still connected to his body, I knew I would never hear the end of it.

One of the first things a young intern learns is not to show up the attending physician, especially in front of a crowd. They were sure he was dead, and I was only there to verify what they already knew.

Well, it had been a long day and since I was forty-years-old at the time and not really in the mood to play games, I gathered my courage and said, "He's not dead." They looked at me as if I was an idiot. I felt like I should crawl from the room. Just when I was seriously considering doing that, the most amazing thing happened. Dr. Smith took a deep breath and moved. Now that got everyone's attention!

I knew from experience he was not long for this world and had about twenty more minutes. I told them it would be soon and left the room.

It is very hard to be humble when you go from despair to what I was feeling, but I did manage to keep from grinning until I had left the room.

The osteopathic profession has been trying for years to explain the cranial rhythmic impulse, that motion that I and others feel. All attempts to explain its rhythm and its origin have failed. It has failed because the medical community refuses to acknowledge that we are spiritual beings at our core. Each individual's cranial rhythmic impulse is driven by a force that at least in part helps to energize their individual spirit as it interfaces with their physical body. The resulting motion is palpable. It is possible to reciprocally use the body to treat the spirit and, to use the spirit through that interface to treat the body. It's a two way street!

Death is an interesting process. As the years go by, I have learned a lot about it. In olden times, when someone died, the body was allowed to "lie in state" for several days before it was buried. Nowadays, the body is whisked away by the mortician so that an autopsy or embalming can take place. I am not sure that is a good idea.

From what I have learned, it takes awhile for the spirit to fully disengage from the body and then it takes a few days for it to leave the immediate vicinity of the body.

When my wife passed away, after a lengthy illness, I was about forty-five minutes away, helping one of our children. When I arrived, I placed my hand on her head and felt her spirit trying to disengage from her body. I then treated her and gently guided her spirit through the release. If I had not done that, I don't know how long the process would have taken. I have been told it can take up to three days.

Perhaps the practice of allowing the body to "lie in state" is one that we should bring back. I know that we are almost never alone. This is not a matter of "I see dead people" but more a matter of understanding that there is a larger reality.

The Bible contains many references to demons and evil spirits. This concept was indelibly affixed to my mind when I was about 16-years-old. One night I awoke fully aware that there was something standing at the foot of my bed. Though the room was dark, there was still some ambient light from the streetlight outside. That personage was totally black and evil beyond description. I was so frightened I could not move and prayed for deliverance. Occasionally I have mentioned this incident to others who have also encountered this individual. Unlike this experience, the vast majority of "spirits" we encounter are not malevolent; nevertheless, I firmly believe we are not alone. Good and bad spirits abound plentifully.

Malevolent entities can cause physical harm. We have ample accounts of such in the Bible and New Testament. One of my favorite New Testament stories involves a time when the disciples were going about healing people by casting out evil spirits. They came across a boy who had been vexed since he was a youth and tried to heal him but failed. In frustration, they went to the Savior and asked why they had been unable to heal the lad. "Then Jesus answered and said, O faithless and perverse generation, how long shall I be with you? How long shall I suffer you?" (St. Matthew 17:17)

This passage has fascinated me for several reasons. The first is that the disciples were being taught to heal. It was not a secret. It was a skill that could and can be learned and apparently Christ was teaching his disciples to do just that.

The second and most obvious thing that fascinates me about this instance is that they were aware that malevolent spirits could influence our health but equally important was the fact that they were being taught to deal with the situation and it was not a "secret." Furthermore, they were not afraid to deal with these entities.

The next thing that strikes me is that the Savior got mad at His disciples. Why would He get mad? I have seven children and I used to teach pilot training. I have some experience in getting mad at those who I'm trying to teach. The question and perhaps the answer is: Why in the world would He get mad unless perhaps there was a principle that He had been trying to teach them that they obviously were not learning?

The scriptures say, "And Jesus rebuked the devil; and he departed out of him: and the child was cured from that very hour." (St. Matthew 17:18) That in and of itself is incredible and a worthy lesson but the real crux of the matter comes when the disciples ask why they could not heal the child. "And Jesus said unto them, Because of your unbelief: for verily I say unto you, If ye have faith as a grain of mustard seed, ye shall say unto this mountain, Remove hence to yonder place; and it shall remove; <u>and nothing shall be impossible unto you</u>." (St. Matthew 17:20)

Imagine having the power to not only heal but to move mountains. What power we must have within each of us. Remember they were not being rebuked for healing but rather for not having enough faith and perhaps understanding.

But why was He angry? Weren't they doing what He had asked them to do? Hadn't they already been using faith to heal people by casting out evil spirits? There has to be a reason for the anger displayed by the Savior. In the next breath, however, the Savior softens his stance and again becomes the teacher when he says, "Howbeit <u>this kind</u> goeth not out but by prayer and fasting." (St. Matthew 17:21)

What "kind" is He talking about? What kind goeth not out but by prayer and fasting? I think the "kind" that he is talking about is the "kind" that is not an evil spirit. The kind that He was also trying to teach them about, i.e., the plain old every-day illnesses that are <u>not</u> the result of evil entities; the kind that great faith can heal; the kind that yields to an understanding of what we are and the power we can tap into.

I think that the "devil" referred to in this instance was not an evil spirit but rather a generic term for illness or disease. Furthermore, I think the passage may have been incorrectly translated because the Savior did not fast and pray before laying His hands on the lad. He just laid his hands on him and healed him. He did not take time to fast and pray. Remember, "*...and greater works than these shall he do...*" *(John 14:12)*

Years later we see that Peter had mastered the lessons taught to him to the extent that when he visited the people of Corinth they recognized his ability to heal. "Insomuch that they brought forth the sick into the streets, and laid [them] on beds and couches, that at the least *the shadow of Peter passing by might overshadow some of them*. There came also a multitude [out] of the cities round about unto Jerusalem, bringing sick folks, <u>and</u> them which were vexed with unclean spirits: and they were healed every one." (Acts 5: Verse 15-16). Apparently, Peter had learned his lessons well and had developed his healing abilities to the point where just being in his presence was "curative."

I have to make sure you understand that we have that same ability. If Peter could learn it, then we can learn it. It was something that we were supposed to learn but somewhere through the ages, it was perverted and people were taught that only the kings, priests, and physicians had the right to "heal." Obviously, the ability to fully harness the power of faith has been lost to most people in "the West." The challenge is to regain that which we have lost. Obviously, first we have to believe.

A close friend sent me a videotape taken in a clinic in China where a form of healing called Chi Lel Qigong is practiced. On the video, a woman is lying on her back on a medical gurney. Her abdomen is exposed as an ultrasound transducer is moved across her abdomen just like is done to pregnant women to see how their unborn child is developing. This woman, however, had a large cancerous tumor in her bladder.

Half the screen is frozen to show the "before" picture of the tumor. The other half of the screen is "real-time" ultrasonography. Several Qigong masters are in the room chanting. Within a couple of minutes the tumor has started to vibrate and then simply dissolves into nothingness. No trace was left that it had ever existed. They had literally created a reality, through the use of thought, feeling, and emotion, where the tumor did not exist!

The real important thing to learn from all this is that we are a lot more complex than that which we have generally been led to believe. We exist in an energy matrix that is incomprehensible. We have to look at not only what we are but also at our environment and that which is contained therein.

Many people are aware of "spirit guides" and "guardian angels" in their lives. Seldom does someone come to me for treatment who is not accompanied by some unseen spirit/entities. Fortunately, the vast, vast majority of such entities are there to help. Unfortunately, that's not always the case and it's one of the reasons for me writing the third and fourth editions of this book.

We are spiritual beings having a physical experience. We've all heard of "near death" experiences where a person has died on the operating table and then is revived some time later. Once revived, the person can describe what happened while they were "dead." Though there was no heart or brain-wave activity, they often can describe what happened as they stood across the room and watched efforts to revive them take place. If there was no electrical activity in the heart or brain it is impossible for them to know what was going on **unless** what we are, i.e., our conscious "self" is not a part of our body but merely resides within our body while we are "alive."

How many of you believe you have to be a priest or ordained member of the clergy to cast out evil spirits? It doesn't say that in the Bible. We are not alone.

Evil entities do still create disease. It happens all the time. I was working with a medical student one day when a patient came into my treatment room. I noticed the student's eyes get big and he gave me a strange look. I don't have the ability to see spirits or entities but I can feel them. I treated the patient and when I was done and the patient had left the room, I discussed what had happened to the patient with the student.

What had happened, and what the student saw, was that as the patient entered the treatment room, an evil spirit stepped out of the patient's body, went to a corner of my treatment room, and stood there. About half way through the treatment, the evil entity left.

Most entities don't make it through the front door of my office. Some make it as far as the treatment room door. Few last through a treatment. In this case it figured it would wait until the treatment was done and then reenter the patient. About half way through the treatment it figured not only that it didn't have a chance but it was not able to stay in the room. They get real uncomfortable in my presence, especially when I'm treating. Not all evil entities or evil spirits are alike. Some are very powerful and some are little more than a nuisance. The small ones are more like parasites.

Almost two years ago, a patient called me and told me she had just been told that she had three months to live and she needed "a miracle." She had been diagnosed with breast cancer that had metastasized (spread) throughout her body. I told her to come in the next day, Saturday, for a treatment. About half way through the treatment she got very tense and acted strangely.

I had been working on extracting an evil entity from her and at that point it had left her body and was standing beside the treatment table. I couldn't see it but she could see it and was afraid. Eventually, it gave up and left. It's a blessing that I can't see such entities. For her, she received her miracle. She is disease free.

I've always had to deal with these evil forces but have not always been willing to recognize them for what they are. As for what they look like, most are described to me by seers as appearing like ferrets. Some, however, are gigantic horrible multi-headed beasts.

As luck would have it, the first time I battled a demon, it was huge. The patient's family was oblivious to his peril and of no help whatsoever. I looked all over and read everything I could in an effort to figure out what to do. An exorcism was the obvious answer but they don't teach that in medical school and very few religious leaders perform exorcisms.

There are so many superstitions surrounding evil entities that fear is the overwhelming obstacle. Indeed fear is literally the medium in which they are fostered.

Interestingly enough, almost everyone I've encountered who has a demon is on an anti-depression medicine or has an addiction to tobacco, alcohol, or drugs (including prescription medicines).

Much debate has been had on whether or not fear is the opposite of love. If it's not, it's close but neither fear nor evil entities can exist when God is present. The references that state that God wants us to fear him I believe are incorrectly translated. I say that because He wants us to be like Him and that would require us to become "love." The one time I encountered Satan, fear, not hate, was the overwhelming emotion present.

Nevertheless, Christ taught His disciples how to deal with these entities. I don't believe in coincidence so I figured this was just one of those lessons I was supposed to learn.

I don't "see" spirits, etc. I feel them. I decided to confirm my suspicions by asking three people I know, who are "seers," to "look" at him and tell me what they saw. They all described the same beast. They warned me not to try to deal with this particular beast since it would literally kill me.

Most people are loath to admit they have bad breath so admitting that they have an evil spirit or demon is unthinkable. People that are infested with evil spirits or demons generally don't know it and if they do, they don't admit it. They may feel something is wrong but that's it. The problem is that those closest to them don't think in those terms either. They may go to church on Sunday but what they hear about evil spirits no longer applies for some reason.

Often evil spirits inhabit families and they work together to preserve themselves from those who can harm them or cast them out. It works very effectively.

In this case, rather than face the problem, he went into hiding with the full support of his family. Fear is the breeding ground for evil and some families and cultures foster fear. Faulty family values or cultural morals and paradigms contribute to this and then it's perpetuated from generation to generation. Since love is the antithesis of fear, it's not uncommon for these people to not feel that they are loved. Their sense of self-worth is often very low.

Nevertheless, when I couldn't find someone to handle the problem for me, I decided it was up to me to do what needed to be done. Fear is an illusion. In my life, when I've faced my fears, I've always prevailed and I figured this would be the same.

One seer told me it would take three hours of battle to get rid of it and since I didn't know where he was, this would have to be done remotely. I prepared myself through fasting and prayer. Supposedly, it is easier to cast demons out at sunset so at the appropriate time, I laid down on my treatment table and reached out energetically until I energetically contacted him and the demon.

Throughout the day, during my breaks between patients, I had done this in an effort to see if I could actually contact the beast. Each time I could remove it from him but as soon as I withdrew, it reentered him. I probably shouldn't have done that because it was waiting for me, and I had forewarned it of my intention.

My goal was to hold it away from him for three hours which was supposed to be long enough that his spirit could recover by itself and the demon would leave. It would be physically draining. Since this was being done at a distance it takes a lot more energy. Furthermore, the demon knew where I was so it came to me at my office, so there were battles at two separate locations going on. It started at a distance and ended up in my office.

The battle was intense. It was like an energetic wrestling match. I had to energetically hold on to it and keep it out of him for three hours. (I've since learned an easier way to do it.) At an hour and a half the demon had come to me and I was holding my own but I didn't know if I could keep it up for another hour and a half, which I really hoped would be enough. It was like holding a rabid wolf by the throat and trying to keep it from ripping me to shreds.

At that point a violet cloud with a cherub in it appeared in the room. The cherub just smiled at me. The battle lessened to a small degree and I thought help had arrived. Boy was I wrong! After about twenty seconds it disappeared and the demon came at me with twice the strength and ferocity it had previously displayed. After about forty more minutes I was starting to realize that I might not survive the struggle and was doing some serious praying. Then God showed up.

When I did my psychiatric training, one of the questions we learned to ask was "Do you see or hear things other people don't see?" If they have, then they're "a keeper."

The problem is that many "normal" people see things but have been trained not to speak of them. If I ease into it, people who have "second sight," as it is called, will tell me many fascinating things. That's how I found out about the kahuna that helps out in my office.

God exists. I won't go into it, but I KNOW God exists. I've heard His voice and have felt His presence.

Anyway, God showed up, the room filled with light, and the tide of the battle changed. The power of God poured from my hands as I've never felt it flow. The battle didn't take the full three hours.

I was spent. I was drenched in sweat and ached. I could hardly move. It took about thirty minutes to get enough strength to get off the table. Within hours my patient called me. He had felt the change take place and was no longer constrained to hiding out.

The next day I called one of my seer friends to inquire if the demon had indeed been expelled. It had, but was nearby because it too had a lair and they had not been expelled. The demon was waiting to get back with its "children." At this point, the name "Legion" comes to mind.

I again started preparation to finish the job. I had planned on doing it the next evening. However, about 1:30 a.m. that morning, God woke me up and said it was "time to go to work." That which had taken hours to perform earlier, only took minutes to do with His help and it was done and finished.

I'm not an exorcist. People so infested do not generally know they are infested. Most of the time, their families don't even know a demon is involved. They recognize aberrant behavior, but it's common and definitely easier to blame outside influences or people for someone's behavior or rather misbehavior. In this case there was no one willing to do anything more than to pray for him. I'm sure prayer helps but someone had to step up to the plate and take a swing and nobody else was willing to do that. In this case, his family helped to create an atmosphere of fear not love.

The demon did not want to be removed but, someone had to step up to the plate.

I wasn't looking for that lesson but lessons come when it's time to learn them. I had avoided the subject of demons and evil spirits in terms of health but it was time to learn what I needed. Like most people, I'd gone to church on Sunday and had hoped on Monday that the stories about demons were myths. They aren't!

Since that time, I have developed an even closer relationship with God and it has gotten much easier to do that which needs to be done. Now that I'm willing to acknowledge the existence of such entities, I'm amazed at how many people are infested by one or more demons. It is very common.

Well, I feel I have taken a bold step in discussing the issues in this chapter. Having said all this, **please don't call me or ask me to remove a demon from you or someone else**. You are all capable of doing what I did.

9

Balance

*"Come to me, all that are weary and that suffer in strife and affliction! For my peace will strengthen you and comfort you. For my peace is exceeding full of joy. Wherefore do I always greet you after this manner: **'Peace be with you'**. Do you always, therefore, so greet one another..."* (Atttributable to Jesus Christ in *The Essene Gospel of Peace*, book one pg. 48)

"Humankind has not learned about balance, let alone practice it. It is guided by greed and ambition, steered by fear. In this way it will eventually destroy itself. But nature will survive; at least the plants will..."Happiness is really rooted in simplicity. The tendency to excessiveness in thought and action diminishes happiness. Excesses cloud basic values" (*Many Lives Many Masters*, Brian L. Weiss, M.D. p. 209)

"What does peace have to do with balance? Everything!" (RCB)

When I was a kid, I used to play on the teeter-totter. Occasionally I'd race to the teeter-totter and plunk myself down on the seat and wait for someone else to plunk themselves down on the opposite seat. As luck would have it, occasionally "Fat Albert" would be the first to arrive. As could be expected, his seat would be glued to the ground and I'd be up in the air at his mercy. Did he really expect me to balance him out enough so that it would be fun? My point is, however, that with his butt planted firmly against the ground and me suspended in the air, there was nonetheless balance.

Balance occurs all the time. Almost everyone is "balanced." If that were not the case, we'd all fall over but even that would result in a type of balance even though it would require the ground to achieve it. When a patient asks me if they are in balance, I will often bend forward and extend one arm out in front of me and then stick a leg out in the other direction to balance me. I will then ask them if I'm balanced. Of course I am but it's not very functional since I can't walk or do much of anything in that "balanced" posture.

"Balance" is an interesting concept. I like the concept of balance and I've often used the term to indicate the idea that someone is "straight" or "well" but in the purest sense that is not necessarily true.

Nowadays, physicians like to prescribe antidepressants for patients who they think have a "chemical imbalance." Many patients like to take those medications and if the patient doesn't like taking them, their family certainly likes the patient taking them because it makes the patient easier to deal with. The patient becomes luke-warm and non-threatening. They have no highs or lows because their spirit becomes partially disengaged from their body. The question is: Are they balanced? Yes. Were they balanced before taking the medications? Yes.

The plethora of antipsychotic medications available today would make Aldous Huxley or George Orwell proud. Physicians are taught that when someone is depressed there is an imbalance in the brain's neurochemicals that is helped by taking such medications. I'd love to know what test these other docs have been ordering to determine that there is such an imbalance. There is no such test. It's not true. Those drugs (I don't want to call them medicines) lead to further psychological and physical imbalances. Those drugs do not help achieve a healthy balance.

"Yes, there is a need in emergency situations to have drugs available. BUT the vast majority of prescribed medications are given electively for POSSIBLE benefits. When compared with safe alternatives, very few drugs can compete. Remember that the placebo effect averages 35%. There is virtually no drug! that is 70% effective. Most are 2 to 15% "better" than placebo, with complications ranging from minor rashes to death. The Congressional Office of Technological Assessment determined some years ago that 86% of the drugs approved by the FDA did not have scientific validity for their recommended use!...And of course the two leading drug groups—statins and antidepressants-have the worst safety and efficacy science!" (*PHARMACOMAFIA LIES: 94% of the PharmacoMafia's advertising is NON-Scientific!!*, C. Norman Shealy, M.D., Ph.D., http://www.normshealy.net)

When Prozac came out, we were told that the patient should be on the drug for no more than 6 months. We're now told that a patient can take it and probably will have to take it for the rest of their life because it <u>permanently</u> alters the homeostatic mechanism within their brain, i.e., it permanently causes a chemical imbalance. That mechanism measures how much of each chemical is available. We were also told that in clinical studies, 5 milligrams of Prozac was only slightly less "effective" than 20 milligrams of Prozac but Eli Lilly, the manufacturer of Prozac, decided to go with 20 milligrams as the dosage and physicians went along with it. If a little is "good" is a lot "better?" Folks, physicians are lazy! It's easier to drug someone than to work with them to get them back to health and most patients go along with that approach because it's cheaper! I said physicians are lazy but patients are even lazier. Everyone wants a "pill" to make them better.

Depression is very real and very serious. The causes of depression are many. When the body starts to show the symptoms of depression most physicians are only trained to treat the symptoms. Some physicians will search for the cause.

I'm not going to rest the blame solely on physicians. The truth is that you, not your physician, are responsible for your health. When you become "out of balance" for one reason or another, it's initially not your physicians' fault. Granted, most physicians will be more than happy to help you along that path but you don't have to go there without "kicking and screaming" unless you're just plain lazy.

When something happens to the body or to the spirit that causes either to be moved out of balance, there is a corresponding counterbalance mechanism that kicks in to provide a sort of balance that allows us to continue to function while we heal. That counterbalance can involve the spirit or the body or both. The problem is that we have to allow the body to do what it's designed to do.

We were spiritual/energetic beings before we came to this existence and we will be spiritual/energetic beings when we leave. The problem with that entire "truism" is a very substantial reality, i.e., we are physical/energetic beings right now. No matter what we were or what we will once again become, we are experiencing a different reality at this time, a reality more important than we can comprehend. To be truly in "balance" we have to embrace the larger reality of who and what we are at this time.

Balance is very important but it's not the whole answer. Strain or rather the generalized lack thereof is also very important. I often work on patients by unwinding them. During that process, I attempt to keep the part being unwound in a position where there is no strain. Sometimes that is relatively easy to do but at other times it's very difficult. It's difficult because almost as soon as I place a tissue in a position in which the strain is neutralized, the tissues will move to a new position where there is strain. It can happen so rapidly that there is a seeming fluidity to the motion that is occurring as the head, neck, arm or leg is "unwound." It may indeed involve the whole body. Eventually the affected area or areas will return to neutral. Often with the release of strain, heat will be given off and the patient may become very emotional.

Balance and strain are important but there is more. Remember, the tissues often flow into an energetic "mold" that your spirit forms. If that mold is bent, the tissues will be bent. It's important to make sure that both the physical body and the energetic body are balanced and relatively free of strain. I say relatively free since some strain is necessary for us to stand erect and to move. We call that strain "tone." The postural muscles of our neck act in concert with one another to balance the head and keep the neck and head erect.

At a strictly anatomical level, the musculoskeletal system works fairly well to keep us erect. That system requires an active spiritual/energetic input to keep it functioning. That input functions as more than just the battery that keeps the system activated.

Applied Kinesiology

Applied kinesiology fascinates me. It fascinates me because it deals with our energetic being as it relates to our physical being. Often I will have a patient stand erect and extend their non-dominate arm out to their side. I will then place their other hand on their chest and stabilize the dominate shoulder with my corresponding hand as I face them. I will then ask them to not allow me to push down on their extended arm. I will then push down on the extended arm and notice how much resistance they can muster.

I will then ask them to say "I am a man/woman" and will again push down on the extended arm when they answer. This is a test of "truth." I will then ask them to say just the opposite and will test their arm strength to see how much weaker they are when they lie. Our thoughts, feelings, and emotions can also create strain especially if those thoughts and feelings are out of balance. I will also test muscle strength with a known toxin such as air freshener to see how much weaker they become. For this test, I simply have the patient hold the substance being treated with their dominate hand against the middle of their chest. I will then repeat this procedure and test the various medicines and nutritional supplements they are taking to see which ones make them weaker.

You'd be surprised how many nutritional supplements make people weaker. You'd be surprised how many very popular nutritional supplements make people weaker. It's important to understand that a product that makes a person weaker today may not make them weaker tomorrow even though the really bad ones will never result in a favorable response.

Sometimes I'll have a patient stand erect with both arms extended out to their sides. I will then push down on both wrists and notice how strong they are. I'll then put a thin book on the floor and have them put one foot on it while the other is on the floor. One arm will become weaker.

Why does this work? It works because we are energetic/physical beings. Balance is very important. Some substances are toxic to the body's balance and some substances are toxic to the spirit's balance. Whatever the cause, the result is that the interface between the body and the spirit becomes unbalanced and disease results. Initially, we become weaker.

If we ignore our physical self, we become ill and can die. If we ignore our spiritual/energetic being we will also become ill and can indeed die. There is a balance that has to take place between the two. At this point in our existence, we are a duality and that duality exists in a sort of balance.

Bruce is a very capable, intelligent, handsome man. He has several college degrees and comes from an ethnic family where there exists a plethora of physicians, dentists, and attorneys. He is trim and is well spoken. In spite of all of this, he has not found his "niche" in life. His family thinks he should be an attorney. Even though he has a "pre-law" degree he never applied to law school. He has confided to me that he feels like he is a fraud. He doesn't think he's capable of achieving what he's told his family he wants to do and he thinks that if he tries and fails everyone will know he's a fraud. He's afraid.

Bruce's mom is one of those intellectual types that made sure her kids were tested for IQ and when Bruce excelled she set out to "train" him and then show him off. When Bruce was in his pre-teen years, his mom ran off with another man leaving him and a younger sibling with an emotionally distant father. The shock to his spirit was horrible. Eventually he chose to go to a boarding school rather than continue in that environment.

Rather than direct his anger towards his former wife, Bruce's father often was mean and unresponsive to Bruce. Eventually, to further distance himself, his father chose to marry a woman who made him miserable whenever he had contact with Bruce. Though Bruce states otherwise, I seriously doubt Bruce really believes either parent loves him. Bruce continues to try to seek their approval.

Bruce has severe, unrelenting back and shoulder pain. MRIs, X-rays and laboratory tests have all revealed no physical problem. Bruce "doctor shops" looking for a physician who can "fix" him. I've treated him but he says he feels funny afterwards so he does not want to be treated bioenergetically but only wants to be "adjusted." His fear attracts demons and they do have their way with him and they don't like what I do. Demons are real—very real. We have a saying for this: "He has inner demons." They don't like to be worked on.

Inner demons aren't always truly demons. Our own spirit is more than capable of making us miserable all by itself. We talk to ourselves all the time. Sometimes those thoughts are influenced by demons, sometimes they come directly from demons, and sometimes they are our own thoughts, i.e., the product of "stinkin' thinking". The problem is that if we believe something to be true, our bodies follow that "truth" whether it is true or not. If it is not true and it results in an imbalance, disease can occur.

Drugs can help dull the pain but they also make it easier for demons to inflict the body. Bruce takes antidepressants and anti-anxiety medications in an effort to help with the pain. He often takes more than the prescribed amount of medicine because he says the medicines are ineffective. Bowel problems persist and he has been diagnosed with depression, generalized anxiety, and irritable bowel syndrome. When stress is removed from his life the pain gets better but then he suffers from depression because he feels like he's not performing up to his and his family's expectations. He's depressed because he believes he is a failure and he's afraid to try because if he does fail, it will just cement his suspicions that he is a fraud. It's a tough cycle. Bruce keeps going back to his family for support because he believes that families are supposed to help. The problem is that they can't help. They are too broken to help. Subconsciously, I think Bruce knows this.

Sooner or later, most dysfunctional families expect their kids to grow up and go away. After years of telling his family that he's going to be an attorney, they all realize that Bruce isn't going to be one but they won't let him forget that he could be. Bruce thinks that being an attorney is something that will make him acceptable to his family and at this point he feels it's the only way to regain their respect and, in all candor, it probably is the only way Bruce will respect himself unless a major paradigm shift occurs. It's a no win situation, i.e., anything short of that to Bruce means he is a failure even though to the rest of us, that is absurd. Bruce is stuck in a paradigm that has never served him well. He has tried to break free but his fears keep pulling him back.

Bruce has attempted suicide. It's easier for him to kill himself than it is to pay the price and do whatever it takes to succeed at finding peace even if it means trying and failing a few times along the way or even "turning his back on his family". At this point, I really don't know what Bruce truly wants other than to hide out. The fear of failure is very real and fear is like blood in the water. Blood attracts sharks and fear attracts demons. Bruce has them. I've removed them several times but he keeps allowing them back in.

Edwin Arlington Robinson once penned:

Richard Cory

> Whenever Richard Cory went down town,
> We people on the pavement looked at him:
> He was a gentleman from sole to crown,
> Clean favored, and imperially slim.
>
> And he was always quietly arrayed,
> And he was always human when he talked;
> But still he fluttered pulses when he said,
> "Good-morning," and he glittered when he walked.
>
> And he was rich—yes, richer than a king,
> And admirably schooled in every grace:
> In fine, we thought that he was everything
> To make us wish that we were in his place.
>
> So on we worked, and waited for the light,
> And went without the meat, and cursed the bread;
> And Richard Cory, one calm summer night,
> Went home and put a bullet through his head.

I first became aware of this poem when I was a senior in high school. A musical group called the *Three D's* had put the poem to music. It was beautiful. Their voices harmonized wonderfully and then there was the punch line—wow. The struggle with personal demons can indeed be fatal.

Both Bruce and Richard Cory are/were out of balance energetically. It has come close to ending Bruce's life and it did end Richard Cory's life. Not all outcomes are as severe.

Pain is an interesting beast. Most of us have experienced pain at one time or another. Fortunately, most of the time pain goes away fairly quickly. Some people, however, experience chronic pain. Medical professionals know that pain, depression, and anxiety go hand in hand. We know that pain that is not resolved in a reasonable period of time can become self-perpetuating. Essentially, pain makes spasm which makes more pain and so on...there is no balance. It's much like falling. To break the cycle, however, requires much more than simply treating the initial cause. You have to treat the cause <u>and</u> the effect. If demons are involved or have become involved, they also have to be removed and they will probably have to be removed several times.

People so inflicted don't want to admit that they have demons. It's embarrassing! It certainly requires you to admit that the Twilight Zone may exist! At this point the phrase "Pride goeth before the fall…" comes to mind. Indeed pride and fear are dangerous playmates.

When I examine a patient, I go through an initial discussion of why they have come to see me. I take what they say with a "grain of salt" because it's seldom the real reason. That doesn't mean that they lie to me, but they might, but it means that they may not really know or want to admit why they have come to see me. They may feel pain but they may not know why there is pain. They just know they hurt or they feel bad.

My job is to put my hands on them and decide if what I feel and what I intuit matches what they tell me. Initially I try to sense where the balance points are. A balance point doesn't necessarily mean a place of maximum health. It means a point where a fulcrum has been established. That fulcrum will shift and change as I treat the patient. More often than not, if I push on that fulcrum, it will be painful and when it releases the pain will stop. Sometimes, that fulcrum exists outside the physical body.

Louise Hay has written a book that I love. Its title is *Heal Your Body*. It is 83 pages long and points out ways the body outwardly manifests spiritual imbalance. An example is: "Jaw Problems (Temporomandibular Joint, TMJ Syndrome)—Anger, Resentment, Desire for revenge." Another example is: "Shoulders—Represent our ability to carry our experiences in life joyously. We make life a burden by our attitude." If we look under back problems, specifically upper back problems we read "Lack of emotional support. Feeling unloved. Holding back love." Louise may not be 100% correct but she hits in the ballpark most of the time. What we think affects our health.

What we say also influences our health. If a person says something that is a lie, they will become weaker even if they want to believe that what they are saying isn't a lie. I find it useful to muscle test patients that seem stuck and aren't getting better. I simply ask if they want to be healed. A lot of those folks fail the test.

Likewise, "positive affirmations" seem to be the rage. The theory is that we can program ourselves by saying something that we are something that we are not. Unfortunately, if we know it's a lie, we will become weaker. If you're going to say affirmations, make sure that you are affirming things that are true to your soul. Start small and build up.

There is a new butter-like spread called "Healthy Balance." It's not butter but it's also not margarine and it contains no trans-fatty acids. I'm not sure it's a good thing but I'm also not sure it's a bad thing. What I do like is its name. We need to not just be balanced; we need a "healthy balance."

Past Lives

I was raised with fundamental Christian paradigms. Life goes on, however, and paradigms that don't make sense have to be modified if not discarded. Having said all that, I have to address the possibility of past lives. I am reticent to do this but I have to because there are "lesions" or strains and behaviors that I can't explain any other way. As I've said, I can usually place an "age" on a lesion. Sometimes those lesions feel much older than the individual I'm working on.

By definition, "past life" lesions are unresolved injuries to your energy/spirit being that occurred during a "past life" which are then carried into this life. These energetic lesions can generate physical pain that may initially have no underlying physical/pathological condition. Sometimes these lesions don't manifest until later in life but that is not always the case. I think many phobias and irrational fears are manifestations of "past life" experiences. The physical manifestations of such are many.

In the book *Many Lives, Many Masters,* Brian L. Weiss's, M.D. presents a very compelling argument for the possibility of past lives. I can't mirror what Dr. Weiss writes about but there are things that patients present with that I can't explain any other way. I have had a few patients report "past life" experiences after being treated. As I said, some lesions feel much older than the patient. An example is a woman I know who will occasionally speak in tongues at her church. Theoretically, that can either be a manifestation of "the spirit" or a demon. Supposedly, such manifestations are supposed to be for the edification of others and there should be someone around to interpret what is said. When that happens, everyone gets a "warm fuzzy" and life goes on.

The problem is that she will often speak in tongues when sleeping and she appears to be very fluent in whatever language she is speaking. Since she is asleep, it's probably not a manifestation of the spirit and there are no demonic overtones. Additionally, as mentioned in Dr. Weiss's book, she too has physical pain that cannot be explained medically. Perhaps as Louise Hay says it's due to a "lack of emotional support" or "feeling unloved" or "holding back love." Perhaps her pain is due to a past life experience. I don't know the answer but I love it when paradigms that have not served us well change. All truth comes from one source. We used to believe that the earth was flat but that didn't serve us well either.

I have discovered that if I look for and find a "past life" lesion and address it as such with my patient, they can be treated. I used to not look for such lesions. It was only after reading Dr. Weiss's book that I have done so. Previously, it was like walking down a hallway and hearing a noise behind a door but not opening the door to see what was happening. I now open the door.

Soon after I had decided to look for past life lesions, I was examining a patient and felt a lesion in her neck that felt like a past life lesion. It felt like her head had been cut off. I asked her if she had ever experienced a past life experience. She said she had experienced two such experiences. The first involved her working as a physician in France. She did something wrong and ended up at the guillotine. Hello!

This past week, a patient came in with a pain in her back. As I examined it, I became aware that this was a past life lesion. I told her such and volunteered that it felt like a long time ago, she had been a man and had been run through with a javelin. She immediately said that she had been to a local psychic who had told her that in a past life she had been a man and had been run through with a javelin while protecting her current husband, who was with her at that time in history as a fellow warrior. Since I've decided to look for past life lesions, seldom does a patient show up without some form of past life trauma.

For those of you who need a bit more, I found the following article (one of many) doing a simple word search on the web. The following is portion of the article "Reincarnation as Taught by Early Christians" By I. M. Oderberg (From Sunrise magazine, May 1973. Copyright © 1973 by Theosophical University Press)

"Actually, the idea is found in the oldest traditions of Western civilization, as well as being taught throughout the ancient Near East and Orient. And there is solid evidence that during its first centuries, Christianity did indeed impart what it had learned about the pre-existence of souls and their reimbodiment.

"Josephus, the Jewish historian who lived during most of the first century AD, records in his *Jewish War* (3, 8, 5) and in his *Antiquities of the Jews* (18, 1, 3) that reincarnation was taught widely in his day, while his contemporary in Alexandria, Philo Judaeus, in various of his writings, also refers to reimbodiment in one or another form. Moreover, there are passages of the New Testament that can be understood only if seen against the background of pre-existence of souls as a generally held belief. For instance, *Matthew* (16:13-14) records that when Jesus asked his disciples "Whom do men say that I am?" they replied that some people said he was John the Baptist (who had been executed only a few years before the question was asked). Others thought he was Elijah, or Jeremiah, or another of the prophets. Later in *Matthew* (17:13), far from rejecting the concept of rebirth Jesus tells his disciples that John the Baptist was Elijah.

"John (9:2-4) reports that the disciples asked Jesus whether a blind man had sinned or his parents that he had been *born* blind. Jesus replied that it was in order that the works of God may be made manifest in the blind man, that is, that the law of cause and effect might be fulfilled. Or, as St. Paul phrased the thought: we reap what we sow. The blind man could not have sown the seeds of his blindness in his present body, but must have done so in a previous lifetime."

Paradigms

Merriam-Webster's Unabridged Dictionary says a paradigm is "a philosophical and theoretical framework of a scientific school or discipline within which theories, laws, and generalizations and the experiments performed in support of them are formulated." In other words, it's how we think things are supposed to be, based on experience and/or beliefs. Paradigms are not cast in stone. The principles upon which they are formulated often change. It's rare to find a paradigm that can stand the test of time.

When we were children, our parents taught us patterns of behavior based upon that which they were taught and upon that which they had learned yet even at that, they often taught us less than the whole truth. Sometimes that was because it was a way to keep us "safe." "Don't ever cross that street" gives way as we get older to "go wherever you want to go but be safe."

During my obstetrics and gynecology training, I had a fourteen years old girl come to the clinic because she was sure she was pregnant. I asked her if she had ever had sexual intercourse and the answer was "yes." I then asked her if she was using any form of birth control and again the answer was "yes, the pill." I then asked if she had missed any of her periods and the answer was "no." I then asked if she had ever gone a day without taking the pill and the answer was "no."

At that point, curiosity was getting the best of me so I had to ask the obvious "Why do you think you're pregnant?" Her reply was "I didn't take it on time."

"What time did you take it?"

"7:30 a.m."

"What time do you normally take it?"

"7:00 a.m."

The physician who had prescribed her birth control pills had told her that if she had sex and did not take the pill at 7:00 a.m. every day, she would become pregnant.

I had an opportunity to have a long talk with her about several things that morning. The physician that had prescribed her the medicine had done her a tremendous favor but he had also lied to her in the process. Much of what we are taught as children is based on myth.

I remember being in my high school gymnasium listening to a speaker tell us that by 1985 we would no longer be able to raise enough food to feed us. As we mature, we have the opportunity to learn that the stove is not always hot, that sometimes it's safe to cross the street, and that not eating everything on our plate won't affect starving children in Africa. We learn that our parents did/do not have all the answers. We learn to put aside paradigms that have not served us well.

When I went to medical school, I will always remember the speech the dean of the college gave us on our first day. He said that ten years from then, one-third of what we would be taught would be proven to be false; another third would be proven to be of questionable value; and another third would be of value. He said our challenge would be to figure out the difference. All these years later, I've discovered that he was correct. Times change. Paradigms change. We all remember when margarine was good and butter was bad. When I was much younger tobacco ads said that smoking was good for our health.

When I turned fifty, I decided that I needed to stop and analyze my life. I had accomplished much more than I ever imagined but I'd also suffered mightily along the way. The previous year, my wife of eighteen years had developed colon cancer and had passed on. I'd like to blame her death on a fondness for cigarettes that she had developed a few years earlier but I'm not sure that caused it. Needless to say, we had different views on how to remain healthy. I think cancer is perhaps more a spiritual disease than a physical disease.

I was raised in a very fundamentalist Christian religion and thought I needed a change. I met a very nice woman who introduced me to a few other churches but the more I studied the more it felt like I was being taught the teachings of men mingled with scripture. Truth has a familiar ring to it. Some of what I heard had that "ring" but a lot of what I heard didn't. Eventually, she chose to embrace the Pentecostal faith, I didn't.

For awhile I floundered as I tried to start over. I didn't know which part of the paradigms with which I was raised were worth keeping and which needed to be discarded and it made me wishy-washy and luke warm. Fervent prayer and meditation seemed to be the answer.

Slowly, piece by piece I reassembled a system of beliefs upon which I would base the rest of my life. The process continues. The important thing is that I'm now open to truth that has existed outside of those paradigms which had sustained and in some ways harmed me up until then.

Don't get me wrong, I am definitely still a Christian. If that offends some of you, then that's your paradigm but it's not mine. That doesn't, however, mean I don't look for truth wherever it exists even if it's in a far Eastern religion or in some other religious sect.

When I graduated from high school, I was set on becoming an attorney. The thought of that now makes me shudder. Fate intervened as did the war in Vietnam. I joined the Air Force ROTC program and scored very high on the aptitude test for flying. When I graduated with a degree in Political Science, I went immediately into the Air Force as a pilot. Thirteen years later I emerged and went to medical school.

What happened? For me, paradigms had changed. Perhaps somewhere along the way I had learned to listen to my heart. I no longer believe in coincidences. I look for them in my life. I look for soul recognition in those chance meetings with others. Things happen for a reason.

As for my journey, I ended up at the only osteopathic medical school that taught what I was looking for when I sent out to become a physician. It wasn't so much the school but the fact that they allowed Jim Jealous, DO to come in one weekend a month, along with a group of committed physicians, to teach the students that which he knew about intuitive craniosacral osteopathic medicine.

Since then, it has been my patients who have taught me and I've tried to listen and learn the lessons they bring to me. I've learned a lot and seen and experienced far more than most osteopathic physicians have or will ever experience but there's more.

The saying goes that when the student is ready, the teacher will appear. Usually that teacher is a patient. As the years have gone by, the lessons have gone from the physical realm to the spiritual realm. I've learned that the spiritual is more real than the physical and that if one or the other is ignored, the patient suffers. Still, not everyone is "cured." That bothers me.

As I said, I'm a Christian so I look for scriptural references to help me when I get stuck. When I was growing up, the predominant belief was that the Bible was the "word of God". It was translated correctly and was infallible. The problem is that nowadays there are many different translations of the Bible, all of which claim to be correct yet all say things differently. We also know that there was a time when forty-three different texts were just thrown out in an effort to put the Bible together in a "palatable" form. The Dead Sea and Nag Hammadi texts (discovered in December 1945 near Nag Hammadi in Upper Egypt, this collection of 13 ancient codices dating from AD 390 contains the "Gnostic Gospels") contain more information. When the vaults of the Vatican are eventually opened, who knows how our paradigms will have to change to accommodate the truth contained therein.

What about truth contained in the other major religions of the world? What about books such as the Sefer Yetzirah? What about the Koran? What about the Book of Mormon? What about the Tanakh, Kabbalah, and Talmud? What about the four Vedas? I've only just scratched the surface but all of these teach truth. The problem is that some of these will evoke conditioned responses based on the paradigms you have adopted.

Do you really want to know the truth or do you just want to feel warm and fuzzy about what you already believe? That's an important question. Much of what I will write in this book will never have been written about before and will be from my own personal experience with healing. The bottom line is, however, it is still truth.

Today, a young boy came to my office. His mom brought him to me on the recommendation of a friend whose son I had also treated. Her son was in relatively good physical shape but energetically he was shutdown. His spirit and body were not interfacing well. There was a huge strain in the middle of his chest that was very old, i.e., older than he. I treated him osteopathically and then treated him energetically but the strain persisted. I then went into the strain and examined it. It was obvious that if I left it untreated he would eventually develop heart disease and die so I treated the strain. It was like grabbing hold of a live electrical wire and just holding on. I shook as blast after blast rocked my body. Sweat poured down my chest and back but eventually it released and his spirit and body were able to mesh.

This was the first time I'd treated this boy. His mom sat in the room witnessing the event. When I was done she said she had no idea what she had just witnessed. I referred her to the third edition of this book. I didn't tell her she had just witnessed a miracle. Perhaps she thought I was nuts. I didn't tell her about his heart. There was no longer a need to do so.

A year ago, I would not have looked for that lesion. A year ago, I was not willing to admit the possibility of past lives let alone go looking for remnants of injuries sustained while living them. For years I've listened to patients talk about past lives (reincarnation) but since it didn't fit the paradigms I believed in, I just didn't go there mentally or when I was treating. For years while examining patients I've been aware of injuries that seemed older than the patient but did not look for their origin. I stopped with this life. My results were good because the vast majority of lesions come from this life and I was willing to accept the "few that got away."

The problem I have is that I believe I ought to be able to treat all lesions because I believe Christ when he said "Truly, truly, I say to you, he who believes in me, the works that I do shall he do also; **and greater works than these shall he do…**" (John 14:12) Does that make me an egomaniac? No. It means I believe. It means that through the years I have gone from wanting to believe (not just on Sunday) to believing. Paradigms change.

10

The Cranial Rhythmic Impulse

"Where there is great love, there are always miracles." (Willa Cather)

In the book <u>Siddhartha</u> by Herman Hesse, Siddhartha travels from one extreme to another in his search for inner peace and knowledge, eventually finding what he has been looking for as a ferryman who learns and gains knowledge from the river with which he constantly interacts. As the river did for Siddhartha, I am constantly amazed by what the body is able to teach me; seldom has a day gone by that I haven't learned something new.

In medical school, we learned to examine the inside of our patient's eyes with an ophthalmoscope to see the pulsations of the arteries inside the eye. We can see the effects of atherosclerotic plaques and know that some of the arteries have hardened. Those who develop skills in "funduscopic" examination can know many other things.

Cardiologists are noted for their skill in listening to the heart and knowing what the different sounds mean. Gastroenterologists can feel an abdomen and know if a liver or spleen is enlarged. Whole books are written on the external manifestations of internal disease. Not all physicians develop the same skills in each of these areas. To do so would be an astronomical feat.

In osteopathic medicine, we are taught about the most basic "motions" in the body. Nevertheless, while the knowledge can be taught, the skill in feeling the motions cannot. It appears, however, to be a gift that can be cultivated.

The most basic motion that is displayed by all of the body's tissues is the cranial rhythmic impulse. It is simply a marvelous manifestation of the interaction between the spirit and the body. This motion permeates every tissue and fluid of the body. None are exempt, all are included. This motion fluctuates about eight to fourteen cycles per minute when a person is healthy, and it feels much as though the tissues and fluids are breathing. This fluctuation can be faster or slower if a person is not well. Not only does it fluctuate, but variations can also appear in the intensity, amplitude, tone, force, or strength of the cranial rhythmic impulse. In addition, there are many other qualities to this motion, which go beyond our normal senses.

Sarah was one of the most rewarding, yet sad cases I have experienced. She was about eighteen months old when she came into my life. Her mother was one of my patients. I still remember the telephone call. Her mom said that she wanted me to treat her daughter but there were a few things I needed to know. Sarah had been brain dead for the past nine months. She had been born with the inability to properly metabolize calcium. She was dying.

There was nothing anybody could do for her, but her mom was looking for a miracle. It was not the standard miracle that you would expect. Sarah appeared to be in terrible pain. She would constantly grind her teeth together and would screech all night long. She was being fed through a tube that was placed through her nose and then down her throat and into her stomach. She was totally unresponsive to those around her. Her mom wanted Sarah to be comfortable during her last few months of life.

The first time I saw the child, my heart went out to her. She was in such agony. Her mechanism was terrible. There was no harmony in her system. She was so small that I could almost cover her with my two hands. I placed one hand under her sacrum and the other under her head and waited for something to happen.

Sometimes, it is not what you do but what you don't do that is most important in treating someone. I once heard Roland Becker, D.O., talk on his "water bug" theory of treating. This principle proposes that it's sometimes best to just sit back and watch the "mechanism" without being judgmental of what it's doing. Don't try to make it move one way or the other, just watch it, and see what will happen. I decided that perhaps this would be the best approach. Sarah certainly did not need me intruding into her body. She needed relief and compassion.

For about thirty minutes I just observed the turmoil in her body as only someone who can feel the cranial rhythmic impulse and the other energies associated with the body can do. Nevertheless, gradually a change started to take place and her entire body relaxed and softened. She smiled and fell asleep. The change was profound.

There is a difference between being in a coma and being asleep and there is a difference between brain dead and being in a coma. Sarah was brain dead. Her body's tissues and her soul were in agony. Eventually, I felt the cranial rhythmic impulse expand and contract and then I felt the "tide" flow through her.

The "tide" is not the cranial rhythmic impulse. It is a very significant and powerful force that exists independent of the body, permeating everything. Others have called it the "breath of life." It fluctuates much as the ocean's tide but it fluctuates and cycles about every minute and a half.

That evening, Sarah started taking food by mouth for the first time in six months. She stopped grinding her teeth immediately after the treatment, and she stopped screeching during the night.

I wish I could say that she fully recovered brain function and is doing well today, but I can't. Four months after the treatment, her mother called to tell me that Sarah had passed on. She appeared to be at peace throughout that period and her mother was grateful.

I used to be almost embarrassed when discussing the cranial rhythmic impulse, or the mechanism, with others. Very few patients are aware of it and even fewer physicians know about it, but the information relayed by the body's subtle energy fields can surpass what is gained by any test or imaging process such as x-rays, MRI, etc. With time, I have reached the point where the self-doubts I used to have about these impulses and energies have vanished. They exist. They are real and powerful. I say powerful because they can be used to diagnose and also to treat. Remember, we are spiritual beings having a physical experience. Dealing with the mechanism is dealing with the energetic/spiritual being directly.

Those who doubt the existence of the mechanism are on "solid ground" because scientists only believe in that which they can quantify. Presently, we don't have the technology to measure these energies. But, that doesn't mean they aren't real.

Like Sarah, I had treated Liz's father and that is how she came to me. This little girl was four months old and was still at birth weight. Of a four-ounce feeding, she would throw up about three-and-a-half ounces.

Since we live in the Indianapolis area, she was seen at the I.U. Medical Center's Riley Hospital for Children. After four months of tests and a battery of physicians, her parents decided to "try something else." They took her out of the hospital and brought her to me.

I must say that I enjoy working on children. They are so pure and innocent. Their mechanisms are fantastic to work on. The flow of their cranial rhythmic impulse and associated energies, when they are working, are incredible.

When I examined her, I noted that her cranial rhythmic impulse was not working as it should and there was a major restriction in her pleural diaphragm (the area in the uppermost part of her abdomen). Other than that, she really was not too bad.

Once I was able to release her diaphragm, it was just a matter of running the mechanism back and forth through her body until her tissues relaxed and the mechanism came to its full potency. To me, it feels a lot like sitting in a bathtub and then scooting forward and backward until a big wave is formed. When you stop, the wave keeps going...

To those experienced with working with these energies, it makes sense. As I mentioned earlier, the cranial rhythmic impulse and the mechanism have different qualities by which they can be evaluated. When all of these qualities are added together and appraised as one unit, the sum is called "potency."

I have seen many interesting phenomena associated with the potency of the mechanism, but I do not think I have come anywhere near seeing a limit to its power. I have heard stories of wonderful healings that inspire me to continue my studies.

As for Liz, once she reached her full potency, I gave her back to her parents and asked them to call me the next day. I also told them to bring her back in a week.

The next day they called and said she'd had seven bowel movements in the first hour after the treatment. They thought she was never going to quit! More importantly, they fed her a half-hour after the treatment and she kept it all down.

They returned in a week and said she had kept all her feedings down during that period. A recheck of her mechanism showed a slight tightening of her diaphragm, which released readily. Furthermore, her mechanism was doing quite well. I again treated her and told her parents to bring her back if she started spitting up again.

A month later, her grandparents rushed her in and said that she had thrown up. I think it was more that they overfed her, but it was nice to see Liz again and treat her. The propensity for her diaphragm to tighten was gone and she was doing fine. That was over ten years ago and I have not seen her since, but reports indicate that she is a normal, healthy little girl.

Several years ago, one of my daughters gave birth to my 5th grandchild. He too was having trouble and was throwing up his feedings. His physician wanted to operate. My daughter thought differently and flew with him from Arizona to Indianapolis so I could treat him. Immediately after being treated, he stopped throwing up and started gaining weight. The amazing thing is that when she returned my grandson to Arizona, his physician still wanted to operate even though nothing was now wrong! Incredible! His rationale was that unless he operated, he couldn't be sure things were okay. She told the physician that he should have his head operated on to see if something was wrong with him.

One of the major complaints I have with medicine is that it fails to acknowledge that there is a force emanating from within the body, which is very significant. I choose to call this force the spirit while others may want to call it the soul. Furthermore, I do not believe that the spirit resides passively within the body during its mortal life.

Our spirits, like our bodies, can become diseased. They, just as the body, need to be nurtured, exercised, and fed good things. If your body wallows in filth, it becomes dirty and prone to disease. If your spirit is immersed in filth, environmental or otherwise, it will be affected.

Additionally, if your spirit struggles with faulty paradigms or beliefs too long, it can become ill and once the spirit becomes "ill" the body follows. If the spirit becomes ill, your body's health will be affected. It is just that simple. There are lots of things that affect our spirits for good or bad.

Our spirits "know" even if our conscious mind does not remember. I call that "soul recognition" though others have a different meaning for that phrase. I've heard Gregg Braden say that the difference between the angels in heaven and us is that they remember. Sometimes we remember.

From what I have observed, patterns form first in the subtle and not so subtle energies of the body. Though the spirit is included in these "energies," it is not limited to the spirit. The tissues flow into the mold set by those energies. It is vital that we guard ourselves from anything that will influence how our own energy patterns are influenced. That includes among other things, who we associate with, what we read, what we eat, and most importantly, what thoughts, feelings, and emotions we have about others and ourselves. Sometimes those thoughts, feelings, and emotions are based on beliefs or paradigms that we were taught by our families or they are based on cultural beliefs. When what we do or who we feel we are conflicts with that which our family or culture says we should do or be, disease often results.

As I said earlier, have you ever been around someone who makes you feel so good you want to just stay in his or her presence and bask in the feeling? Have you ever been in the presence of someone who is so bad that you cannot wait to get away from them because you feel they are draining your body's energies? We all have. That is not a "body" experience. It is a "spirit" experience. Unfortunately, things are not always so "black and white." We need to pattern our lives to optimize our good experiences. It is not easy.

We are not just bodies. We are not just spirits. We are a combination of the two. Some will say that we exist as mind/body/spirit but I do not agree. I think the brain, a unique organ in the body, is a major part of the interface between the "conscious" spirit and the body, i.e., we exist as a duality. Each affects the other and is dependent on the other for its well-being. Shouldn't a physician treat you as both a physical and a spiritual being?

I wish I could say that I am always successful in treating patients on all levels. The truth is that I am not. Sometimes I forget. To be very effective, the patient has to be involved. Unfortunately and all too often it is extremely difficult to get the patient to be an active participant in the process. Most patients never think of themselves as being spiritual and if they do, it's fleeting. "Give me a pill" is what they say or at least what they think.

I once had a fellow physician call and ask me to treat one of her patients for free. The patient was out of work and had no insurance and could not afford my fees but definitely needed my skill according to his physician. The fellow had been working when a crate that weighed a ton had fallen on his head and he was in a lot of pain.

When I first examined this fellow, I noticed that he had the sole of one shoe built up to where it was three inches thicker than the other shoe. He said his body was experiencing intense pain and that he had intractable headaches.

I had him remove his shoes and examined his legs and body. He was indeed bent. He had no energetic midline. His pelvis was bent. One leg appeared to be three inches longer than the other.

Within a few treatments, I had him wearing normal shoes with only a quarter-inch heel lift in one shoe. His headaches were almost gone and those that he did have were of much shorter duration and a lot less intense. What happened next surprised me, i.e., he called and canceled further treatments.

Why would someone in such debilitating pain; that was receiving treatments at no cost to him; that was getting better, stop being treated? I told you, I forgot to treat the whole person. He was dependent on his disability checks and I was threatening his livelihood.

11

Choosing a Physician

"To a man with a hammer, everything looks like a nail." (Mark Twain)

Hardly a day goes by that I don't see someone who has been told by another physician they don't know what's wrong with them, and they'll just have to live with whatever problem they're experiencing. Some patients have seen 50 or more doctors and some have been to famous medical clinics. The patient knows something is wrong but their doctor either thinks it's all in their head or doesn't know what else to do.

To be honest, I do not think anyone has all the truth when it comes to healing people. I certainly don't, but I believe that in the medical community, osteopathic and allopathic physicians who treat "osteopathically," and who have received osteopathic training in cranial, have something to offer which exceeds anything else being offered today in the "medical community."

Going to an osteopathic physician is not the answer to everything, but it should at least tell you that the physician is not only skilled in diagnosis comparable to a MD but possibly also has additional skills and knowledge.

Whatever type of physician you choose; the important thing to remember is that healing comes from within. There are exceptions but generally, patients heal themselves. Physicians as a group are only facilitators (I say group because there are a few who are also "healers") of that which is very powerful within each of our patients. We, as health care professionals, merely help the patient along the path toward their maximum health. With few exceptions, it is wrong to accept the credit for what happens, good or bad, to the patient. One of those exceptions is where the physician was not paying attention or was not skilled enough to realize what was happening, and they "jammed" the cranial rhythmic impulse or the mechanism and made the person worse.

I remember attending my first Sutherland Cranial Teaching Foundation (S.C.T.F) basic course. A physician who had been in practice in California for more than two years was paired up with me. We were at a treatment table, and he was holding my head. I started to feel bad and got a terrible headache. I asked the table trainer to examine me and see what was going on. It turned out that the physician who was treating me was feeling his own cranial rhythmic impulse and was treating me according to what he was feeling in himself. This was not what I needed. As a result, he had jammed my "mechanism." Unfortunately, this has happened to me at just about every course I have attended.

Additionally, it is possible to have someone "jam" your mechanism without even touching you. Strong energy patterns can play havoc with the mechanism. I have trouble just sitting in a lecture at the "advanced" courses because the thought patterns are so strong in the room that I get a headache. Normally, I almost never get a headache unless I get one from a patient and then I can usually get rid of it by simply taking my hands off the patient. It's an "empathic" thing that I have to deal with that is somewhat unique to me. Nevertheless, the point I am trying to make to you is that you need to make certain the person who is treating you is skilled in what he or she is doing. It takes years of practice and, even then, the physician may not be completely skilled. It is easy enough to simply ask your doctor if he or she has ever attended a cranial course sponsored by either the S.C.T.F or the Cranial Academy. That does not guarantee that they know what they are doing but it is a start.

Several years ago, the Cranial Academy started offering certification in "cranial" to those who pass their proficiency exam. If your doctor has been certified, that is a good sign. The Sutherland Cranial Teaching Foundation and the Cranial Academy are the only officially sanctioned bodies for teaching craniosacral manipulative medicine.

Even if they are "certified" and have attended officially sanctioned courses, there is no guarantee. Having said that, I am not "certified" by the Cranial Academy. Until recently, I have chosen not to submit myself to any certification process other than the national medical boards. I have certain hermit-like tendencies. I know what I am capable of, and I do not need a proficiency exam or a certification to make myself feel warm and fuzzy about it. It goes beyond that, however. Being board certified would not mean that I am any more qualified to do what I do and it would not affect how I practice medicine. Unfortunately, it would however lower my malpractice insurance rates and it would allow me to once again teach at osteopathic colleges.

Since there is no "board" for what I do in my practice, to become "board certified" would mean that I have to become board certified in another specialty to gain those benefits. It might make my life a little easier in the future but even that is doubtful. It is all part of the game that I do not and choose not to play. Additionally, part of my hesitancy is that I don't like being around physicians. Go figure…

Having said all that, about a year ago, I started the process to become board certified in neuromusculoskeletal medicine. I lost a lot of sleep and my soul was not happy with the decision. Essentially, my heart was not in it and I ended up writing a letter to the board and withdrawing my application. They do a good job of doing what they do but it is a long way from what I do.

One of the toughest things I have to deal with is the name "cranial" or "craniosacral treatment." Just as osteopathy is a terrible name for the medicine I practice, those names are extremely inaccurate when it comes to describing what I do in my practice. It is far more suited to what therapists do.

That brings me back to trying to put a name on that which I do in the practice of medicine. At one time, I tried to come up with a name. I must admit my favorite title is "osteopathic physician" and at one time it sufficed, but nowadays everyone has to have a specialty. I do not know who made up that rule but if I tell someone I am an osteopathic physician, I have yet to find someone who did not ask for my specialty. In my search for a proper name, I settled on osteopathic neuromusculoskeletal medicine. It was general enough to be somewhat vague but specific enough to give an idea that I worked pretty much with the body but still included that fact that I am an osteopath. Within a few weeks of settling on that name, the national osteopathic folks published that they were changing the name of osteopathic manipulative medicine to osteopathic neuromusculoskeletal medicine. That pretty well squelched my desire to use that description.

Presently, I say that I practice osteopathic bioenergetic medicine. The description works well, but if I am pressed further, I just say I am a healer.

No matter what you call it, the bottom line is that you need to be careful and you need to listen to your intuition when it is time to find a doctor. Training and experience matter.

12

My Practice

"Work like you don't need the money,
Love like you'll never get hurt,
Dance like no one's watching,
Sing like no one's listening,
And live every day as if it were your last."
(Unknown)

"Pythagoras said that the most divine art was that of healing. And if the healing art is most divine, it must occupt itself with the soul as well as the body; for no creature can be sound so long as the higher part in it is sickly." (Apollonius to Tyana)

As I said in the last chapter, I now say I specialize in "osteopathic bioenergetic medicine" when asked what my specialty is. Is that the whole truth? No. The difficult part is in getting to the whole truth. I remember going to my initial courses in "cranial." The techniques taught were all very mechanical in nature. They did not require intuition or instinct. These courses were designed so that anyone could be taught about "cranial."

Basic instruction involves a lot of anatomy. It also involves lengthy discussions on how each of the bones in the cranium (head) move within its own sphere of influence. Even the "advanced" courses go on and on discussing how the bones move. The advanced courses also include the movement of other tissues but even those are basic. Patterns are named and if you want to become certified in cranial, you have to be able to name the patterns.

Andrew Weil, MD, rose to fame by writing the book "Spontaneous Healing." The first chapter of that book is about Robert Fulford, D.O., who taught him about wholistic medicine. Many years ago, after corresponding with Dr. Fulford for about a year, he invited me to his home in Ohio. Dr. Fulford was quite aged at that time. I spent a day conversing one on one with him about osteopathic medicine. At one point, I asked why he was no longer associated with the Sutherland Cranial Teaching Foundation (S.C.T.F) on an active basis. His reply was most interesting. Essentially, he had gone beyond that which they were willing to acknowledge existed. He felt that he had his own path to follow. I know what he meant. I too feel that my path is not the common one. Perhaps that is because I am not willing to accept only what I have been taught.

I remember being taught that if I am doing a myofascial release that I should not allow the tissues to backtrack along the path they just took. On the other hand, we were also taught that the body has an inherent wisdom and knows how to heal itself. If the latter is true and the tissues want to backtrack, then shouldn't we allow them to backtrack? Of course, we should. The whole secret is to listen to the tissues and then allow the inherent wisdom to manifest itself for health. I was also told that once our patient reaches a still point, the treatment is done. That just does not make sense to me. Treat until the mechanism says to quit. A still point has little or nothing to do with when a treatment is complete.

A syndrome that I have named occurs in the "cranial community." I call it the "just kidding" syndrome. The basics behind this are that we are taught that the bones in the cranium move in certain patterns and when things go wrong, they are always in certain patterns that can be named. It is all very tidy. The problem is that the bones in the head do not always move that way; in fact, quite often they don't move that way. We go to great lengths to teach and critique each other on something that is a fallacy. I just don't get it and never will. I figure they are "just kidding."

Furthermore, experienced physicians all know that the act of simply acknowledging that a pattern exists starts the process of healing that pattern so that once it's named, it no longer exists. It's like taking a picture of a person who is running and saying that is what the person looks like all the time. But, the reality is that a fraction of a second later, the picture is totally different. Life is motion! We should be less involved with naming patterns and more involved with recognizing health.

A while ago, at one of the advanced courses held each fall at the University of New England, College of Osteopathic Medicine, Dr. Jealous distributed a handout titled "The Other Pair of Hands." It is mentioned later in this book. The introduction of that document caused quite a stir among some of the "rank and file" in attendance.

I have to admit that there were times in my training that I really wondered what Dr. Jealous was talking about, but I never doubted his sincerity. Even when I thought he had flown over the rainbow, his sincerity made me think and indeed consider that perhaps I was the one on the wrong side of the rainbow. I firmly believe that Dr. Jealous is one of the foremost authorities on craniosacral osteopathic medicine alive today. Having said that, I am not sure I have done him a service in so saying since he now teaches courses in "Biodynamics." I think he too has found that traditional names are lacking and too restrictive. He is a healer.

Indeed, each of us left the "path" a long time ago. We now walk separate paths. I have not talked to him in years, but I will always be grateful to him for introducing me to the journey.

We both used to call what we do "cranial." Too many other people, however, use the same term to describe something a whole lot different from that which we do. It would be like saying a butterfly and a caterpillar are the same. The origin is the same but the shape, grandeur and capabilities of the butterfly dwarf the caterpillar. With that metamorphosis a lot has changed in my life and in my practice of medicine and I'm sure it has changed for Dr. Jealous as well.

Most of the people who come to me for treatment are referred by word of mouth. Because of this, there is usually some preconceived notion as to what they will experience. Sometimes the person referring them will go into great detail about what I do. They may even talk about personal things they know about me. No matter what the new patient has been told, each person has individual needs and will experience the treatment differently.

I have tried to make my practice as comfortable as possible for both my patients and myself. When compared to most medical practices, the pace is slow but it affords me the time needed to do what I feel needs to be done. I do not like to rush. The "mechanism" does not like to be rushed either.

I like to have music playing, but it's not easy to find music to treat by. What works for one person may not be suitable for another. Sometimes one selection will ruin the whole CD. On an average, I go through about eight CDs for every one I keep. Occasionally, I will play Native American flute music or violin music by Drew Tretick. I love Enya's music as well.

I always tell new patients to wear comfortable clothing. Jeans are very hard to treat through and hurt my fingers if I have to work on the sacroiliac joints. Tight clothing restricts the motion of the tissues. Generally, it's smart to just wear one or two thin layers of clothing. Some of my colleagues have their patients disrobe or change to gowns, but I don't. I find most people are uncomfortable when they do this, and I need them to be comfortable during the treatment.

Working in Maine was a good experience. There, people have learned to wear layers of clothing to keep warm. Even in the dead of winter, they may not wear a coat if they have enough shirts on. Because they wear so many clothes, they often become uneasy when they get down to just two or three layers. As a result, I learned to treat through several thicknesses of clothing.

Many years ago, I moved my office to a location in Zionsville, Indiana. It is a great area. When I first found the office, it "felt" strange. A friend suggested she "smudge" the office. I had never heard of this but decided it could not hurt anything. She lit some sage, blew it out, and then walked through the entire space moving her arms in circles as the smoke lightly filled the office.

This is a ritual used by Native Americans to dispel evil spirits and entities. It works. The actual procedure involves going to each corner of the room and then moving the sage in circles from high to low and then going to the middle of the room and doing the same. This is repeated in each room. It's not necessary to have "thick" smoke.

I recently moved to a larger office in the same building and had to go through the same process all over again. My patients initially commented that the space did not feel the same. It took three months to get the space to vibrate right.

As I mentioned earlier, I have a patient who is a wonderful woman in her 80's, who came to me when another D.O. left town. She suffered from Trigeminal Neuralgia which made her face feel like it was on fire. I helped put the fire out. She has expressed her gratitude by painting Southwestern theme pictures for me. They hang all over my office.

One day she said she wanted to make a painting of me so she brought in her camera and took several photos. A while later she brought in a painting of me dressed like a Native American shaman kneeling over a fire (see the back cover). I am wearing a headdress made from the skins of a coyote. I told her I didn't remember wearing that to the office that day. She just laughed and said that is how she sees me. I like it a lot.

I have added several Native American pieces to the overall décor so that my office definitely has a Southwestern flavor. The bottom line is it feels good to me and to my patients.

My patients supplied the final changes. When good people frequent a place, their energies rub off and leave a flavor behind. Gregg Braden talks about an experiment that was done where photons were examined in a vacuum to see how they were arranged. As was expected, they were arranged at random. Then some human DNA was introduced into the vacuum and the photons arranged themselves in concert with the DNA. When the DNA was removed, the pattern remained. What this demonstrates is that what we are influences everything and everyone. Those affects remains even when we are no longer in the vicinity. Theoretically, the influence could be world wide.

Since some people like to bring a friend when they are being treated, there is a chair in my treatment room for the friend to sit on. Because of the negative feelings emanating from some of them, I have only had to ask a visitor to leave on a couple of occasions. Sometimes, not because of negative feelings but because of the strong intent of the visitor, I will have them move to the opposite side of the room from where I am sitting.

Unless little children are being treated, I discourage bringing them along. They usually interfere with the quality of the treatment as their presence affects my concentration and distracts the patient.

I dress very casually, as do most physicians who do manipulative medicine and have lately taken to wearing blue jeans, my cowboy boots, and a shirt. If I'm comfortable, I think I do better work. When I'm not working, I usually wear T-shirts or sleeveless T-shirts and have joked that someday I may wear those to the office instead.

From time to time, especially when I used to see patients in the hospital, a patient would ask if I was a doctor. The hospital actually gave me a white lab coat with my name embroidered on it in an effort to improve my "professional image," but I have never worn it. It used to hang in the back of my closet at home. Occasionally, one of my kids would bring it out and ask to wear it for Halloween. Somehow, that seemed appropriate. I tried to find it the other day and it was gone. I do not know how long it has been gone. I figure it is a sign that things have indeed changed.

13

The Treatment

"Healing is something that passes through us." (RCB)

A new prospective patient called me two days ago. It wasn't the first time she had called. She called about two months ago. She doesn't have a clue as to what I do but people keep telling her to come to me for treatment. She really wants to know if I do "cranial." That's what she wants. She set up an appointment but still had no idea what she was doing. She actually asked me to describe what I do in a few brief sentences. That's impossible.

When I first examine and treat a patient, there are always questions asked concerning the type of medicine I practice. It is difficult to describe exactly what happens during a treatment. The traditional medical approach is to take a history and then examine the patient. As I understand more and more about the mechanism, it is less important to get that history first. In fact, it may be detrimental, predisposing me to a particular judgment or diagnosis.

In terms of "traditional medicine" most medical diagnoses are bogus. By that I mean that they are little more than a description of symptoms and may have little to do with the root cause. If given improperly, they can markedly affect the ability of a patient to recover. With that in mind, I try to avoid making a diagnosis until I've had a chance to feel the patient and sense what is going on. Even after doing that, I may still be reticent to make a diagnosis other than at a very rudimentary level.

There are arguments to be made for either way of running an initial examination. Sometimes it's better to take a history at first and at other times it's better to jump right in and ask questions as the treatment unfolds. I tend to bounce back and forth, and then let my instincts take over to help me decide what I need to do.

I play a dual role as physician/healer; the physician part of me does need the history. The healer part of me does not need the history.

My examination of a patient on both levels starts the moment I first see them. It goes beyond what I see, however, and includes what I feel or perceive. I watch patients as they walk to my treatment room. I also watch the way they take off their shoes and empty their pockets. I listen to how they talk about what is afflicting them.

Sometimes we talk briefly. Sometimes a patient wants to talk at depth. I know what I am good at and that is using my hands. It's hard to stop myself from hastening the "talking" along so I can get to what I feel the patient came for, but I know that sometimes "talking" is the most important part of the treatment. Most patients have been to several physicians and they may have been to one or more of the major medical clinics. Remember, most patients do not come to me first.

If they talk too long, it may mean that the patient will have to come back another time but that is okay. As I said, sometimes it is important to let the patient talk even though it slows the process down; the patient is still being treated, albeit at another level.

At a medical course I just attended, I was standing at the back of the room talking to a medical resident who was also in attendance. At the middle of the room, the course instructors were examining another physician as they demonstrated how they evaluate a patient. I turned to the resident and asked him to sense the "patient" and tell me what he sensed. He wasn't quite sure what I was asking so I repeated the request. He then said that he sensed that the "patient" was "dying faster than anyone else in the room." It was an excellent observation so I asked him what he meant. He reiterated that he had said. He added: "That is the best answer I can give."

I then told him that his observation was correct and that I sensed that the "patient" had a major problem with his heart. He asked what I would do with that information. I told him that we had to at least offer to treat him and leave the decision to treat up to him.

Once the instructors were done demonstrating what they were doing and the "patient" was alone, we walked up to him and I asked if I could touch him and treat him. I didn't tell him why. He accepted.

I placed my right hand on his chest, over his heart, and sensed what was energetically happening within him. Without asking him any other questions, I then said "What have they done to your heart?" His answer was that he had coronary artery bypass grafting done on five major coronary vessels fifteen years earlier. I treated him until his mechanism came back to life.

Sensing our patients before we touch them is very important.

Should I have told him that he was "dying faster than anyone else in the room?" Nope. I have to be aware that if I tell the patient something that would perhaps taint his thought patterns, it might dramatically alter that which I want to happen. What we say to others cannot be taken back no matter how much we apologize.

Gregg Braden does a marvelous job of laying out the scientific research that clearly shows that our thoughts, feelings, and emotions influence everything around and within us. He describes an experiment where a person was placed in one room and some of their DNA was placed in another room. The person was shown various movies to elicit various responses. When the response elicited joy, happiness, gratitude, and love the DNA instantaneously uncoiled to expose previously unexposed binding sites. When they were exposed to the opposite emotions the DNA shortened and coiled tighter. If the DNA was moved several hundred miles away from the donor and the experiment was repeated, the same instantaneous result occurred. We must guard our thoughts for they are indeed powerful.

After the medical history has been completed, I ask the patient to either sit or lie down on their back on my treatment table. The lighting is subdued and soft music is playing. I like to work from the head, but I do not restrict myself to that area if I feel I need to be somewhere else on the body, and I often do spend most of my time somewhere else.

An unfortunate misconception with the cranial concept is that it only deals with the head. Sure, the head needs to be examined and treated but what about the rest of the body? It all has to be examined and it is, <u>even if it is not physically touched</u>. It's one of the reasons I now refer to what I do as bioenergetic medicine. Indeed, most of my patients will tell me that they feel areas, other than the head, being affected during a treatment even if I only touch the head.

I stay away from the genitals and work around rather than on the breasts, unless they have to be treated, but the bottom line is that when it comes to actually treating someone, it involves more than bones and their movement. It is also about fascia, soft tissue, muscles, fluids, and energies.

Having said that, it's important, vitally important, to "get permission" from the patient before you touch him or her. This can be verbal or implied. You might think that if someone is lying on my treatment table, he or she has "given" me permission to touch them, but that is not always the case. Their body and spirit have to be in agreement and willing to "let me in." I've placed my hands on patients and waited and waited and waited until I finally said, "Anytime you want to let me in will be fine." They will inevitably ask what I mean and I say, "When you're ready to let me work with you, let your tissues know so we can begin." That is usually all it takes.

While I'm on this subject, it's common to be treating someone and find there are areas of their body they don't want me working with. I'm not talking about erogenous zones, but rather parts or regions of the body where there is something buried in the tissues that the person doesn't want me to treat. It may be any portion of the body such as the abdomen, the mid-portion of the chest, or an ankle. It could be anywhere, but what's important is to understand we must respect the fact these areas can exist and no doctor should force their way into them.

Once I have established that it is okay for me to work on someone, there are several different ways to start. Sometimes, I check out their leg lengths or put a hand under their buttocks to feel the movement of their sacrum. I might place a hand on their abdomen or just sit and gently cradle their head between my hands.

The other day I started by simply lifting the outstretched legs of a patient. It was not what she expected so she asked what I was doing. I had to confess that I was trying to get a sense of where I should start.

I am skilled in all forms of osteopathic manipulative medicine. People come to me for many reasons. Some come because "their D.O." has moved or passed on and they want to be manipulated the way they are used to being manipulated. I try to do some "cranial" on everyone, but many times it's not as deep or extensive as I would like simply because it's not what the patient came to me for. Even William G. Sutherland, D.O., the founder of "cranial," "cracked" a neck from time to time as an adjunct to his cranial treatments. Sometimes it helps. Everyone, however, gets treated bioenergetically.

At the most basic level of a treatment, it is important to feel the tissues to see if they are moving. All of the tissues of the body should expand and contract eight to fourteen times a minute much like your chest expands and contracts when you breathe. It is also important to determine that, if the tissues are moving, they are doing it like they're supposed to.

Sometimes I find that the tissues are so tight and locked up that the inherent forces that exist within our energetic body are struggling to overcome those restrictive forces locked within the tissues. At such times, it's very efficient to simply articulate or stretch out the thoracic and lumbar spinal areas and then go back to doing a bioenergetic treatment or as I like to call it, "working on the mechanism."

Even if the tissues are not moving, it does not stop me from proceeding forward with the treatment. Often I will just make a note of the deficit and press on to see what the tissues want to do. Generally, they will unwind if I allow them to do so. If they will do that, I will follow the tissues as they unwind and see if something deeper or at another level wants to release. Rarely will it take more than thirty minutes for this to play itself out to the point where the outward tissues will start to move.

Conversely, if the tissues are okay at the start, the fluids and membranes should be examined to see if they are doing what they should. I will also examine if the "energies" are flowing through the body. Generally, I work to reestablish normal motion throughout. It's then vitally important to wait, watch, and listen to the patient's tissues and energies. Gradually a story will unfold, and with the telling I learn what I need to do to help bring all these functions into harmony, so the patient can move toward greater health. During some treatments, I never leave a patient's head. It is not imperative to do so but it is imperative that if I work from the head I make sure I treat the whole body. From time to time, I may move to the chest or abdomen or to an extremity. The reason I like working from the head is that it is easier for me to feel what is going on with the tissues when I hold the head. It is more of a straight shot. If I am treating from a leg, I have to run up to the abdomen and then backtrack to the other leg. If I treat from the head, it is a straight shot to any other part of the body.

Having said that, there is another reason I treat from the head. Many times when I am treating someone, I have to rely on what "feels right." I have spent many years treating patients. It is easier to evaluate each patient if I have a common point of reference to judge him or her by. When I change my position, I have to learn the subtle nuances associated with that new point of reference. That is not too difficult for me at this stage of my training, but for a new practitioner, it would be a lot more difficult. Sometimes I treat with my eyes closed to help me concentrate but it is not imperative.

Finally, yet importantly, I like to treat from the head because I feel that I can, for lack of a better phrase, hug their spirit or energies better. It just feels like I can get a better grip. When I treat from the head, it's like a firm handshake versus a limp-wristed handshake.

Many years ago, I became aware that I treat from my fourth (heart) chakra. When I am sitting on my treatment stool at the head of the treatment table, cradling a patient's head in my hands, their head is inches from my fourth chakra, and it is easy to tie into their subtle energy patterns and "feel" them. Depending on the intent and intensity, I may even start to vibrate if there is a turbulent pattern with which I am interacting. Over the past few years, I've noticed that since I now wear my hair fairly short, my scalp will tingle when the patient releases bursts of energy.

Through the years, I have developed the ability to sense what is out of balance in a patient without even touching them. A few years ago, I attended a course where several in attendance had developed that ability. This included those who were teaching the course. It was nice to be able to openly ask questions from the back of the room about lesions and strains that were being worked with at the front of the room without being questioned on how I knew that those lesions existed.

When I started learning "cranial," many of the instructors would walk around the room telling people to close their eyes as they treated. I tried that; sometimes it worked for me, and at other times, it did not. Sometimes it felt like I could sense more if I had my eyes open. That goes against what most would think, but it has only been during the past few years that I have started to understand why sometimes it is important to have my eyes open.

I think I see things that do not register in the visual spectrum but that register with my spiritual being and my spiritual insight. I know I am seeing something that for me and for most people is invisible and I am starting to recognize when I do that. Now, all I have to do is figure out what it is that I see. I know that sounds strange but I know it is real. It is a sense of things unseen that respond to what I am doing.

I've noticed that when I treat with my eyes closed, I'm still looking at my patient but I'm looking out through the area in the middle of my forehead. Perhaps that is what is referred to as the "third eye."

I believe we all have clairvoyant capabilities that develop when it is important to do so. Some people have a real talent for it, however. I'm getting better at it.

I have said that I do not see auras, spirit guides, spirits, or any such thing. If it is not "physical," I just do not see it. I can feel such things, but I just do not see them. Sometimes it takes several occurrences of phenomena to happen before it dawns on me to pay attention. Something is happening all the time. Perhaps I should rephrase that, i.e., something important is happening all the time. The task is to figure out what it is and how to feel/sense it.

Some patients want to see me do more than cradle their head in my hands. One patient, in particular, does not feel she has been treated unless I touch each of her arms and legs, place a hand under her sacrum, and "crack/adjust" her neck.

I humor her by doing that knowing that her overall care suffers due to the amount of time it takes to do so. I have discussed this with her but it just does not sink in. Eventually, I gave up and referred her to another health care provider who tells her the things she wants to hear.

Some of my most "powerful" treatments have been the ones where I seldom moved from the head. It is not always necessary to touch a leg to treat it. The same goes for most of the other areas. The forces within each patient tell me where to be. Having said that, remember, I don't have to treat from the head.

If a patient will be still and pay attention, they will feel the energies flow into their body. They will feel their arms and hands start to tingle and then they will feel their legs and feet do the same. It will be obvious that something is going on. Sometimes, if they keep their eyes shut, they will see "the colors." All these are obvious manifestations that something wonderful is happening and almost all of my patients now experience these things if they will be still and know.

The colors I am referring to seem to be the chakral colors. The first chakra is associated with the color red. The second is associated with the color orange and it then proceeds to yellow, green, blue, violet, and then white at the seventh or crown chakra. Sometimes these colors are faint and sometimes they are brilliant and like a kaleidoscope. The bottom line is that many of my patients actually see these colors during a treatment and the colors seen correspond to the areas being affected. Most see them when their eyes are closed but many see them even with their eyes open.

It is important to remember that the "physician within" does the treating. It goes beyond that, however. The truth is that most physicians are just facilitators. As I said before, I have a gift. Nevertheless, in very basic ways, those who do this work are like house guests. We want to help, but we have to be respectful of the person whose home we are in. Do not go where you are not invited and always say please. In other words, be on your good behavior and leave your own agenda at the doorstep. Show up prepared to learn, and you will learn more than you can process in one treatment.

The amount of force used varies from area to area. It also varies on how "stuck" an area might be. Generally, if an area is small, I will use a small amount of localized force to get something to move if it will not move by using bioenergetic techniques alone. Bear in mind, though, that if force is put into the body, I have to spend time to make sure to take it out before the patient leaves my office. Too often, patients who have been to other "health care professionals" are worse off because their tissues have been traumatized in the name of "healing."

A seminar I just attended was taught by a D.O. and a chiropractor. I was fascinated by the amount of physical force used by the latter in order to attain a correction. It also fascinated me that he never took time to take the force out of the tissues. It was plain and simply a high velocity, high amplitude approach to fixing things. When asked why his patients required so many treatments, he said he "chips away" at the problem.

Sometimes, I need to physically "crunch" or "crack" (adjust) some region that is particularly stubborn. This may be similar to what most correlate with chiropractic treatment, but as I have discussed before, it is not the same. When I have to resort to such modalities it is generally a low velocity, low amplitude approach and I generally find that it is just as effective and leaves less trauma and energy in the tissues. Quite often it looks and feels like I am stretching the patient and in fact that is probably a good description of low velocity, low amplitude manipulation.

Direct force is not always the answer. Sometimes I need to only hold an arm or leg and just run the "mechanism" through it until the tissues catch on and start moving. Sometimes a percussion hammer (a vibrator, of sorts) is used to help give me enough energy to do what needs to be done. I am learning that force is not the answer, however. As I said earlier, turning up the power is not necessarily the answer.

Robert Fulford D.O. is credited with using the percussion hammer to facilitate a treatment. I asked him if the percussion hammer enabled him to do that which he couldn't do by himself. "No" was his reply. It only helped to conserve his own energy.

Once I find something that is not correct, treating is like prayer in that I first feel within me what I want to happen within the patient and then by acknowledging that it has already happened, the change can then take place. Gregg Braden's book "The Isaiah Effect, Decoding the Lost Science of Prayer and Prophecy" goes into wonderful detail on this lost technology. I say lost because in the "West," we do not "believe" and as such, certain "technologies" are lost to us. To me, most of my treatments feel like I'm meditating. My mind is blank. I'm not contemplating anything.

In his book, Gregg Braden describes three separate instances where thought, feeling, and emotion join in an atmosphere of peace and acceptance to harness a power strong enough to possibly move mountains. The first example was mentioned earlier in this book but it bears repeating. In the first example, he describes seeing a video taken in China at a medicineless clinic. I mentioned this to a friend who said she had a copy of the video and gave it to me. The video shows a woman laying on a gurney with her abdomen exposed as an ultrasound transducer is passed over her belly much like would be done to image a baby if the woman were pregnant.

The image shows a two-inch cancerous tumor in the woman's bladder. In the room with the woman are several Qigong Chi Lel practitioners who start to chant softly in the background as the camera zooms in on the ultrasound monitor. The monitor shows a still frame of the original image of the tumor on the left half of the screen while "real-time" ultrasonography is displayed on the right half of the screen.

After about one and a half minutes, the tumor starts to vibrate and at about two minutes, it collapses like a building that has been leveled by explosives. By two and a half minutes, the bladder is normal in appearance without any residue or debris in the bladder. The practitioners then applaud.

It sounds incredible but these people expect this type of response and they achieve it. Thought, feeling, and emotion are brought into play and "miracles" happen on a daily basis. Reality changed to match their expectation. Reality changed to match what they felt had already happened.

The other two examples Mr. Braden mentions in his book involve an account he personally witnessed in which a head wound was completely healed within a few minutes by simply stroking the wound. I have heard similar stories of Native American shaman wiping away knife wounds. The third event was where he participated as a friend of his "prayed rain" during a drought and it rained that evening.

In the "West," we act as if this is sacrilege. Some even say such events are satanic. Nothing could be further from the truth.

Sometimes, while my hands are gently resting on the patient, they will start to vibrate or shake. The vibration produced is very similar to that produced by a percussion hammer. The motion is totally involuntary and can occur in one or both hands. I am not sure why they do that, but I assume it has to do with the vibration of the energy field they are in. I have heard that shaman will sometimes experience the same phenomenon.

Generally, with a release from the tissues, I will twitch. Sometimes this gets quite abrupt. Once while treating a patient, what appeared to be a bolt of lightning about one and one-half-inch thick and about two feet long, jumped out of her chest, ran down her arm, and hit me in the middle of my chest. The force threw me backward against the wall. I really thought I would see a smoldering black mark on my shirt, but there was none.

This has only happened once. I cannot explain it, but I have a colleague that witnessed a similar event many years ago. I assume that it was some form of photonic energy but I am not sure.

An interesting note is that this woman (my patient) has been struck by lightening four and one-half times. The last time was while standing in the doorway of her house. The one-half time is where it struck near her and she lost consciousness but it was not a direct strike. She says that she feels that she projects something out of her body that attracts the lightening. Perhaps that is what happened to me.

A similar event happened a little while ago. This time I was staring, for lack of a better word, into the area about twelve inches above my patient. I was concentrating on what I was feeling with my hands and senses so my vision was in "park" so to speak. I became aware that a cloud about ten inches in diameter was forming in the space I was staring into. It was similar to the distortion that appears above a hot road on a summer day. About as soon as I realized that there was something important occurring outside the body the cloud sped toward me. The blast was second only to the strike by the bolt of energy mentioned above, and it shocked the heck out of me. It also made my vision become so blurry that I could not see for about fifteen minutes.

Occasionally, those who accompany the patient will also feel what is going on and be affected. When attending my most recent "basic" course, a woman was sitting just behind and to the left of me while I was treating my table partner. At one point, the energy blast from the release from the patient hit her. She turned around. No one was there but she definitely felt as though someone had hit her in the back. Sometimes, a visitor will feel dizzy or lightheaded after just sitting in the room where I was treating someone else.

A few years ago, I received an e-mail from a massage therapist. She had been massaging one of my patients and had twitched. My patient commented, "You twitch just like Dr. Brooksby." This precipitated an e-mail she sent to me. She indicated that she was one of a few people that she knew who twitched while working on their "clients." Essentially, she thought she was accomplishing more because she twitched and that somehow it was therapeutic but that's not true. There is nothing therapeutic about twitching in response to a release of energy from the patient. It's simply an outward manifestation of that which is happening within the patient. That applies whether it is the physician responding to the release or the patient responding to the release.

Similarly, as I said a few pages back, now that I wear my hair cut short, my scalp will often tingle when a patient's energies start to flow. This will occur even if I am not touching the patient and can occur even if I am standing several feet away from the patient but it's not therapeutic.

As for the "twitch," it is actually more of a jerk. It feels and appears as though I am being shocked or had touched something very hot. Sometimes the releases are so powerful that they take their toll on me and I'm worn out by the end of a treatment. Sometimes there are rapid releases from within the patient that elicit a series of many twitches from me. Sometimes it feels like the energy I have been running into the patient has bounced back at me and there are times when I just have to just keep running the energy until I feel the release that I want even though it's uncomfortable.

Many years ago, I heard that Robert Fulford, D.O. twitched when treating patients so I wrote him and asked him if he did indeed twitch. He responded that he did not twitch but rather responded to a release from within the tissues. I wrote back and said that I too responded to a release from within the tissues. This started a long period of correspondence between the two of us which eventually led to us meeting. After his death, I attended a seminar where one of his protégés commented that he aspired to be good enough that he too would twitch. Having experienced this phenomena almost since I started medical school, I thought then and still think he was nuts.

Again, these "twitches" are more of a jerking motion. There is another type of "twitch," however, that is quite different. Sometimes one or both hand(s) will start to vibrate or shake in response to the healing forces at work within the patient. This may continue for a few seconds to many minutes. I've heard of a level of shamanism where the shaman experiences "shaky hands." I think this may be what is happening. This phenomenon is always associated with healing and is therapeutic but totally involuntary.

My job is to treat the patient and then determine the necessity of further treatments. When treating, my goal is to get their tissues working well for twenty-one days. This is based on the idea that it takes twenty-one days to form a habit and twenty-one days to break a habit. Sometimes, it is not always that easy. Not everyone who comes to see me walks out healed. Additionally, depending on how long the problem has existed and the severity of the problem, I may have them return in four days, a week, or anywhere up to eight weeks.

Most problems resolve or get substantially better within three to four treatments. Some take a lot longer and some only require one treatment. It always depends on the individual case. I have even had some "failures."

I do not like telling patients to return for another treatment. From experience, I know that most patients improve more than I thought they would. That has led me to the point where I may overestimate how much healing has taken place during any one treatment. Remember that healing can take place on several planes including the physical, emotional, energetic, and etheric (now called the quantum hologram but I like etheric). All will be affected but to what extent is unknown.

If I put the responsibility of deciding when to come back on the patient, it brings them into the process and does not allow them to be passive. If they want to get better and participate in the process, they will heal more quickly than if they were simply along for the ride. A patient has to participate. They have to feel and acknowledge that they are getting better. We are what we think we are. Once again, if a person says that they have a certain disease such as cancer or fibromyalgia; they are programming their body to have/maintain that disease. Our thoughts, feelings, and emotions are very important.

A couple of years ago, I was at a wrestling tournament and was cheering on the local high school's wrestling team and one wrestler, Tommy, a friend of the family, in particular. Tommy was doing great until the opposing wrestler performed an illegal maneuver severely injuring Tommy's knee. The match was called and Tommy won by default. He was in excruciating pain. I sat in the stands as his father worked his way out of the bleacher seats and across the floor to where the trainers were working on Tommy's knee.

My family then started in on me. They wanted me to see if I could help. I do not like to call attention to myself. When I leave work, I don't even want to think of myself as a physician, and I really didn't want to walk across the floor to interject myself, uninvited, into this extremely bad situation, but I did.

The strangest thing happened however, when I walked up to Tommy, who was lying on the floor in agony. Without a word being said, the trainers, who had him surrounded, stepped aside. Kneeling beside him, I placed my hands on his knee and continued until the inherent healing potency within him was manifest. He was then able to stand. I asked his father to bring him by my house after the meet. Later that night, I thoroughly treated him and applied arnica gel and DMSO to his knee.

Though the coach told the team that Tommy was going to be out the rest of the season, he never missed a day of practice and walked without crutches the next day. He went on to compete in the Indiana State semi-finals for high school wrestling.

A while ago, another young friend of the family injured his ankle while playing basketball. Later that day, he came to our house for dinner. After dinner, I offered to look at the injured ankle. The ankle was swollen, and black and blue.

The injury was in a place where it's very common to break the tip off a bone and all indications were that was what had happened.

I applied arnica gel and DMSO and then treated the ankle until the inherent healing potency manifested itself. I was, however, convinced that the ankle was broken and would need time to heal and wrote a prescription to have the ankle x-rayed.

I saw him at church one week later and asked how he was doing since I had not received the x-ray report. He said, "I don't know what you did but my ankle was pain free the next day and the bruising was totally gone" and he demonstrated that the ankle was healed by jumping up and down. He never got an x-ray. I was convinced it was broken but he accepted the healing. Powers were brought into play far greater than I, and he was healed. His thoughts, feelings, and emotions were focused and he believed he was healed and indeed he was.

I really didn't know he would be that well, I just knew he would be better. Once the process of healing is set in motion, phenomenal things can and often do happen. I see miracles all the time.

One last example may help drive the point home. A new patient whom I had seen for back problems, called to say that he had a broken toe and that his orthopedic surgeon wanted to operate to put screws into the toe since it appeared that healing had stopped and it would never heal without "internal fixation." He asked if I could possibly help.

I know that there are three phases of the healing process and that the most rapid phase takes place in the first six to ten days after the injury. Each of the other phases of healing takes longer and involves other aspects of the healing process. Basically, however, once the second phase, which lasts six to eight weeks, has occurred, if healing has not started, it generally will not take place, and internal fixation might be necessary. An interesting thing about "bioenergetic medicine" is that it seems to start the initial rapid phase of healing all over again.

He wanted to know if I might be able to help. I told him it would be worth trying. Two weeks later, I received a call saying that a new x-ray has shown new growth and that the toe was mending. He was happy. (Note: The toe healed within six weeks of the initial treatment after a year of no healing having taken place.)

I know some of my patients get a bit exasperated by me when I do not tell them to come back. As I said, I leave it up to them to be active participants in what I/we do. Some have figured it out and will not leave until I do schedule another appointment for them. Eventually they learn to listen to their bodies and learn to estimate how long it will be before they will need to come back.

If they do want another appointment and I didn't tell them when I want to see them again (I do tell some patients when to come back), I will ask them when they feel they will need another treatment. This is a joint effort as we both learn to be still and know.

I should also say that if the patient says that they want to come back "tomorrow" or in a few days, I will discourage it since it takes time (about three days) for what I do to run through their tissues and then it takes a few days for the tissues to respond to the treatment. That essentially means that one treatment a week is more than sufficient and even that may be too much.

14

Unwinding

"When you possess great treasures within you, and try to tell others of them, seldom are you believed." (The Alchemist, by Paulo Coelho p. 135)

Having already described the unwinding process to a small degree, I need to discuss it in more detail to keep you from misunderstanding its importance. An unwinding occurs when the body is placed in a position where it can spontaneously release that which has been held within. Normally, what needs to be released is some form of trauma or stress the body did not deal with at the time of the occurrence even if the time of the injury was extremely distant. Notice, I said trauma or stress. They are not synonymous. The bottom line is that the body has stored the effect of the incident or event in the tissues or in the subtle energies associated with the body.

For example, let's say you have received a blow to your thigh that the body didn't resolve. A bruise may or may not have formed and you may or may not have experienced pain. If this insult was not dealt with and not healed by the body, it may be stored in the tissues. When this insult is released, by whatever means, a bruise may form and you may experience pain as if you had just hurt your thigh, even if it is years or decades later.

I have seen bruises form on the face and back of a woman who had been slapped and then beaten with a belt even though this abuse happened many years earlier. Unfortunately, the pain will quite often also manifest itself.

Something else I have observed is that the physical pain of abuse is usually easier for the patient to deal with than the emotional pain. That's one of the reasons that once a person decides to sue over an injury, they have more difficulty healing because their soul/spirit is now vested in the injury. The result is that they cannot completely heal because energetically the person is not letting go of the trauma. There is no way for the tissues to complete the healing process. It is impossible.

People who have been abused as children will often have incredible emotional pain and they usually have physical pain as well. When the strain is released, it may be very traumatic for the individual. The patient may start to cry and experience many feelings including that of pain, fear, or anger. At the same time that they experience this, they may not know where it is coming from or the cause. The conscious memory of the event may not manifest itself. Great care, caution, and compassion for the patient are needed. You need to understand the importance of this if you are serious about learning how to work with the cranial rhythmic impulse and the various healing energies.

Unfortunately, the ready availability of anti-depressants makes it easy for physicians to prescribe them for these patients. Depression often goes hand in hand with such trauma. Who wouldn't be depressed? Does it require being placed on antidepressants for years on end? It shouldn't. When the spirit becomes stuck in an unhealthy pattern, medicine is not the answer. Medicines may help ease the stress so the body does not become so overwhelmed that it cannot heal but often, it's not enough.

I think many "mid-life crises" are the result of the spontaneous release of such trauma/stress with the resultant acting out in response to feelings that have long been suppressed. Indeed, psychological counseling may be needed to help address issues that are suddenly remembered or that can no longer be ignored.

Tissues are much like rubber bands. If you wind a rubber band clockwise, you must unwind it counterclockwise. The same is essentially true for the tissues of the body, but it is not just a clockwise/counterclockwise motion. It can run in any direction and in any plane of motion. "Unwinding" varies from person to person. Some are so mild, only the most experienced practitioner would recognize that an unwinding is taking place. Others are erratic and violent.

Occasionally, when I am treating a patient, they will "unwind." Generally, this starts with a gentle side-to-side rocking or a gentle movement of the head to one side or the other as though it is searching out something. This motion may last for a brief moment or for most of the treatment. Generally, the patient thinks I am moving their head because I have my hands on their head. If allowed to build up momentum I can just leave one or two fingertips lightly touching their head or even move my hands away from their head and the motion will continue.

Unwinding is therapeutically beneficial though many people who do "cranial" view it as an annoyance. Nevertheless, it is important to remember that the "physician within" knows what needs to be done and if allowed to manifest itself, the patient will heal more quickly than if I impose my own agenda. The better I get at "doing" the more I have to figure out how to stay out of the way. Even if I am utilizing thought, feeling, and emotion to treat, I still have to stay out of the way. Perhaps some day we will understand the full power that we have available to us through our feelings.

Sometimes an unwinding will get very active. Indeed, it may lead to a patient leaping from the table. I have seen it get to the point where I have had to lie across the patient to keep them from bouncing off the treatment table.

During my sophomore year in medical school, I was attending one of the monthly weekend cranial seminars when an unwinding happened to me. Dr. Jealous was treating me after someone had "jammed" my "mechanism." As he treated me, I started to twitch. It started more like a jerk that occasionally happens just as you begin to fall asleep, but it was my right arm that moved. I really didn't pay much attention to it until it happened again. Then my stomach muscles started to vibrate, and then twitch, and then it just hit me. There was no pain. There were no emotions being released. My body just started twitching. It looked like I was shivering only it was a bit more intense.

I could force myself to stop twitching but as soon as I relaxed, it started up again. I found it easier to just relax and go with the flow. Dr. Jealous told some of the other students to cover me with their coats and they went on with the seminar while I lied there twitching for the best part of an hour. Gradually it just slowed down and stopped. I didn't see visions, relive past experiences, see colors, feel pain, or anything else. I just shook for about fifty minutes. This was a somatic release pure and simple. Of all the "releases," these are the least complicated.

I see this type a lot in my practice. Most of the time the patient stops it from progressing even if I tell them it's okay and that they should allow it to progress. It feels weird to have your body doing things you are not telling it to do.

There are many different types of releases. These include but are not limited to somatoemotional (where the physical release triggers an emotional response), somato-visceral (where the physical release triggers a response in the viscera (gut, etc.), and visceral-somato (where the strain in the viscera triggers a muscular release) releases. They occur because something has affected the tissues and left an imprint.

When my kids were younger, from time to time they would damage something that was near and dear to me. If they didn't totally destroy the item so that it was unusable, whenever I would see the mark, it would elicit in me the memory of what had happened. If I had the item repaired, there was nothing to trigger a memory. We all have memories that come to mind when we see or do things that are tied to these memories. Our tissues are much the same. They remember until they are allowed to forget.

I once attended a seminar where Viola Frymann, D.O., was the guest lecturer. She talked about unwinding the tissues and demonstrated a procedure to do this.

After the seminar, I asked her to "unwind" me. While I sat on the treatment table, she came behind me, placed her hands on my head, and started the procedure. She turned me every which way but loose. I felt things happening in my body and closed my eyes. It felt like I was in an airplane. I could see the sky, clouds, and ground in my mind's eye as though I was reliving the experience in my mind. It was incredible! Specifically, I remembered the flight where I was subjected to the forces she was releasing. It was a training sortie and I was teaching my student how to fly in formation with another jet. My student was from Finland and was quite aggressive and we pulled many G-forces during that sortie and my neck had not been the same since. The specific technique she used I now call a compressive unwind because she seemed to use a slight compressive force on the top of my head.

Generally, there are a set of circumstances that when added together generate enough energy to facilitate an unwinding. Obviously, the patient must be in a position emotionally, spiritually, and physically that will allow this to take place. That does not mean that they have consciously made that decision, but it is more a process that has taken place either before they came to my office or during the treatment.

Most of the time, it is also dependent on where I place my hands. Once the unwinding commences, it will probably stop if I move my hands even a few inches since the therapeutic fulcrum established requires a certain amount of balance. Having said that, many times it will continue long after I remove my hands from the patient, if I allow the entire mechanism to become involved.

Sometimes it is the close proximity to my energies that facilitates the release and subsequent unwind. An unwinding may continue if I withdraw my hands a fraction of an inch or more away from the body but when I increase the distance or lessen my intent the unwinding may grind to a halt.

Another thing that I have noticed is that some of my patients can feel my energy as they approach my office. Many times, I have had patients, who were sitting in my waiting room at the front of my office, start to unwind. It is all a matter of how much energy is involved and how close the patient is to a therapeutic fulcrum.

In a way, it is like trying to start a bonfire. It takes a bit of effort to reach the energy of activation. If the resulting flames are nurtured, it will build to the point where there is essentially nothing required other than to sit back and watch the blaze explode. Generally, the more a patient has been worked on, the closer they will be to the therapeutic fulcrum.

Since I like to work from the head, that is generally the area where an unwinding starts. That does not mean that it will only occur if I am working on the head. It can occur while working on any part of the body and it can occur in other areas of the body. Having said that, it usually starts in the area of the head and neck, the place I am working on has nothing to do with the "size" of the unwinding or the area of the body that unwinds. Remember, when I unwound, they were touching my head but my arm started to twitch. Most of the time, I can encourage an unwinding by simply allowing the tissues to move wherever they want to go.

I have had instructors tell me that if I am following the tissues, I should not let them backtrack. As I mentioned before, I do not agree. If the "physician within" knows what the body needs, I feel it is terribly arrogant to suppose that in this one instance, the "physician without" knows better. I allow the tissues to go wherever they want to go.

"Osteopathy by the numbers" isn't the best way to treat yet our profession is moving more and more towards that approach. Indeed, it won't be long before we kill ourselves off in an effort to become "standardized." The beauty of osteopathic medicine lies in the "art" of osteopathy not the "science." Miracles happen because of the art not the science involved. What if all artists painted the same way? What a terrible thought.

Sometimes, when an unwinding occurs, my hands are not on the body but rather on what I will call the auric/energy fields around the body. Occasionally a treatment will proceed to completion, the patient will leave, and then hours or days later, an unwinding will spontaneously take place. The important thing to know is that you do not have to unwind to be healed. It may be fun or interesting but it is not necessary unless the physician within you feels it is necessary at that point in time to initiate an unwinding. Most people never experience a noticeable (to them) unwinding. Remember, for you to be healed, you may not need it. We are all different.

I do not practice medicine the way most physicians practice medicine. As such, coming to me for treatment is a very different experience for most patients.

If they can remain open enough to allow their body to heal, most of my patients get better.

A year ago, a woman came to me for a treatment. Normally, I will not take on a new patient who is involved in suing someone. I asked her to fill out some paperwork and I took her MRI's back to my treatment room to look at them on my film reader. The films weren't that bad.

As I said earlier, the examination of a patient starts when I first meet them. When I went back to my waiting room to collect the paperwork, I noticed that she had written on every available space and had further written up the side of the paper in the margins in an effort to plead her case.

When someone does that, they really don't want to be healed. They are building a case and I don't have time for that. I decided to cut to the chase and asked her to stand while I "muscle tested" her. I asked her if she wanted to be healed and she said "yes" and she got weaker. She failed the test! I told her she failed and she argued with me. That's nuts! I told her to go away and to do some forgiving. She didn't get it and probably never will. Indeed, she called back the next day and left three messages on my answering machine telling me that I'd made a mistake and she really did want to get better. Go figure!

The point is that our bodies know when we're lying. They know what they need to be healed. If the physician doesn't listen to what the patient's tissues are telling him/her, the desired result will probably not be achieved.

One of my patients told his wife in regards to me, "I don't care if he comes in and swings a dead chicken over my head as long as I feel better." Now I should say that I have never swung a dead chicken in the air in the process of treating a patient, nor have I done anything even remotely similar to that but you get his point.

Pete had been plagued by severe unrelenting back pain for years. He walked like the "tin-man" and was on some very potent pain medications. It hurt for him to simply lie on his back on my treatment table. A friend told him to see me.

Since he was desperate for relief, the path for him to see me was opened. After the first treatment, I was not sure he would come back but he did.

On the third or fourth treatment, Pete unwound a bit. Most of the outward motion was in the upper chest, neck, and head. Remember an unwinding is a total body experience even if the outward manifestation is only in one part of the body.

I have seen unwindings where only one arm or a leg "flopped in the breeze." One such patient made sure she wrote her check out before the treatment because she knew she would be unable to do so afterward. In Pete's case, eventually, after several treatments, the unwinding progressed to an active, total body experience.

When I saw him again, he said he didn't feel any better. He also said he "twitched" for over a week. The next treatment went without him unwinding at all. Progress was still made and he continued to improve but, it was obvious to me that I needed to see him again fairly soon.

When he returned a week later, he started to unwind almost as soon as I put my hands on him. As occurs with most "unwindings," it started almost imperceptibly with a gentle side to side motion of his head. It was not like he was rocking his head from side to side but it was almost a seeking motion. He continued to unwind. Gradually, more and more tissues were incorporated into the process until all were involved. Legs and arms moved and twitched. His body convulsed.

While this was going on, his wife sat behind me on a chair in a corner of the treatment room. I knew that both were concerned and perhaps a bit scared about what was happening. It was an excellent opportunity to discuss what was happening so we talked about it.

Initially, I was positioned at the head of the table cradling his head in my hands. As the process picked up momentum, I moved my hands to where only my fingertips were lightly touching his neck. As the unwinding picked up more momentum, I moved my hands to where they were cradling Pete's head but were about four inches to either side so I was not touching his physical body but was still in touch with his energetic body. This slowed down the progression and velocity of the motion to where it wasn't too "violent" but it continued to progress.

I then moved to the left side of his body. While sitting on my treatment stool, I placed my right hand lightly on his chest and my left hand lightly on his lower abdomen. We continued to talk and to joke around a bit. I tried to keep things light since it can be scary to have your body doing things that you are not telling it to do. I showed them that if I stopped monitoring with my hands but instinctively slipped into the "treatment" mode the intensity of the unwinding increased.

I showed them that he could consciously stop the unwinding at any time but as soon as he relaxed it would start again. I also showed them that when he relaxed into it, it was more comfortable and less stressful on his nerves. I showed them that if I took my hands off of his body and placed them in the air about eight inches above his chest, I could increase the intensity of the unwind if I increased my "intent."

Generally, we had a good time. Unfortunately, I was supposed to treat his wife next but it took about seventy-five minutes for this whole process to run so I did not have time to treat her. A treatment should take about 30 minutes but I allow forty-five minutes per patient so that I can finish without rushing. Obviously, "unwindings" can put a major damper on an orderly schedule. I dislike having patients wait since I know how much I dislike waiting. Sometimes it cannot be helped.

Back to Pete, after about seventy-five minutes he stopped twitching and took one deep breath after another. The energetic midline opened and there was a very nice flow of energies up through the midline chakras. He smiled and said his back felt better. I cautioned him that it takes about seventy-two hours for a treatment to run its course through the body so he might unwind again during that period and that it would likely happen the next time when he laid down and relaxed.

I remember unwinding at a course in Tulsa, Oklahoma many years ago after Drs. Herb Yates and Dan Moore had treated me together. Each night for the next three nights, as I reclined in my bed, it felt like I was on one of those hotel beds that you put a quarter into and it vibrates. I vibrated for three days.

In Pete's case, he said he vibrated and unwound, whenever he was still, for about five days. Generally, I tell a patient that they will not know the effect of a treatment for seventy-two hours.

Most patients notice a change after a treatment but occasionally one will say they feel no change. What I feel happening within the tissues and what they feel are usually two entirely different things. Even after seventy-two hours, they may not notice a change. That is just the way it is.

Pete unwound like a champion but when I saw him again, he said that his overall pain was the same. The important part was that even though he did not feel better his tissues had changed. He was easier to treat and at the end of the next treatment, he said he noticed a definite change for the better.

A colleague of mine schedules a new patient for three successive treatments before he sees them for the first time. These appointments are scheduled a week apart. It is not a bad idea though I do not do that. I like to get my hands on someone before I make the decision on whether or not they will need another treatment. Sometimes it only takes one treatment and sometimes (rarely) it takes forty and sometimes (even more rarely) it never works. It depends on many factors.

I am not solely responsible for whether a patient gets better. That would be a terrible burden. The fact is that the patient is, for the most part, the responsible party. Their nutritional and mental statuses as well as how well they have taken care of their body, throughout their life, are significant factors. The list goes on from there. It is important to remember that we are the sum total of all that our forefathers and we have experienced and thought about. We are also influenced by those with whom we come into contact, directly or indirectly. The net result is that each of us is different.

There is another type of unwind as I mentioned earlier in this chapter that I call a compressive unwind (the type Dr. Frymann used on me) and it is much as the name implies. I will have the patient sit on one of the sides of the treatment table and will run the table up to its full height. I then stand on the other side of the table facing their back and will have them lean back against my chest. I then interlace my fingers, place the palms of both hands on the top of their head, and apply about a pound or less worth of downward pressure. The head and neck will then start to move out from underneath my hands. I continue the pressure and "ride" their head as it moves.

The problem with this type of unwinding is that it is not very comfortable for the patient. It can be painful. For some reason, the head will search out troubled areas that are very painful. I always tell the patient that is what will happen so they will be prepared.

If the head stops in some position other than upright, I'm not done. After a little while, I will usually tell the patient to relax and let it go. To the patient, it will feel as though something will break if they do not stop the motion so I assure them that nothing will break. Usually that is enough to get them moving again.

I have seen this type of unwind go on for over forty minutes and I have seen them last under a minute. The important thing to remember is to allow their tissues to go where they want to go and not where I want them to go. It is okay if they backtrack. Let the physician within run the show.

Sometimes I will do these two types of unwindings in succession. I let instinct tell me what to do and in what order. Our bodies remember things in a variety of ways. Technically, when our body responds to something without our mind becoming consciously aware of the input or of forming a deliberate response, it is called a reflex. How we eat, walk, comb our hair, speak, write, and do all manner of things that we do not consciously think about falls into the category of "reflex." If I poke you with a pin, you will respond by withdrawing unless you consciously override the reflex to withdraw. The pathway that the stimulus must take usually requires it to go to the spinal cord and then returns to the muscle or tissue. A reflex does not require the stimulus to make a trip to the brain. Tissue memory is very similar to a reflex.

Another way for tissue memory to manifest itself is when a "lesion," or as I like to call it, "a goober," occurs. Unless you are a physician and understand the phrase "segmental somatic dysfunction," the name goober is more descriptive of a lesion. The problem with the term "segmental somatic dysfunction" is that the lesion may occur in the middle of a muscle or any other type of tissue. It may even occur in the middle of one of the "long bones" of the body, such as the tibia, which is located in the leg.

Anyway, when a goober occurs, something has happened that has settled in your tissues. This "something" can be emotional, psychological, and/or physical in nature but it is not limited to just that. For some reason, your body has not dealt with this input properly and has isolated it from the body and there it sits until it is released. Unwindings deal with unresolved goobers.

15

The Fascia

"When you look into the eyes of another, any other, and you see your own soul looking back at you, then you will know you have reached another level of consciousness."
(Brian Weiss, M.D., *Messages From The Masters*.)

Immediately underneath your skin are two layers of fascia. In anatomy courses, we normally blast through these layers and view them as an annoyance. The fascia is very thin and very hard to dissect intact. If you have ever seen an animal that has been skinned, fascia is the white glistening material that also covers the meat/muscle. It allows the skin to slide on top of the deeper tissues. There are actually four layers of fascia, which include the two superficial layers and the layers that wrap the muscles. Embryologically, these four layers consist of one sheet which folds back and forth on itself.

I used to work under the hypothesis that when people talk about tissue memory, a major portion of this memory exists in the fascia. Of course, there is no way to prove this theory, but I used to believe the fascia acts as the body's magnetic tape. When something happens to you, for the most part, it is recorded in your tissues. Everything good, bad, or indifferent is recorded.

I would like to be able to say that all of this is recorded only in the fascia, but from what I have felt during treatments, this cannot be the case. I would also like to say the portion that is not recorded in the fascia is recorded in other tissues and that may be true, but I doubt that is entirely correct. Memory also exists in the body's "energies" and in your spirit. Indeed, as the years have gone by, it has become more and more evident that the latter is probably the real answer and that there is an interface with the tissues and fascia.

As I've said before, it hasn't been that many years ago that "cranial" was viewed as unacceptable by most osteopathic physicians. There were a lot of rumors and stories about those who practiced cranial, which sounded pretty farfetched. The more I learned, however, the less and less far fetched they sounded. Those of us who have gone on to the bioenergetic realm have a view from a vista that is truly amazing. We live in the Twilight Zone.

Early in my career, as a means to ease the workload of the hospital's emergency room, a decision was made by our hospital's administrator to send non-emergency patients to the hospital's outpatient clinic for treatment. In anticipation of the increased workload, I was hired to work in the clinic.

The physician, who already worked in the clinic, primarily did osteopathic manipulative medicine. She arranged for those who wanted osteopathic manipulative treatment to see her and not me. Since Sydney had a "sprained ankle" she was referred to me. That's how I met Sydney. She had gone to the emergency room and was referred to me to handle.

Through the years, I have concluded that if something is supposed to happen, it will. It is wrong to try to force someone to come and see me but when the time is right, they show up. In Melvin's case, it was time so I was put in a position where I could help him. I think the same happened with Sydney.

She had a sprained left ankle and even had the air splint and crutches to prove it. I had her lie on her back on my treatment table and felt her ankle. It was definitely sprained but that was not the whole story. That was only the tip of the iceberg.

As I held her ankle, I tried to get a sense of what happened during the injury and how old it was. Normally, I would expect a new sprain to be somewhat warm, but her tissues were cold and hard. This was an old injury, but she claimed that she had just sprained it!

Whenever I am stuck for an answer, I have found a particular Biblical phrase helpful, "Be still and know…" So, I figured I would just hold on to her ankle and try to sense what had happened. I didn't judge the injury. I just sensed what was happening without being critical and without trying to get it to move the way I thought it should move. Within minutes things started to happen.

The first thing I noticed was the strain seemed to come from within her whole body rather than just from within her ankle. As I watched this unfold, Sydney's arms started to shake. Then her body started to twitch. When I thought I had things figured out, the whole pattern changed! It was still a total body strain, but it was different even though there were things that felt similar. Sydney continued to shake but then the pattern changed again.

In all, about five distinct patterns cycled through the tissues several times. I told her that her tissues were doing strange things. She said, "There's something I should tell you. I have multiple personalities."

Though this was the first time I had actually encountered it, I had often wondered what affect multiple personalities would have on the tissues. This is not the only time I have seen the tissues indicate something hidden within. Our tissues reflect everything. In fact, it has been said that our inner self is a mirror of our outer world and that our outer world is a reflection of our inner self.

In addition, certain medical conditions often manifest themselves in a consistent manner. An example of this would be hypothyroidism. We often think of this as being solely manifested by a goiter, an enlargement of the thyroid gland located in the front of the neck, but it may also be manifested by a basic body temperature below 98.6, which we commonly think of as being "normal." Additionally, longitudinal ridges running the length of the nails may be the only manifestation of a low thyroid output. All of these are signs or manifestations of an internal disease process. The same is true for many diseases. It is up to the physician to learn to read these signs.

It is important to say that Sydney really did have a sprained ankle. It was a bad sprain but the sprain pattern was ensnared in her other patterns. It was impossible to treat one without treating the other. When I work on the mechanism, it is a total body experience. The entire body is treated not just the affected area.

It's also important to state that if you have been injured in a past life and the strain was not resolved energetically, you may carry that into another life. There seems to be a propensity to re-injure the same area over and over again until the initial and all subsequent injuries have been resolved.

It is very important for you to understand that if you have a bad knee but forget to tell me about it and for some reason I do not mention it myself, it will still end up being treated in the process of receiving a treatment even if I never touch the knee. You are hooked together, and as I often tell my patients, "If I pull your toe hard enough, your head will follow." If I treat one part, all parts are treated. It's much like taking a cup of water out of a bucket of water. If I do that often enough, sooner or later the bucket will be empty. Having said that, sometimes it's very important to hold the affected area and treat it directly. I'll talk more about that later. In Sydney's case, by treating the sprain, a total body release was accomplished.

Recently, a woman called me to make an appointment. She said that she was having headaches and was in a lot of pain. She then went on to ask if I would be restricting my treatment to just her head or if I would be working on her back as well. I told her that until I examined her, there was no way to know what I would have to treat. She then told me that her chiropractor had her back in pretty good shape and that she didn't want me to work on that area.

I did not schedule an appointment for her. I am convinced she would have benefited from a treatment but she had essentially told me that she did not want a treatment.

Often, when a new patient comes back for a second treatment, they will report improvement in some area other than the one for which they sought my help. Again, think of a strain pattern like a bucket of water. You cannot take out a cup of water without influencing what is left in the bucket and without lowering the entire water level. By treating any portion of the body, the entire body is treated.

In Sydney's case, it took a long time and many treatments. She had been undergoing psychological counseling and started improving dramatically. Most people undergoing psychological counseling benefit from being treated. The two work very synergistically together.

Eventually, the strain pattern in her ankle resolved but things still didn't feel "right." As the strain continued to decrease, the epicenter shifted to her left wrist and hand. Then it shifted to her right wrist and hand.

One day, while treating her, the release was exceptionally active and seemed to be building to a peak. She had been shaking, moaning, and rocking back and forth, as she gripped her clothing. She seemed to be trying to rip them from her body. Suddenly, it all stopped. She took a long, deep breath and smiled. It was over.

Sydney always used to dress totally in black. The next time I saw her, she wore a white dress with a floral print. The personalities had integrated themselves and she was whole. There was still some strain and she needed a few treatments from time to time but the difference was remarkable. I have not seen her in years.

16

The Boundary

One day, they were meditating in a quiet garden when one of the disciples, deep in a meditative state, began to levitate. Feeling his body lifting itself up from the ground, he became very excited, and very proud of his accomplishment. He stirred himself from his meditation and felt himself back on the ground. He stood up and walked over to Buddha.
"I have mastered levitation," the disciple announced.
"That's nice," Buddha responded, "But don't let it distract you from your meditation."

During my freshman year in medical school, I remember going to Dr. Jealous' octagon shaped house many times to study with him. It was located in a beautiful wooded setting in the hills surrounding North Bridgton, Maine.

On one occasion, about twenty students had gathered so we decided to do "multiple-hand" technique. This is where more than one person works on a patient. In this case, a student was assigned to each arm and leg and another was assigned to the head. The person working on the head was given the task of being in charge to make certain we were not working at odds with each other.

Please do not misunderstand; there is little benefit to having multiple people working on a patient. The treatment is seldom more profound and it can be risky. Personally, I don't like having someone else working on the same patient when I'm working. It distracts me because I have to divide my attention to make sure they aren't interfering with what I'm doing. When I am training someone, I understand that it's part of the price I have to pay to train but it is fatiguing.

Anyway, I was working on the left arm. My task was to simply observe the cranial rhythmic impulse but not to try to judge it or do anything with it. I remember that after awhile I felt I was gripping the arm too firmly so I lightened my grip. After a while, I again felt I was gripping too firmly so I again loosened my grip. Repeatedly this happened. All the while, our eyes were closed to heighten our sense of touch. Eventually, I peeked.

I thought I was touching his arm but in reality, my hands were about four inches away from it. What was I feeling? Was I imagining things? Was I feeling my own cranial rhythmic impulse (which, by the way, is very common among inexperienced and occasionally experienced practitioners)? It is vital that the physician knows what his or her own cranial rhythmic impulse feels like and makes sure they are not treating themselves. After careful consideration, I found I was indeed feeling his cranial rhythmic impulse.

What this led me to discover is that you can feel the cranial rhythmic impulse without actually touching the body. Moreover, you can treat it without touching it as well. This sounds incredible and if I had not experienced it myself, I would be skeptical. These many years later, it's an every day occurrence and something I can do with relative ease.

There are energy fields that radiate around and through us, influencing our health. My ability to see "auras" is very limited at this time. Some of my patients have said there is an intense, deep violet/purple light about me and that my hands radiate a brilliant white light when I treat. At this time, I have to take their word for it.

Not only are energy fields all around us but they also penetrate everything including us. The most massive or all encompassing of these energies pulses about every 1½ minutes and when it comes into sync with that which defines us incredible things occur within our bodies. That energy is tangible and very powerful. It is also very subtle. It gives light and life to that which we are. Some call it Prana. Others call it the "Breath of Life." Others call it the "Light of Christ."

A few years ago, I gave a talk to a group of people in Martinsville, Indiana. In the course of that presentation, I referred to the Tide. Afterward, one of the people present came up to me and asked how long I had been involved in "new age" religion. This is not "new age" it is just life as I have observed it. I do not read "new age" "how to" books or go to "new age" seminars. I have a very fundamental Christian background. What I present herein is that which I have personally experienced and have tried to make sense of. Truth is truth even if you've never heard it from the pulpit. If not saying what you personally believe to be true makes me "New Age" then that's what I am.

Within us are other energy patterns, all of which are part of us. Each is there for a specific purpose. They are very powerful and very subtle. I've seen masters of the martial arts, who are in their eighties, demonstrate their knowledge of these energies as younger, much larger martial artists tried to lift or physically move them but failed as the master calmly stood before them.

Legends and folklore are made of this stuff. Often dismissed as fable, these sound too incredible to be true. I am not sure why we are so ready to dismiss such phenomena. Why are we so eager to depreciate the power that resides untapped within each of us?

Awhile ago, at the insistence of one of my patients, I read a pamphlet by one of the New Age guru's which are so popular now days. In it, he states that God is that which resides within us. I think that's silly because it underestimates and demeans the power of God and it underestimates the innate power within each of us to not only heal ourselves but to do other "miraculous" things.

I have definite religious beliefs. I believe that all things are played out according to a "plan" and that it is up to us to see the wisdom in that plan. If God's influence is everywhere, and if all things, past/present/future are before Him/Her, and if not even a sparrow can fall without Him/Her knowing of the event, then the possibility that He/She exists in another dimension has to be taken into consideration.

I heard a CD by Gregg Braden wherein he stated that scientists now believe that there are at least eleven dimensions. That would help explain how non-corporeal spirits exist and operate and might possibly explain such future events as the "Rapture." It would also help to explain how His/Her influence can exist within each of us regardless of how worthy we feel. Furthermore, that influence is palpable. It can be felt. It can also be utilized for healing.

17

Liquid Light

"True love is giving until it hurts. It is not how much we give—but how much love we put into the giving." (Mother Teresa)

My first "regulation" basic course in cranial was sponsored by the Sutherland Cranial Teaching Foundation (S.C.T.F), in Tulsa, Oklahoma. Though I had been schooled/mentored by Dr. Jealous, who was a member of the S.C.T.F. for several years prior to that time, I had also taken an abbreviated course taught by Viola Frymann, D.O., at the University of New England, College of Osteopathic Medicine.

The Tulsa course was held at the Embassy Suites Hotel. After the day's work was done, the faculty would gather at the restaurant at the hotel to eat and to renew old acquaintances. Since I was staying at that hotel, I would join them as often as was possible.

I remember one evening when many doctors including Drs. John Harakal, Roland Becker, Jim Jealous, Edna Lay, Dan Moore, Louis Hasbrook, and Ed Miller were sitting at several tables that were pushed together. I am sure there were other members of the S.C.T.F at the table but I cannot remember whom. Nevertheless, I made the best use of that time by asking question after question to Dr. Becker, who was sitting almost directly across from me.

I am not sure what the original question was but Dr. Harakal told me of two experiences of somewhat miraculous healings that he had experienced from the hands of Dr. Roland Becker. The first occurred when Dr. Harakal had a massive heart attack. Dr. Becker lived in the same town as Dr. Harakal and they would often exchange treatments with each other. After Dr. Harakal had his heart attack, each day for five days Dr. Becker treated Dr. Harakal in his hospital room.

Dr. Harakal said that his physicians had never had someone with such high cardiac enzyme levels (a sign of significant damage to the heart) and as low a cardiac output (the amount of blood the heart can pump) live. Not only did he live, but he was able to function normally.

The second miracle occurred when Dr. Harakal's knee was bothering him. He had Dr. Becker treat him and it got better but after several days it started to hurt again. This happened about five times before Dr. Harakal told Dr. Becker to "just turn up the juice and heal it." I will always remember that he said, "It felt like Dr. Becker had taken a white hot poker and had jammed it into my (his) knee. I would have given him any amount of money to quit but when he was done the pain never came back." Since Dr. Becker's touch was very light, the pain was coming from something other than physical pressure.

Several years ago, a patient came to me with pain in her right shoulder. After examining her, I was certain that she had a partial rotator cuff tear. It takes a long time for these to heal but treating them can speed up the process so I treated it. After a short time, I became aware that I was sensing/feeling something in her shoulder that can only be described as liquid light. It was palpable and powerful.

I also noticed that though my touch was very light, my patient was squirming under my touch and was vocally expressing the pain she was feeling. It was awesome! I wanted to check something else in her abdomen but didn't want to move my hands for fear that I might not be able to find the liquid light again so I stayed put and just watched.

After awhile, she calmed down and the "liquid light" withdrew into her tissues. I knew we were done so I asked her to sit up. The shoulder was healed. I cannot explain it in other terms. At that time, I had felt other manifestations of similar energies but nothing exactly like this. I wonder if that is what Dr. Harakal was describing. Unfortunately, both of these extremely dedicated fine physicians have since passed so we will never know. Since that treatment, however, I have felt the same phenomenon several times, always with profound results.

Most people experience a "learning curve" when they learn how to do new things. Healing is no exception. Depending on where I am on that curve, the length of time it takes to treat a patient varies. Each level of expertise has its own learning curve. Generally, the more skills I have acquired at a certain level the less time it takes to treat a patient. When I reach a certain skill level, new knowledge or abilities are revealed to me and it affects the amount of time it takes me to treat the patient as I learn how to incorporate this new knowledge into my treatment regime. As my skill increases, the time shortens and then the cycle starts over.

It is an interesting process since the increased skill/ability to treat and the increased ability to sense what is happening don't usually happen at the same time. Usually, I first receive the increased ability, which shortens the time to treat a patient, but within a short period of time my ability to sense more will then increase, which essentially allows me to sense more that has to be treated and as such increases the time needed for a treatment.

In mid December 2000, I became aware of a quantum increase in my abilities when I noticed that it was taking me about twenty minutes to do what normally took forty minutes to do. This change happened over night. It is unfortunate but people judge the quality of the treatment partially or in large part by the amount of time spent working on them. I was almost embarrassed to tell my patients that I was done treating them after twenty minutes.

I do not know why I experienced this jump in ability, but as has happened in the past, with the subsequent increase in my ability to sense what needs to be treated, other areas have been revealed to me for treating. This quantum increase in ability may have something to do with the vibrational changes in the energies around us. Indeed, at about the time of the Winter Solstice 2003, another huge change occurred. It felt like we had moved into a different dimension energetically.

Two of my clairvoyant patients told me a few years ago that there was an obstacle that I needed to overcome but once that was accomplished; I would jump many levels in my ability to heal. I think that obstacle had to do with faith. Though I am still too much in my "left" brain, once I became comfortable taking my own path, let go of "traditional" osteopathic and allopathic beliefs, and trusted that I am being led by a power that knows clearly what I need to be doing, I was free to learn. That required a lot of faith. Though that applies to me, you are also subject to "faith restrictions."

For me, my patient "mix" varies depending on that which I need to learn. Obviously, I feel that I am on a path and am being taught things by the hand of someone infinitely smarter than I. It's a lot of fun. We're all on a "path" and though your path is different than mine, the hand that is guiding me is also guiding you. Just as my "mix" varies, your experiences vary according to what you need to learn and know. It's important to learn to look for the lessons that are presented to you.

18

Children

"We must always remember that where we have already formed a conclusion we cannot learn anything. If we desire only to judge, we can learn nothing."
(Rudolph Steiner)

A few years ago, one of my patients called to see what I thought should be done with her son. He was experiencing headaches and was dizzy. When he looked at vertical objects, they appeared to tilt. He also said that his vision was blurred. All of these symptoms had started within the previous week. He had seen his pediatrician the day before the call and was told he was okay.

I hate it when someone, especially a child, goes to a physician and is told they are fine when things obviously are not fine. Assuming the pediatrician checked his eyes, ears, nose, and throat, and found no evidence of infection or disease, why didn't he or she listen to what his or her patient was saying and then figure out if there was something wrong? I had the parent bring the child in to be checked.

I examined him, did a brief neurological exam, and was not thrilled with the results. I then checked out his mechanism, and again was not thrilled. It was terrible and there was an area in the left temporal/parietal/occipital region, on his head, that was considerably jammed.

The cranial rhythmic impulse in a child is usually unencumbered by the restrictions that adults carry around. If the cranium is not moving freely, it can usually be made to do so relatively easily. That was not the case this time. His mechanism eventually opened up and started to move, but I still was not happy.

I must say that the amount of information gained in the new imaging techniques such as CAT scans and MRIs are marvelous, but I have my concerns about the safety of these. I'm not sure there isn't something harmful happening that we are not aware of. Sometimes, though, the benefit outweighs the risks of the procedure.

When I was treating the child, I was very concerned that he might have developed a brain tumor. Having said that, however, I could not feel one. I only felt a "disturbance in the force" that could have been one.

When I was in the Air Force, we used to have check-rides where we would be evaluated on our instrument flying procedures. This required us to fly with a hood that blocked our ability to look outside the aircraft to become visually oriented. This forced us to believe our flight instruments even though our bodies told us we were badly tilted and obviously experiencing vertigo.

J.F.K. Jr. died because of inexperience in such a situation in real life. During a check-ride, however, we had a saying, "One peek is worth a thousand cross-checks." If you tilted your head up, looked out the corner of your eye, you could see where you actually were in relationship to up and down, and that one peek would reset your internal senses and help you overcome the vertigo.

Nevertheless, though my hands told me there was no tumor, when it came to the life of this boy, I needed a peek. If there was a tumor present, I was not sure we had the time to wait. I treated him and then set up an appointment for an MRI for the next day. I sweated bullets until I got the results.

I did not receive the results until early in the morning the day after the MRI. It was negative. I called his parents to tell them. His mom didn't act too surprised though she was pleased with the results. She said that he had been significantly better since the treatment.

I saw the boy again a few months later. His tissues were better but there was still a significant strain pattern. I was able to get further with the second treatment and it was gone by the time he had received three treatments.

What was it? I don't know. Was it bad? Yes. Could it possibly have been the energy pattern of a tumor in embryo? Probably.

A year ago, a young mother brought her toddler son in for a treatment just to make sure he was all right. He was off a bit but his tissues were working well by time I was finished. A week or so later, she took him in for his "shots." Immediately thereafter he started acting strangely. His mom picked up on it and brought him in for me to check him over.

There was an overall "darkness" in his energy pattern. I treated him and told his mom that I was very concerned. She did some research and found a group in Chicago that deals with vaccination reactions in children. I don't think they are totally correct in their approach but they helped. I treated him a few times and he was able to fight off what was happening and he is back to being his old self again. It was scary. I had heard of kids developing autism as a reaction to pediatric immunizations but I had never personally seen it happen. I'm sure that is what was happening and then a miracle happened. His mom called several months later, just to thank me. I think the mom deserves the credit.

Another child who came to me with severe problems was Melanie and this book wouldn't be complete without her story. I don't think any patient has triggered so many diverse emotions within me.

Melanie was referred to me by another health care professional. She was thirteen. The previous fall, her family physician had diagnosed her as having a "slight scoliosis." That means her back had a slight curve to the side so she was bent. She was referred to an orthopedic surgeon who confirmed the diagnosis and told her parents to bring her back in the spring for a recheck. For a variety of reasons, they did not get back to him until July.

A lot can happen in a nine-month period. In this case, Melanie had started her growth spurt and had grown three inches. This translated into a huge lateral deviation of her spinal column. When they did return for another examination, the orthopedic surgeon had an opportunity to turn a bad situation into one that was at least tolerable, but he blew it. He used the opportunity to overreact and scare Melanie and her parents. He made them feel terrible.

He told them that Melanie had to be immediately fitted for a body brace and that if the scoliosis got any worse, she would have to be taken to surgery to attach a metal rod to her spinal column to keep it from deviating any further. The problem is that it would also prevent her spine from correcting back toward the midline.

I would like to believe that medicine has progressed beyond the Dark Ages, but in some areas it has not. Affixing metal rods to the spines of children with scoliosis is barbaric! I can't say I know the reason why some kids have spinal columns that become bent, but I haven't found one yet which hasn't responded very well to treatment if treated in a timely manner.

In Melanie's case, her right leg was about one and one half inches longer than the left and her left hip was higher than her right. Her spinal column was deviated about four inches to the left of center.

When I met her, she was wearing a semi-rigid plastic body brace and was accompanied by her mom, dad, and a friend. None of these folks were happy. They looked like they were going to a funeral.

I've seen a lot of people with scoliosis. Until a few years ago, the worst case I had worked on was a man in his late fifties. His spine looked like an "S." I never did get it to become completely straight, but it got better and he was one happy camper.

Generally, kids respond very well to treatment. In fact, most get better within just a few treatments. This was the worst example of scoliosis I had run across in a child though I have since seen worse. The good news is she responded very well to treatment. By the end of the first treatment, her legs were essentially the same length and her spine was almost straight.

I wish I could say I felt good about all that but her parents were still less than pleased. That orthopedic surgeon had really done a number on them. They were scared! They wanted to know if they should keep their next appointment with him. I figured, sure, go ahead and keep the appointment. If the surgeon is ignorant then he needs to be educated.

I was not prepared for the next question. "What happens if he tells us not to come back for further treatments from you?" My reply was, "If he's ignorant, then educate him. If he's stupid, fire him."

A week later, Melanie came back with her mother. At that time, her spine was deviated to the left about one inch and the torsional twist of her pelvis had come back but there was only a one-half-inch difference in the apparent length of her legs.

Melanie's tissues were twisted all over the place. When I felt her cranium, there was a huge strain pattern coming from her mouth and jaw. I asked if she wore a dental appliance and was told she had a retainer. I was almost sure this was the culprit.

A few years ago, I had a young boy as a patient who was having seizures. When I examined him, there was a significant strain pattern coming from his mouth. I asked him to open his mouth and saw he had braces. In questioning his parents, I discovered the seizures had started within two weeks of their installation. I told them to talk to the orthodontist and have him cut the wire between the front two teeth. After that was done, it only took one more treatment and the seizures stopped. Even subtle changes in the pressure applied to the delicate membranes and bones of the skull can influence dramatic changes in the health of a patient.

In Melanie's case, I was sure her scoliosis was the result of her dental appliance. I asked her to bring it the next time she came to see me since she didn't bring it the first time I treated her. As I said, when she returned she was still bent but it wasn't bad. Two things bothered me, however. The first was that when I had her place her retainer in her mouth, it didn't change her cranial rhythmic impulse one bit nor did it affect the way things were moving in her head and body. This meant that the retainer wasn't a "player" in terms of trying to place the blame on why she was bent.

The second thing that bothered me was that her mother said she'd feel better if I could show her some case studies of children I had worked on, who had progressed through puberty into adulthood. I told her that I had not been practicing medicine that long.

Fear is a funny thing. The changes that occurred in Melanie's body were miraculous if measured by what traditional medicine could have accomplished in a similar period of time but the miraculous is routine in my practice, so I reserve that term for the things that really "wow" me.

Her mother decided to stick with the treatments and I saw Melanie about every 2 months for several years. She has stopped growing and still has a slight scoliosis but it is very slight. I now see her perhaps once a year. She avoided needless surgery.

Each child/patient is different. Each patient with a scoliosis responds differently. Some totally resolve. Generally, they all get better to one degree or another. If treated properly and early enough, none have progressed. That means that affixing a metal rod to their spine would have been of no benefit yet I had one patient tell me that her orthopedic surgeon was very concerned that the degree of curvature had only lessened from 32 degrees to 20 degrees. If he had his way, she would have been permanently fixed at 32 degrees and never have lived a normal life.

Sometimes I am embarrassed to be a physician when I encounter such stupidity from a member of my own profession. Just because you are a physician does not mean you have "common sense." If your doctor tells you to do something that does not make sense, make sure you understand what he/she is saying and agree that it makes sense before you do it.

I'm going to cover a very touchy subject, i.e., cancer. Specifically, I will discuss two patients who have experienced breast cancer. The first had a lumpectomy, no chemotherapy, and no radiation. She changed her diet, stopped smoking, and took care of herself. That was ten years ago and she is disease free and very happy.

The second was diagnosed with a small tumor. She elected for chemotherapy, which shrunk the lump to the point where it was difficult to find. At that point, the lump was removed and they removed lymph nodes in her armpit and checked them to see if any cancer cells were present. None were. In my mind, removing the lymph nodes and chemotherapy were not good choices. Removal of the lymph nodes will alter her lymph flow pattern for the rest of her life. She then underwent radiation therapy.

This has frightened her to the extreme. Will it change anything for the better? I don't think so. Radiation causes mutation or cell death. It doesn't stabilize anything. If she has no sign of cancer, which is now her state of being, why use radiation? It's all guesswork. What I am telling you is not the "party line" in medicine today. Part of the problem is that the "party line" will be different a year from now.

Cancer is scary business and the medical profession is very good at scaring patients who experience cancer. I wish I had the answer. I think I know what I would do if I were faced with temporary cellular dysfunction, i.e., cancer, but fortunately I have not been placed in that situation.

The worst problem I had to face with the second patient was the fear. She would have cut off her arm if they had told her it would have helped. Unfortunately, the legal system weighs heavily on a physician. We deal with what is called the "Standard of Care." I am not sure who sets the "standard" but if an "unsatisfactory" outcome results from a physician's care (even if it's not their fault) the physician can be sued.

In a courtroom, various "experts" will be called to testify whether or not the physicians' care matched what the experts would have done. If not, then the physician may be judged at fault. Generally, that means that patients are subjected to being treated by established procedures and recommendations rather than "cutting edge" technology or alternative methods because it keeps the physician safe from being sued.

Patients get scared and physicians get scared. I wish there was a way to avoid it. Perhaps if we talked to each other it would help. The biggest problem I have with physicians is their egos. Having said that, I am sure I fall into the same trap from time to time.

19

Congenital Disorders

Remember: You are a spiritual being having a physical experience. You are neither a spiritual being nor a physical being. At this point in time, you are both.

One of the most frustrating aspects of my practice has to do with treating patients with "congenital disorders." These disorders have existed in the patient since birth though the reality may prove to be that they existed well before that since, as I pointed out in Chapter Eight, if we are carrying around unresolved "past life" strains, they will influence our mental and physical health. Genetic anomalies have often existed in the gene pool for many generations as well. Sometimes the disease associated with the genetic defect manifests itself from birth. At other times, the disease may remain dormant for years before manifesting itself. I feel that there is a way to heal these patients but I am still working on how to do it. Sometimes I have great success and at other times we're not that fortunate.

Presently, I am trying to figure out what part our thoughts, feelings, and emotions have on who and what we are. As a physician, I've seen cancerous tumors disappear without surgery, chemotherapy, or radiation therapies. My belief is that we are equipped with everything we need to heal ourselves. Some people are able to do so all by themselves. Some people are never healed. Other people require a "group effort" to be healed. Perhaps the latter is because they lack the faith to do it themselves. Perhaps it is not a matter of faith.

A few years ago, a young man came into my office because his mother is a patient of mine and she made him show up for the treatment. He had blood in his urine. X-rays revealed a "tumor" on one kidney. His color was ashen. Until proven otherwise, that is a sign of an underlying cancerous condition. Mind you, this is a young man.

Is this a congenital disease? Does he have a familial predisposition for cancer? I don't think so. He smokes and says he "can't" quit. That's malarky. I questioned him about whether or not he wants to die and he essentially told me he is tired of the consequences of his bad decisions and wouldn't mind dying. He has a "death wish."

I treated him and removed a demon that was plaguing his body. I suggested several nutritional supplements to help his body restore itself to health. His mom was there and offered to pay for the supplements. He refused. I was surprised when he called a few days later to make another appointment. I treated him several times and his ashen appearance has disappeared but then he withdrew from treatment and moved to another state…

Some of the prevalent congenital disease processes fascinate me. During my training at one small clinic in Maine, a flu epidemic was in full attack and we all worked frantically to stem the onslaught. Within a three-day period, we treated an average of eighty-eight patients per day versus the thirty or so we normally examined and treated.

Within the grip of that epidemic, while rushing from room to room checking each patient, it is difficult not to prejudge each patient but rather to take each on his or her own merit. As I hurried in to one exam room to see the next patient, I checked the notes the nurse had taken during the preliminary work-up. They indicated that this twelve-year-old boy had the flu. I entered the room, without taking the time to acknowledge his mother who was sitting in the corner, and went immediately to his back so that I could listen to his lungs with my stethoscope. His complaints were of a cough, fatigue, runny nose, and feeling bad. I wanted to make sure he did not have pneumonia.

Pulling up his shirt so I could place my stethoscope on his back and listen to his lungs, I noticed several large light brown patches on his back. I remembered from my training a rare disorder called neurofibromatosis or Von Recklinghausen Disease. The patches this boy had are called "café au lait" patches. If a person has six or more, their physician should check the patient for the disease. I thought I had made a dramatic discovery but when I turned to mention this to his mother, I noticed nodules covering her body. She also had the "Elephant Man's Disease." There was no reason to mention to his mother what she already so painfully knew.

In another case, my patient already knew his diagnosis. Bob had Marfan's Syndrome. This genetic disorder manifests itself in very tall people with long slender fingers. The most serious manifestation is a softening and eventual dissection or rupture of the aorta, the main artery leading from the heart.

Bob came to me with chest pain, so I checked this out. I placed my hands on his chest and felt into the tissues. It felt like his tissues were tearing apart. I tried to run the mechanism through his tissues in an attempt to treat them, but it was almost futile. To make things worse, Bob smokes two to three packs of cigarettes a day. I wish I could say that I was able to cure him but I didn't. Perhaps if he quit smoking it would have been more effective, but I really don't know if it would have helped. That was years ago and I wonder what I would have been able to feel and accomplish at my present level of skill.

Another patient of mine with a congenital disorder was Judy. Her disease manifested itself in her legs and feet. They would involuntarily turn in on each other, forcing her to walk on the outer/upper sides of her feet. Other members of her family also have this disorder but it is particularly bad in her.

When I examined Judy, I noticed a spasticity of her legs and ankles. The remarkable thing was that when I felt her cranial rhythmic impulse I noticed it was shutdown in her legs. When I was able to re-establish motion and then get in touch with the tide, her legs would relax and return to a normal posture. The problem was that it took all of my concentration to accomplish this. As soon as I eased my intent, her legs would again spasm and turn inward.

I treated her several times but eventually her parents decided to have her operated on. I am not sure what the result will be. Unfortunately, her family moved to another state and I will probably never know the outcome.

I have to wonder why Judy's tissues recognized health when it was presented to them but did not continue to follow that pattern. Why doesn't what I do always "work?"

I wish I knew the answer. I wish every time I placed my hands on a patient, the mechanism would open up, and the tide would flow through so that their tissues would drink in the tidal energy and breathe life. It just does not happen that way. Sometimes miraculous things happen. Sometimes they don't.

I'm not always the same. Likewise the patient is not always the same and the energies that are available to us are not always the same. The bottom line is, however, there is something within the patient that generally either triggers a spontaneous healing or doesn't. Within any given patient, sometimes things happen and sometimes they don't.

Whether or not a patient is "healed" depends on many variables. Generally, I think it has to do with "energy," understanding, and faith. Remember, we have about 100,000,000,000,000 (one hundred trillion) cells in our bodies and most of those cells produce energy. We usually have all the energy we need. Furthermore, we have the blueprint for health stamped on each cell. It is a hologram of sorts. There are some things we do, however, that limit our ability to tap into various energy sources.

"Energy" is an interesting concept. Sometimes I feel supercharged. Sometimes I feel the presence of spiritual individuals in my treatment room who radiate healing energy and some of my patients have seen these personages. I know that there are times that turning up my own energy helps but I also know that "generally" it is better not to do so but rather to establish balance within the energies present within my treatment room.

Our minds are amazing. When I was in medical school, we learned a technique for compressing the fourth ventricle in the brain. The nickname for that technique is a CV4. To do this procedure, the patient lies on his/her back while the physician gently cradles the back of the patient's head with both of his/her hands.

The tissues and bones of the head normally expand and contract eight to fourteen times a minute. With each contraction, the physician essentially takes up the slack but then does not allow the tissues to expand at the next expansion. With the next contraction, he/she does the same until there is a faint bobbing of the mechanism that fades away into stillness. This stillness is called a "still point" and is a very potent way to induce healing. It's not very precise and elicits a "shotgun" effect on the entire mechanism. The physician then monitors the "still point" until, all of a sudden, the tissues inhale and the procedure is over. The "still point" can last anywhere from a few seconds to many minutes.

One day, while practicing this procedure on one of my classmates, during our lunch break, I was in a bit of a hurry. For some reason I thought, "I wish the still point would come so we can go to class." Almost as soon as those thoughts were formed, a still point occurred. It took me by surprise and at first I thought it was a coincidence.

For some reason, I no longer felt the need to hurry. Once the still point was over, I allowed the mechanism to return to normal function and then again thought, "I want a still point." Again a still point occurred. This was the first time I realized the profound effect thought has on the body. Our thoughts do not just affect our own individual bodies but also the bodies of those around us even if we are not touching them. Conversely, the thoughts, feelings, and emotions of those around us affect us. It's important to associate with honorable/good people because if you crawl around in mud, you will get dirty. That "dirt" can affect your health.

Perhaps I should say that again. Our thoughts influence our bodies and the bodies of those around us. In fact, our thoughts influence a lot more than that. Our thoughts influence everything around us. I highly recommend that you read Gregg Braden's book, "The Isaiah Effect," and then get his tape on the "lost mode of prayer" for more information on this phenomenon. When I read his book and listened to his tapes, it was marvelous to hear and read about things that I have often wondered about and had been experimenting with personally and in my practice. Mr. Braden refers to this as a "technology" that has been lost to those of us in the "West." I think it's time we rediscovered it.

Suffice it to say, we have more influence on what occurs in our lives and in the lives of everyone on this planet than we can comprehend. The search for this knowledge is why I decided to become an osteopathic physician.

During that search for knowledge I've been exposed to "technologies" that are not taught in courses or in institutions, that can help us heal others. The knowledge of those technologies is gained from direct experience in response to vigilant pensive thought and meditation. I think the "ancients" were aware of some of these technologies. Some cultures are more receptive to this than others. Western philosophies have taken away our faith and weakened us. In the medical community, if something cannot be "proven" in a double blinded study, then it is of no value. In some cases that is true but in other cases that is definitely not true.

Sometimes, when I am treating a patient, I cannot get the response I want no matter what I think. Usually, however, if I verbalize what I want, it will happen. It is as though my thought is not enough. The patient has to also think in concert with what I want. That means the patient can also influence their own health by what they think. This is not supposition. It is something I can palpably feel within their bodies.

We are what we think. Our bodies mirror how we think. If we think positively, then our tissues open up and embrace positive healing energies. The power of faith is immense. The opposite is also true. If we lack faith, it's like trying to drive a car without ever starting the engine. You may have four brawny guys pushing you but it is a laborious task unless you start the engine and then it's amazing what can be accomplished. Faith can indeed move mountains, enable the blind to see, the lame to walk, and cure all manner of disorders.

One of my patients was in a motor vehicle accident. In a split second she became "bent" and "twisted." She lost her sense of neutral. If I treat her, she becomes "straight" but she'll return in a week or two and proclaim that "I'm bent." She tells everyone she's bent and twisted. With almost every thought she reaffirms that she is bent and twisted and she is. She has become her disease. Our thoughts, feelings, and emotions markedly influence our health.

20

Abuse

"It is the secret of the world that all things subsist and do not die, but only retire a little from sight and afterwards return again. Nothing is dead; men feign themselves dead, and endure mock funerals and mournful obituaries, and there they stand looking out of the window, sound and well, in some new strange disguise."
(Ralph Waldo Emerson)

There are many forms of abuse. Sexual abuse is one form of abuse, but all forms affect the body. For some reason, when someone has been abused, they may function very well for most of their life.

Experience has shown me that at about the age of forty, plus or minus six years; things start to come "unglued" if insults or trauma to the body have not been resolved. I am not sure why. I have seen it happen earlier and later than that six years window. Depending on the severity of the abuse, many things can happen. In Sydney's case, she developed multiple personalities, which is common where the abuse has been severe and repetitive.

Generally, if sexual abuse has occurred, it will show up in the tissues of the pelvis but it might also include some of the other tissues. It is common for someone to either loose interest in sexual relations or to experience a change in their sexual orientation as the body tries to adjust to the release of old sexual trauma if the deep strain has not been addressed.

Through the years, I have learned there are several areas on the body commonly called chakras. Chakras are not associated with any organ but if the chakra is lesioned, the organs in the area of the lesioned chakra will be affected. Also, specific types of energies gravitate to specific chakras. One area that is extremely powerful is the "heart chakra." It is located in the middle of the chest and is associated with emotions and emotional trauma.

If a person has experienced emotional trauma, the cranial rhythmic impulse and other energies may be diminished in this area. If that area is treated and brought back to its full potency, it is common for the patient to experience vivid dreams and daydreams. They may start to cry while being treated, but just about anything can happen when a release occurs.

Earlier, I described finding a trigger area and the out of balance feeling I felt when my hand was not positioned directly over that area. There are several areas on and around the body where these vortexes or "chakras" seem to occur in everybody. The major chakras are located on the midline of the body.

Have you ever wondered about such sayings as "broken hearted" or "heart ache?" Our bodies, if we will listen to them, will teach us a lot. In this case, these sayings put forth what we all are keenly aware of and what most of us have experienced in the area over the middle of our chest.

Having dissected several cadavers, I can attest that unless you are having a heart attack, there is no organ that relates to heartache, but it happens nonetheless. The question arises that if there is no chakral "organ," then what is the reason for the discomfort?

Some scientists say the heart is a "liquid crystal oscillator." That may well be but when viewed in respect to the other chakras it is evident that it's not the heart that is generating this force. Remember, we are spiritual beings having a physical experience. Just because a chakra is located over a certain organ does not mean that organ is the reason the chakra is located there. Perhaps the converse is true. Remember, we are spiritual/energetic beings having a physical experience. The energetic matrix is laid down long before the tissues flow into that matrix.

There are seven "major" chakras each containing a universal spiritual lesson that we have to learn if we are to evolve into a higher consciousness. Each is located along the midline of the body. The first six extend through body, on each side, and project out a distance. Depending on the origin and nature of the energy field, it may only project out a fraction of an inch or it may project out several feet. Technically speaking, our energy fields can project out hundreds of feet or more. Quantum physics states that the field may well extend hundreds of miles or more.

The first "major" chakra is located approximately over the pubic bone in the pelvis and is associated with the color red. Lesions in this are can be related to our survival instincts, and to our sense of grounding and to the connection of our bodies to the physical plane. The next chakra is the second chakra. It is located about the width of your hand above the first chakra, just below the umbilicus. Its associated color is orange. Problems dealing with insults or conflicts with your "tribal" or "core" values will affect these two chakras. Lesions related to sexuality, work, and physical desire will show up in the second chakra. The third chakra is located in the solar plexus and is associated with the color yellow. Problems with self determination and self-esteem, ego and personality will affect this area and it's common to see teenage or adolescent children with stomach problems if this area is upset. The fourth chakra is located between the breasts in the middle of the chest and is associated with the color green. The fourth chakra deals with emotions, love, forgiveness and compassion. The fifth chakra is located in the throat and is often associated with feeling out of control of one's life, i.e., will and self-expression. It is associated with the color blue. The next is the sixth chakra. It is a located in the middle of the forehead and is associated with the color violet. The "third eye" is associated with this area. When this area is treated, people often develop their "second sight" or clairvoyant abilities. The seventh chakra projects out the top of the head and is associated with the color white though some books depict it as black. It is related to our overall spirituality.

I have also found paired chakras that are slightly lower than the bilateral mid clavicular regions (collarbones). These are very powerful and act as a portal into the energetic/spiritual body. I have yet to see anyone write about these paired chakras.

This has been an interesting week. I saw a woman on Monday who came to me primarily because it was the "thing to do." What I mean is that most of the members of her family had been to me for one reason or another and they were putting pressure on her to share the experience.

Don't get me wrong, she had ample reason to see me. Her back hurt and had been hurting for a long time. When I put my hands on her, it was obvious that her back was in major trouble. The problem in her back was buried under a lot of surrounding trauma. If you bury a bone, you have to remove the dirt first if you want to get to the bone. To get to buried trauma, you have to go through whatever it is buried in.

Though a lot of releasing went on and I bounced a bit, she didn't seem too impressed with the treatment until it came time for her to sit up. She was "buzzing" and commented that it felt like she was on drugs. I told her to call me when she felt that she was in need of another treatment.

She called the next morning to say she felt like a truck ran over her and then the next morning I received the following E-mail:

"I'm not sure where to start with this one, but I think it's important that I share with you my experience. I shut off my TV last night and rolled over to my right side. Just then out of nowhere an old, gray, hairy, arthritic hand came out of the air and touched me on the shoulder. I said, "Grandpa"? It faded and I then rolled onto my back where the entire room was full of something. Mostly to my right and over me were swirling lights (or energy) like that of the tracer a sparkler makes when being twirled around by a kid only without the fire. It was the essence of something like that. At times, I thought there were thousands of "somethings" swirling around, but two would seem to try to take shape and get close to me. I would say, "BACK OFF"! At one point, the one over me seemed to rain down on me and I could feel her or "the" vibration go through me. I actually heard it. I was terrified, but sometimes could make myself feel OK. Now, I'm not a fruit cake and I generally don't go looking for such things even though I consider myself very open. I feel my session with you opened this can of whatever and I would like to understand it better so I'm not so frightened. Perhaps I'll make my appointment sooner as in, as soon as you can get me in."

When I read this E-mail, I was reminded of Judith Orloff's book, "Second Sight," which gives an account of her experience in realizing that she had clairvoyant capabilities beyond that which most of us exhibit. As for my patient, I had a chance to meet and examine her on Friday of the same week. She is evolving. I think we will see a lot of this as we approach the "shift of the ages," and as we do so, I think many more "clairvoyants" will come to the forefront. Gifts of the Spirit come in all shapes and sizes.

The vibrations of the elements around us are increasing in both intensity and frequency. We vibrate in concert with those vibrations. If they increase in vibrational intensity, so do we. One inward manifestation of this is that our sense of time is no more. The days, weeks, months, and years are flying by. Everybody knows it but it just doesn't make sense since the clocks keep ticking away just like they always have. The problem is that we know something is afoot. We sense it and we talk about it. What we don't do is accept it as real.

From the web: "Earth's background base frequency, or "heartbeat," (called Schumann resonance, or SR) is rising dramatically. Though it varies among geographical regions, for decades the overall measurement was 7.8 cycles per second. This was once thought to be a constant; global military communications developed on this frequency. Recent reports set the rate at over 11 cycles, and climbing. Science doesn't know why, or what to make of it." Additionally: "Time will appear to speed up as we approach Zero Point. A 24 hour day will seem to about 16 hours or less. Remember the Schumann Resonance (or "heart beat" of Mother

Earth) has been 7.8 cycles for thousands of years, but has been rising since 1980. It is at about 12 cycles at present. It stops at 13 cycles." (http://www.2012.com.au/SchumannResonance.html)

A few days ago, I was examining a new patient who came to me because her neck hurt. I examined her legs and noticed that they were the same length and that her pelvis was level. I was surprised, however, when I placed a hand under her tailbone and discovered that it was not moving even if she breathed deeply.

I then placed a few fingers on her chest, between and slightly above her breasts and noticed that there was no energy flow in that area. I asked her to take a deep breath and she inhaled only about one third of a normal breath. I then moved up to the head of the table and examined her neck, which felt like a board.

At that point, I told her that I've examined and treated a lot of people and that though I can't read minds I can read tissues and proceeded to tell her that she was afraid to breath into her heart chakra for fear of releasing what was stored therein. I told her that her neck hurt because she felt out of control with her life and that it had no place to relax into because her upper chest was blocked as she tried to hide her emotions.

At that point, I told her that the trauma extended back about five or six years but there was current trauma as well and that since she is married my guess was that she was having marital problems. At that point, she broke down and confided in me concerns about her husband and his infidelities.

As we talked, I continued to treat. Tears flowed but more importantly, her heart chakra opened up and she started to breathe deep breaths, and as she breathed, her neck softened and the strain dissolved. Her vibration increased and she was light headed when she sat up at the end of the treatment. I will see her again in a few weeks to dig a little deeper.

Cindy was one of my first patients. I learned a lot from treating her. I initially treated her for a sore neck and some back pain. Her tissues responded well to treatment, but I had a sense there was something more going on; I just did not know what.

After a couple of years, she suddenly developed abdominal pain that required her to be hospitalized. A week passed and her doctors still didn't know what was causing her pain. Not knowing what else to do, and since she was better, they discharged her from the hospital. She then came to see me for a treatment, which was directed at her upper abdomen. She experienced a lot of relief, but things still didn't feel "right" to me.

During the next few years, she remained fairly stable but occasionally experienced pain in her neck, back, and abdomen. Then, her "patterns" started to change. As one area would be restored to balance, another would go bad. When I treated her, waves of fear and pain would pour forth from her tissues almost like shock waves. These all had very strong sexual overtones.

When I say "sexual overtones," I mean that the energies given off had a sexual flavor. If you go into a home where steak is cooking, you will smell steak. If bread is cooking, you will smell bread. Likewise, when the body releases a trauma, I can sense part of the essence of that which is given off.

As I started to open up the shell that Cindy had developed to protect herself, many things started to happen. During one treatment, she started an unwinding process where she brought up her legs and arched forward in the posture of giving birth. The memory of giving birth was trapped in her tissues and as they released, the muscles were triggered which corresponded to the memory, so she assumed the birthing posture.

The goal of each treatment was to establish peace within her tissues and with each treatment, eventually, she would relax and a different pattern would take over. During this particular treatment, she went through this process twice. By the quality and feel of what was being released, it was apparent these were totally different pregnancies.

At one point, I felt the area that needed treating was about a foot and a half away from her shoulders. I pulled back to about two feet above her shoulders and slowly brought my hands forward. As I got closer, the energy pattern felt more compressed and more vibrant. It eventually reached a peak and then started to diminish as I moved closer to her body. I again slid my stool backward away from her head until I was again on the point where my hands felt the most balance. I then increased my "intent" and concentration.

When I say "intent," I mean that my focus and concentration were more intense and I increased the force/power that comes from within me. For those of you who have had training in the martial arts, it's the same thing you would do to break a brick half way down a stack of bricks without breaking the other bricks.

Anyway, things really started to happen once I did this. Her body shook and she brought her knees to her chest and began moaning. I could feel the energies run through her body as they knocked down obstacles and opened up channels that had been closed off.

Energy work is not easy. Sometimes the sweat pours off of me. Sometimes I have trouble standing after a treatment. At times, it feels like I'm pushing against a building in an attempt to move it. I try to always let the patient's own mechanism show me what needs to be done so that I don't impose what I think needs to happen within the tissues. This keeps us in agreement.

In this case, I continued to input energy until I reached a point of "combustion," a point where the tissues had enough energy to take over and do what needed to be done without my input. When that happened, I backed off and monitored as I would in a normal treatment. Eventually, Cindy calmed down and relaxed.

Seldom does one treatment "cure" a person who has been abused. Often, the patient will get worse as they progress through their healing. Their personality may change several times because it's hard to face the memories that are released from the tissues. Often, those memories are repressed and, when they are exposed, it's hard for the patient to deal with them. The patient's soul is placed in turmoil. Occasionally, a patient will withdraw from treatment rather than continue on and face that which is released. Cindy withdrew from many things. Her life changed.

Years later I heard that she was not feeling well so I went to see her and told her I wanted to see her in my office. When I examined her, there was a huge disturbance in the area of her liver so I ordered a scan of her liver and abdomen. She had colon cancer that had spread to her liver. She died several months later. I have to wonder if unresolved trauma manifested itself as cancer in her case.

I'll use the next case, involving Dolores, only to further illustrate that sometimes the place to treat is not always on the body itself. Dolores is one of several patients who all exhibit similar characteristics. Abuse seems to be a common theme. For some reason, when a mother is involved in the abuse, the tissues can be very disturbed.

Dolores had neck, shoulder, and upper back pain. When I examined her, I noticed her pelvis and chest areas were shutdown. Several trigger points in the area of her left shoulder and on her back, just next to her shoulder blade, were "hot." When I say hot, I mean that if I touched the trigger point, she'd jump off the treatment table.

Dolores had been seeing a therapist to help resolve some abuse issues. This helps if the therapist is a concerned, caring individual, and it certainly can make my work easier. Occasionally, the patient will ask if they can bring their therapist to a treatment session. The problem is that many therapists and associated health care professionals come with their patients not to see what I have to offer but rather to "grandstand."

I have one patient whose therapist insisted on trying to elicit a round table discussion before a treatment. Essentially, she tried to tell me how to treat the patient. This drove me nuts because she didn't have a clue as to what's going on! Additionally, she stole my energy and was distracting, and interfered with the treatment process. I wished she had stayed home but my patient liked having her around, so I tolerated it but eventually had to call a halt to it.

Anyway, Dolores asked if she could bring her therapist with her to a session and I reluctantly agreed. I have tremendous respect for the mechanism. There is no doubt that the forces I deal with are very powerful and, generally, very pure. When someone wants to bring a guest to see what happens, I feel like I am supposed to perform and I don't like feeling that way. This work is too sacred to me.

In this case, though, it worked out well. After about twenty minutes, Dolores was in a full-scale somatoemotional release and was disassociating. What I mean is that she had separated herself from her body. Sometimes this is also associated with regression to an earlier age.

We had reached a point where I could not stop the treatment but Dolores definitely did not want to be touched and told me so. She was so vocal about it that she actually swore at me and she sat upright.

Her therapist was helping her verbally but I could not stop. I backed off her tissues to a point about twelve inches above her most active trigger point and increased my intent. She immediately reacted as though I had jabbed her with a sharp object. I backed off and lessened my intent. She still reacted but not as violently.

About this time, I looked at her therapist and his eyes were as round as saucers. Dolores' back was to me so there was no way she could see what I was doing. Several times, I withdrew my hand and then brought it back toward a spot about twelve inches behind but not on her back. Each time she flinched as I hit the point of maximum intensity. Eventually, the lesioned area relaxed and the energies flowed through the tissues. Later, her therapist said he would not have believed it unless he had seen it with his own eyes. I was "jabbing" a spot in the air behind my patient and the patient was flinching in response.

I had treated Dolores many, many times over the course of several years. I had thrown everything at her that I could think of. I used to think that if I had treated someone three times without achieving a "cure", I should refer him or her to someone else. Truthfully, if I've seen someone five times, I start from square one and reexamine what I know of the case and what I've done to make sure I'm convinced I'm on the right track. I had treated Dolores more than forty times. She kept coming back. The reason was simple—she felt better but it did not last. She also had good insurance.

A few months after that, something strange happened. She called and said she was having headaches and needed to come in for a treatment. I had her lie on my table and I placed my hands on her head. I mentally stepped back and was again reevaluating her mechanism to see if I had missed something. All of a sudden, her mechanism went calm. It didn't stop. It just went calm. I can only liken this to the following experience as presented by Dr. Jim Jealous at the Sutherland Cranial Teaching Foundation's Advanced Course in the fall of 1993:

"As osteopathic physicians, our skills invite us to observe, palpate, and sense with varying degrees of intensity. Often these skills bring us experiences for which there are no concrete explanations. We cannot explain these experiences but they certainly do occur. Osteopathy began because of the courage of Dr. Still to report his findings, and it is our responsibility as clinicians to document the unexplainable. This writing is about one such phenomenon. It is called "The Other Pair of Hands.

"The most essential wisdom that flows from the river of osteopathy is "To be still and know." When the clarity of diagnosis and treatment is opaque, this axiom has helped many physicians remember the importance of not increasing the intensity of their efforts but decreasing the intensity of their efforts by remembering to be still that we might know. Such was the experience that led to the observation of another pair of hands.

"Several years ago, during a treatment, when faced with the dilemma of trying to find a therapeutic fulcrum, around which to balance the inertial tensions within the patient, it became obvious that I had reached the limit of my skill. Everything I knew had been tried, and yet, nothing was happening; there was no way to find a balanced tension anywhere in the body that connected with the healing forces within the whole of the patient's mechanism. I was stressing my own system in trying to discover what might be done. I was beginning to tire from the search. Finally, I took a deep breath, relaxed, and let go of my attention, of my probing mind, of my sense of direction, and just sat still, bewildered, wondering what to do next. I thought maybe I could refer the patient to another therapeutic modality, but intuitively, that did not feel necessary at this time. However, it was clear that I had reached the end of my professional rope. There was a long pause, which represented my unknowing. This pause, this kind of emptiness, this kind of unknowing, remained for a considerable period of time. I found myself just waiting and breathing; there was only the movement of air and time passing. Slowly, the empty became complete. There was absolutely no afferent activity in the perceptual fields of the nervous system. It was still, very still. There was the presence of integrity. My eyes were closed.

"Slowly, it seemed that something was happening; I perceived a vague movement in the patient's body. I was aware only of this motion, and then, as if from nowhere, like a ship appearing out of the fog, another pair of hands appeared in contact with the patient's body. My hands were on the head. This 'other pair of hands' appeared on the sides of the pelvis so that my hands were actually facing this other pair of hands. The background was so empty, so quiet, that there was no real shock at witnessing this phenomenon. It became immediately clear that these hands were establishing a fulcrum that the whole body was responding to as a functional unit. My hands then acknowledged this 'other pair of hands' by assisting and bringing the body to the fulcrum that was being established. There was a very quick, powerful exchange like a spark jumping. The treatment proceeded directly from this moment into automatic shifting. It was a very simple event. It did not last long.

"Following this I did not say anything to the patient. She was very calm. Returning ten days later, she reported resolution of a problem that had been present for a long period of time. Previous treatments had been maintenance, and had not produced an ascending scale of healing. The patient exclaimed that the turning point for her had been the last treatment that she felt that something special had happened. I agreed, with a simplicity that perhaps may have reflected some indifference to the patient, because all I said was, "Yes, that's true." When I examined the patient, there was still a profound 'air' in her mechanism, a synchronicity and wholeness to her system. There did not appear to be different kinds of densities in different kinds of tissues. It felt like the homogenized state we often feel at the end of a still point. It was obvious that the patient was receiving some very deep change.

"What is most evident to me is that I have no idea how it happened, but I know that it did happen and it happened within the context of being still and knowing. It represents an encounter with a quality of healing that obviously is beyond the level of our usual perceptual experiences. It is my firm belief that other clinicians are having similar kinds of experiences and yet may not be forthcoming simply because these events have such an air of mystery. I wish to remind the reader that osteopathy has been cloaked in mystery since its conception and the osteopathic physicians that have 'dug on' after Dr. Still, practitioners such as Dr. Sutherland and some of his followers, have come across very special and mysterious phenomena that have deepened the harbor of Osteopathy. It brings reverence to our work to share these experiences.

"If this were a singular event, I would report it. However, it has happened on a regular basis and is becoming more commonplace. The distance between my hands and the other pair of hands is decreasing and often they appear over my own. The pattern of these events is a process that is completely and always the same. The hands appear in different places, but the precursor to their appearance is always the surrender of frustration to the bewilderment stillness. Even though these events continue to happen, I cannot make them happen. This other pair of hands does not seem to appear until the physician himself has really made **his own effort to the maximum**. This is primordial!

"Sometimes a young student in our profession will come forth with some extraordinary experience and report it. It is important to acknowledge the experience and also make it clear to the student that sometimes these things just happen **because we reach a certain level of sincerity**. It does not mean that we should avoid learning our anatomy or avoid learning our basic fundamental skills because these skills are required in order to follow the process of healing whether it is directed from ourselves or from a higher source.

"Having a complete and thorough knowledge of traditional anatomy and physiology as well as a deep reverence for the mystery of life itself blends and weaves into existence the process of osteopathic medicine.

"These events, however uncanny, have a definite pattern of expression that indicates to me the working of natural order, a process that, however mysterious is, in fact, orderly. Order reflects the influences of natural law. Natural law is the essential core of Osteopathy."

The profound stillness Dr. Jealous speaks about has happened to me many times in my practice and is now almost a daily occurrence. I cannot explain why it happens, but it does. I used to think I had to treat someone for a long period of time to bring about a deep release, but I had only been treating Dolores about fifteen minutes when it happened with her. It's important to understand that time is irrelevant during a treatment. What needs to be done may happen the instant I touch a patient. There is nothing magical about the amount of time you are on my treatment table. If you had a splinter in your foot, would it upset you if I took it out in a minute versus thirty minutes? You're there just to have the splinter removed.

As for Dolores, when I say her mechanism went calm, I mean there was a sense of total peace. Her cranial rhythmic impulse was at peace. Her tissues were at peace. Everything moved at peace. She was in sync with the Breath of Life. Since there was nothing more to do, I told her I was done with her. She looked puzzled but got up and left.

I saw her two months later because she thought she ought to come in for a check-up. She said that since her treatment, she had not even experienced a hint of a headache and that she was again running and exercising without discomfort.

In Dr. Jealous' presentation, a certain phenomenon was mentioned. Only recently have I begun to see auras or any other visual phenomena. Only recently have I seen colors while treating myself. The colors ranged from deep violet to purple and white and were like a shimmering blanket of color. My eyes were closed at the time. Many of my patients have described a similar phenomenon while I have been treating them. The colors they report include gold, red, green, yellow, orange, blue, violet, purple, and white and the various shades thereof.

I wish I could see the same with my eyes open, but I am in the process of developing that ability. I must say, however, at times I see such things without seeing them. It is more than what happens when I feel things. It's as though I truly am seeing something that I recognize, but it is in the invisible spectrum.

The healing that occurred with Dolores came from within and without her, but it required my help. It was profound and thorough and it left an impression on both of us.

A few years ago, while treating a patient, the patient reported hearing a "whooshing" sound during one part of the treatment. A month or so later, while I was working on her, I felt the presence of someone else in the room assisting me.

As I said, I feel these "guests" and sometimes I see them without "seeing." Sometimes it just passes me by. In this case, I just accepted the help and continued. Within a few minutes, the patient said, "What do you mean it's not my fault?" I told her I had not said anything, but she insisted that she heard a voice. Whoever was in the room with me had seen fit to issue encouragement to my patient. Encouragement only she could hear.

Again, a few years ago, at the end of a treatment, a patient remarked that my "kahuna" was powerful. I just let the remark slide, but I couldn't shake it so the next time I saw her I asked what she meant when she said my kahuna was powerful. She replied that "he" was standing in the corner of the room by my desk during the treatment. She went on to describe a large Polynesian appearing holy man covered in feathers and animal skins that stood by my desk and smiled during the treatment. I did not see him, but I am sure he was there. Seven other patients have since "seen" and as such confirmed the presence of the kahuna. I've since learned he is there to help me in the work that I do and to protect my office.

These phenomena occur with greater frequency as the years go by. I cannot explain them. Several years ago, I received a call from a patient who asked if I knew why she was calling me. I gather so much information from the tissues of my patients that many believe I can read their mind. I cannot but I can read the tissues and energies. Nevertheless, I told her I did not have a clue as to why she was calling.

She then told me that the previous night; she awoke and saw an energy being floating over her. The sight frightened her so she yelled and it disappeared. Once the initial shock was over, she realized that the energy being was me and that I had been treating her. That sounds bizarre but there are times when I feel like I have been treating people all night long. Perhaps, indeed, I have been. Again, since that time, many patients have reported a similar experience. Some even call or e-mail to thank me for the treatment.

21

Trauma

"The past must be remembered and then forgotten. Let it go. This is true for childhood traumas and past-life traumas. But this is also true for attitudes, misconceptions, belief systems drummed into you, for all old thoughts." (Brian Weiss, MD, *Only Love is Real*, quoting a Master)

I've run across some fascinating things in my studies. In fact, I have discovered that if I will just sit back and relax, interesting things will beat their way to my doorstep.

Imagine sitting at a stoplight and then being rear-ended by another car. Three weeks later, you are again sitting at a stoplight and are again rear ended, but this time you are also driven into the car in front of you. A month later, while on a whale watching tour, you are standing on the front of the boat when it hits a large swell throwing you and the child next to you into the air. The child lands in the ocean but the bow of the boat is so close to the water that you instinctively reach out and grab hold of the child just as the bow starts up again. This twists you horribly and hurts your arm and shoulder, but you save the child's life. A few months later, you are visiting a friend and are standing in their living room next to a banister when a bolt of lightning breaks the window and strikes the banister, giving you a jolt.

At this point, you should be thinking of that fellow in *Little Abner* who had a thundercloud over his head all the time. It's hard to believe but this is essentially what happened to one of my patients. Each trauma took its toll on Sherrie but the bolt of lightning seemed to fuse them into her tissues. Not only did it fuse them together but it also blurred the boundaries of each injury pattern.

Generally, each injury influences the body as a unit and remains as such though it can be treated and its magnitude decreased. Nevertheless, it remains a distinct unit until it is totally released. As I look at someone's tissues, it is common to feel several different layers or patterns of trauma, each with its own distinction.

When Sherrie was struck by lightning, it was as though her tissues forgot what they were supposed to be doing. They lost their identity. I have seen this happen in cases where the patients were electrocuted, but I have only had a few patients who have been struck by lightning.

In Sherrie's case, treating her was like peeling apart layers of garbage that have been compacted. It was laborious. Neither of us enjoyed it. The good news is that her tissues, just as I have indicated before, knew how to heal when the proper combination of therapies was brought into play.

In this case, I am convinced that what I do had a very important role, but there was more. She started an intensive course in yoga; so intense she immersed herself in it for years. The results were dramatic. What would have taken many years to achieve only took months. The bad news is the fix was not permanent. For some reason, her tissues chose to wander. We have discussed the effect of stress on her tissues and how much better she was at the ashram. It is very frustrating, but we are working on this challenge. On the positive side, as time has gone by, her tissues have calmed down and are much happier. Nevertheless, she is not healed.

Sometimes, I get so annoyed with a body's response that I want to throw everything I know at it. Occasionally, I will treat a patient for a couple of hours to see what happens. Few things are as aggravating as scheduling a patient for a treatment and at the end of that time the tissues are no better than they were when we started.

The option is to either increase my intent or to lighten my touch and back off and watch. I have tried both with Jill and neither seemed to work. She was hurt in a fall that resulted in a compression fracture of her first lumbar vertebrae.

Many people have similar injury patterns and they get better and go on with their lives. In this case, MRIs show no nerve root damage, but the pain she experienced was intense. Working on her was like working on a board.

When I examined her, the most noticeable area of strain was in the area influenced by her heart chakra. She had a lot of emotional baggage that she carried around. I am sure it influenced her health and it slowed down her healing, but the maximum pain was removed from that area. She had tried many things in an effort to rid herself of the pain. She is not a smoker, and should have gotten better, but it did not happening. Treating her did give her some relief, but it did not last.

In her case, however, we were making progress. Life was coming back into her tissues and her energies would flow for about three weeks before she started to shut down. Her pain had dramatically decreased. I think part of the problem was that she was a "workaholic" and hated to slow down. She had learned to ignore her body much like a professional athlete will ignore pain. Then, one day while just watching her mechanism, an overwhelming calm ensued. She was healed. Why?

Everyone is different. We may look the same and our anatomy and physiology may be almost the same, but there are dramatic differences that make us very different from each other. Look at a parking lot. Notice the variety of cars. Do you think that only one person is happy with their car and that everyone else settled for something they did not want? Do you think there is only one man and one woman who are married and happy and that everyone else settled for second best? That's absurd. What works for one person may not work for another because of our differences.

Mary is one more example of how trauma can be stored in our tissues. Mary is a marvelous woman. She is self-assured and very talented. She likes her independence. She came to me because she had severe, unrelenting back pain. She had tried other avenues to gain relief, and then reluctantly came to see me based on the recommendation of several of her friends.

Her gait was stiff and she walked like there was a rod in her back. When I asked her to lie down on my treatment table, it was obvious that she was in a lot of pain but she did not complain. Mary had been in pain for a long, long time.

In Mary's case, I could feel the strain in her back. I could see a picture in my mind of a car hitting something head-on and the tissues as they reacted to the forces of the collision. I asked her about an accident that occurred ten years earlier. She was shocked because she had not mentioned the accident, nor put it on the history form.

I worked on her for a couple of sessions but it became obvious there was more to the story than one accident. As I continued to treat her, the layers started to release a picture of a much earlier pattern of abuse. I told her what I was sensing and she said that I could not know those things. She had not even told her closest friends.

As I went deeper into her tissues, more and more abuse surfaced. As the tissues and energies released the stored trauma, she would often regress to her childhood. Generally, this was in conjunction with some awful repressed memory. As the release occurred, her voice and demeanor changed. Her tissues would soften. She moved without pain. Unfortunately, as she came out of the treatment and returned to her present age, the pain would also return.

During one particularly awful recollection, she sprang from the treatment table, ran to the corner of the room, and crouched down while covering her head. At other times, she would end up arched backward perpendicular to the table, her head almost on the ground and feet almost on the floor on the opposite side. There was no way Mary could have done this as an adult due to her pain, but as a child, there was no discomfort.

During several treatments, her release became increasingly intense and she would suddenly black out and go limp. When this happened, her cranial rhythmic impulse would become smooth, even, and relaxed. Her tissues would also relax.

The point is that until she allowed me to penetrate her tissues, those things which were hidden were going to remain hidden even though I had examined and treated her.

When I first examine a patient, there are many things to see and learn. It is overwhelming. Physicians ask questions to try to hone down their search. It's common for a patient to have many things wrong with them. As a rule, the older the patient, the more things they have wrong with them. They may have high blood pressure. They may have headaches. They may have kidney disease. They may have kidney disease that has caused the high blood pressure, which has given them headaches. Unrelated to this whole process, they might also have leukemia or cancer. So much can go wrong with the body that it is not unusual to miss things unless the physician is specifically looking for something. Even then, it's possible to miss things.

All these years later, I have to wonder if some of what was found within Mary was due to unresolved past life trauma. I will probably never know but I'm thankful that paradigms can change and I'm very thankful for the lessons I've learned.

As for missing things, when I was in my training an eighty-years old woman was admitted to the hospital for chronic obstructive lung disease. In other words, her smoking had turned her lung tissue hard, making it difficult for her to breathe. She was hospitalized so that we could "tune her up."

As an intern, I was assigned to give her a physical when she entered the hospital. I checked for all of the obvious signs of her disease, and I reviewed her old hospital charts to make sure I had a good idea of her health history. I had examined her and was almost done except for the requirement for me to do an exam of her genitals and rectum.

Most interns get around this requirement by simply stating that the patient refused the exam. Most patients will refuse the exam and agree with you if you say, "You don't want me to do a rectal and genital exam do you?" When given the choice, I have yet to have a patient reply, "Sure." On the other hand, if the doctor says, "To make this exam complete, I need to examine your genitals and rectum," I have only had two patients say that they'd rather I didn't.

I could go into details, but it is sufficient to say I noticed the rectal exam did not feel right. I should also say it did not feel wrong either. It just did not feel like I expected it to feel. As I walked down the hall, I passed our resident proctologist and stopped him. I told him of my exam and asked if he would check her out. What didn't feel right was a large cancer of her rectum that would have gone undetected had I not looked and then asked the proctologist to check. It was simply a stroke of luck. What I am saying is that doctors do miss things, especially if we are not looking for them. Even after looking, I could have missed the rectal cancer because I did not know what one "felt" like.

I was at a seminar a week ago. I hate to go to seminars but I'm required to go to seminars to get "CME: continuing medical education". Most of what is taught is bogus. It's like viewing one commercial after another. Drug companies sponsor the speakers so the speakers feel obligated to talk up the benefits of the individual drug company's drug. Nutrition is almost never mentioned. This seminar was sponsored by the Indiana Academy of Osteopathy, a body of physicians who supposedly are more holistic in their approach to medicine.

At one point, we were watching a demonstration on "sequencing" which was happening in the middle of the room. Since this was a medical meeting, we use those in attendance as patients. We were at various treatment tables surrounding the demonstration. As the demonstration proceeded, I turned to the medical resident next to me and whispered "Scan the patient/physician and tell me what you sense." He looked perplexed and said that he wasn't sure what I meant. I repeated my request. He then said that he sensed that the patient was "dying faster than anyone else in the room." This was an amazing observation and very accurate. I then asked him why the patient was dying faster than anyone else in the room. He said that he didn't know. I then told him that the patient's heart was about to fail.

He then asked what we should do about that. I told him that we had to at least offer to treat him; and that's what we did as soon as the demonstration was over and the room's attention was no longer on the patient/physician. We wandered over to him and I asked him if I could touch and then treat him. He said "yes." I placed my hand on his chest over his heart and sensed into his tissues. It was like reaching into a void. He could have had a hole in his chest and it would have felt about the same only it was dark. After a minute or two I asked "What have they done to your heart?" His reply was that he had coronary artery bypass graft x 5 done fifteen years earlier. We treated him until life came back into his tissues.

With "cranial" and/or bioenergetic medicine, the physician has an extra tool with which to scan a patient to see if something is not right. The physician may feel there is a restriction in the frontal lobe of the brain or in the right pelvic region. Then the physician can examine the area further and see if something is wrong. The problem is that it is not always possible to "scan" a patient fully. The patient can block things or hide things from being seen. The patient has to let the physician "in." Remember, we're not sensing tissue, we're sensing the energetic body that resides within the tissues.

Earlier, I mentioned the lady who was concerned about her husband's infidelities and had closed her fourth chakra. In that case I could speculate as to the cause but she had essentially blocked me from looking inside until she acknowledged the cause and let me in.

I have often wondered if a person can be "healed" if these lesions remain hidden. Experience has shown me that, as in Sydney's case, once the hidden strain patterns were uncovered and released, the patient gets better.

Can a person get better if these hidden or repressed lesions are left alone? I don't think so. There has to be a reason that people, who have been abused, start to remember things when they are between thirty-five and forty-five. Our bodies want to get better. They want to be healed. Unfortunately, they learn bad habits that keep them from getting better. Our job as physicians is to teach our patients "good" habits.

When I treat someone, I want to treat their tissues to the point where they feel like the tissues of a child even though I know the process of aging stiffens and strains tissues. When tissues are treated, they often get softer and more pliable. Energy flows more readily within tissues that have been treated.

What I want and what should be done are two different things, however. It is vitally important for the physician to listen to the tissues and recognize the inherent wisdom within the patient's body. This wisdom knows what is needed far better than the physician who is treating the tissues. I may want to do certain things, but I constantly have to put my will in check. If I do not, I could end up hurting the patient.

One of the most difficult things I have to deal with is deciding when to stop a treatment. I love to treat. I love to be in touch with the mechanism. When things are really progressing, it is hard to stop. The problem is that the tissues will reach a point where the treatment needs to stop so they can do what needs to be done and process all that has happened. This may occur before the tissues have fully healed. That's okay. There's always another day.

Most treatments take only twenty to thirty minutes. Occasionally, a treatment will take an hour. Rarely, treatments may take longer and, as I said earlier, it may only take a moment. I find that these longer treatments are usually the ones that involve the energy patterns fostered by abuse.

Headaches

I have not talked a lot about headaches. A major part of my practice involves the treatment of headaches. Cranial works extremely well on all types of headaches. To date, I have only come across two patients whose headaches responded minimally to treatment.

A few years ago an older gentleman, Al, was referred to me by the owner of a local health food store. Ten months earlier, while coming up from his basement, he hit the top of his head. Since then, he had suffered from a constant severe headache. Medications would not touch the pain. He had been to several neurologists and had MRI and CAT scans of his head but everything looked "normal." Eventually, his physician told him he would just have to live with the pain.

When I placed my hands on his head I was amazed at how jammed his head was. Nothing was moving. The cranial rhythmic impulse was shutdown. I have seen worse cases but not many.

I worked on his head for about twenty minutes without apparent improvement. With time, my instinct told me that I should be addressing a restriction in the upper thoracic (chest) region so I moved to that area. Once motion was restored in the chest, I moved back to the head. Within a short period, those tissues started to move. It was like a flower bud unfolding. With that unfolding, motion increased to where normal functioning returned.

I told him that since such a long period had elapsed since he had been injured, one treatment might not cure him, and that he should call if he needed another treatment. He called a week later and said he was still having headaches but they were a lot better and that during the two days immediately after the treatment he had experienced no headaches. I again treated him and told him to call if he needed another treatment.

Because of the way I practice medicine, some people are put off when I tell them to call me if they need another appointment. They would prefer that I schedule them for another appointment at the end of a treatment. They perceive me as saying that I do not want to see them again. Nothing could be further from the truth, but it is also very true that I really do not want to waste their money having them come back if they are better. I prefer my patients to be involved in their own healing. The "down side" to this is that if a patient does not come back, I receive no feedback on how they are doing.

The bottom line is, however, that I do not have a crystal ball that tells me whether what I have done will last. From experience, I can guess if it will last but only the patient will know. The first question I ask a patient is usually "How are you doing?" If they say they feel great, I usually tell them to go away. That is not very good for business but I don't want to waste their time. Telling them to call me if they need another treatment is much more effective.

About a year after treating Al for his headaches, I had a chance to talk to the person who referred Al to me. She said that Al's wife had come into her store and had hugged her with tears in her eyes. Al's headaches were gone. She was grateful for the referral to see me. If I had not talked to that person, I would never have known what had happened to Al.

A similar event occurred a few weeks ago. After several years of low back pain, the son of one of my patients finally listened to his father and came to see me. He said that he had pain 24/7 and that occasionally it was 10 on a scale of 10 (10 being torture) and that it was never less than 4. He walked and moved like he was in pain; however, at the end of the treatment he said he was pain free for the first time in four years. Experience has told me that if someone is in pain that long, his tissues have learned some bad habits and that he'd probably need another treatment. The problem was that his tissues felt good to me so I told him to call me if the pain returned. After a couple of weeks, I was starting to wonder if he was still okay. Fortunately, his mom came in for a treatment and confirmed that he was still okay and had asked her if she was "going to see god today." Such references embarrass me but I'm glad he's still doing well. I wish one treatment was always as fruitful.

22

Fatigue and Fibromyalgia

"Eventually we will understand that all wisdom is within us, and as we remember, practice, and access this wisdom, we will become our own best teacher. At this point, we will find peace and joy in the present time, because the real issue is about how we live our lives right now, being spiritual now, no matter what we have been taught to believe." (Brian Weiss, MD, *Messages From the Masters*)

This book would not be complete without touching on this subject. If there are epidemics in our society, other than obesity and diabetes, they are fatigue and its cousin, fibromyalgia. When I place my hands on a patient and feel their energy level, seldom do I find someone whose energy level is greater than eighty percent of what it should be. Some patients are aware of this deficiency, but many are not.

Fatigue is an interesting beast. From time to time, we all get "fatigued" but when it seems to persist without end and starts to consume your life, it is past the time to do something about it. The problem is that physicians are not taught how to deal with this problem, but we are the ones who get to treat it.

Diagnosing fatigue is not simple and can easily cost a fortune. Those with good insurance are indeed blessed. For those who have to foot the bill themselves, pray that you are never afflicted with this disorder. The good news is that it can be treated and cured in most instances. Unfortunately, most people who are chronically fatigued have seen more physicians than I have relatives.

My approach to the problem is fairly simple. I talk to my patient and ask them to describe their life. Generally, those with fatigue can relate a period in their life when they felt great and they know when they started to feel fatigued. If they can convince me that they are fatigued, I will do a few simple blood tests to determine if they have some sort of blood disorder or blood chemistry disorder. I will also order a thyroid profile that includes a measurement of the thyroid stimulating hormone (TSH) level.

Generally, most fatigue is caused by not getting enough sleep. "Early to bed, early to rise…" is good advice. Next in line is poor nutrition. Most people do not eat properly. The reality is that most of our fruits are picked before they are ripe. Our crops are sprayed with chemicals that we end up ingesting. The soils from which our crops are grown are deficient in minerals. Only "organically" grown foods are properly and sufficiently fertilized, and foods grown under "super organic" conditions are even better. I've heard it said that it takes seventeen ears of corn grown today to equal the nutritional value of one ear of corn grown in 1950. It reminds me of the commercials for "Total" cereal. Even the meats we eat are laden with artificial hormones. Cooking destroys vital enzymes and nutrients. It is a mess. Supplementation is mandatory yet most people do not take supplements. Most "supplements" are less than adequate. "Muscle testing" is an excellent way to determine if a supplement is good for you.

Coenzyme Q10 needs to be added to the diet. This coenzyme is vital in the production and utilization of energy in the body. Cardiac patients, asthma patients, patients experiencing heart failure, <u>any patient taking "statin" drugs,</u> and patients with fatigue respond very well to this nutrient in large doses of 300 mg/day or more.

It gets a bit more difficult from there. Some people are fatigued because they have low levels of thyroid hormone. This is almost of epidemic proportions in our country and is often not diagnosed. Unfortunately, the standard blood tests for thyroid hormone levels aren't accurate enough to diagnose so called "sub-clinical hypothyroidism" even though a new TSH test is available that is a lot better than what we have been using.

Frankly, there has been considerable debate in the medical community as to whether or not there is such a disorder as "sub-clinical hypothyroidism." I firmly believe there is such a disorder.

I think it is interesting that the "standard of care" today has physicians believing that the very sensitive TSH test is sufficient for diagnosing thyroid dysfunction. I think that is absurd. I think it is important to also check Free T3, Free T4, and T7. Only when all of these values are compared can a physician possibly diagnose if the thyroid is functioning properly and even then it's difficult.

Several years ago, "subclinical hypothyroidism" started to be looked at seriously. The idea being that when a physician looks at the lab results from a thyroid profile, the values may be within the "normal" range. The problem with that is that "normal" is based on looking at a lot of people and their lab values and then making a decision as to what is in the middle range and then saying what is "normal." Traditionally, if the lab value then falls in that "normal" range, the physician assumed that there was no problem even if the patient had symptoms of the disease. Unfortunately, when that happens, many physicians are all too eager to assume that the problem is in the patients' head. As I said earlier, none of us are built the same.

Fortunately, thanks largely to the work of Broda O. Barnes M.D., many physicians have realized that if the patient is at the low end of "normal" they might still be low in thyroid. One of the easiest ways to evaluate that problem is to check the patients' temperature. If it is below 98.6°F chronically, there is a chance the patient is hypothyroid. If the patient is given thyroid supplementation (I prefer Armour Thyroid but there are some others based on beef rather than pork that work nicely) and they get better, the diagnosis is made. I prefer a "natural" thyroid supplement rather than the man made ones such as Synthroid.

Naturally, the major thyroid hormones are referred to as T3 (triiodothyronine) and T4 (thyroxin). These are naturally produced in the thyroid gland situated below the Adam's Apple in your neck, however, most T3 is converted outside the thyroid gland from T4. Most physicians will supplement with T4 (levothyroxine) only. Occasionally they will supplement with T3 (liothyronine) only. I figure that a "supplement" should be as close to what nature provides as is possible. That is why I like Armour Thyroid. I'm talking about thyroid supplementation not thyroid replacement which would be necessary if the thyroid gland was removed or totally non-functional.

I have over-simplified this whole process but your family physician should be aware of this information since it has been in every major medical journal at one time or another during the past few years. I get the blood tests but I also check the patient's temperature. I also feel the patient to see what their cranial rhythmic impulse and what their other bioenergetic patterns are doing. I then factor all this together and come up with a diagnosis.

Occasionally, someone will tell me they are fatigued, but all the tests are negative and their cranial rhythmic impulse is terrific. If that is the case, I have a hard time believing they are fatigued. In most cases, and I have seen a few, I have to look for some other disease process or motive.

Treatment for fatigue is geared toward all affected areas. Exercising in the sun is vital. We are too often bombarded with energies from florescent lighting that is not "full spectrum" lighting. I usually work in very subdued incandescent lighting but had all the florescent tubes in my office replaced with full spectrum tubes.

Before I moved to my new office, between patients I would turn on the overhead lights. Doing that always made me feel more energized. Commercially available light boxes that have full spectrum lights at 10,000 lux are a good start for those who feel fatigued and who can't figure out a way to get outside and enjoy the sun. I tell my patients to try to be out in the sun for at least thirty minutes a day between the hours of 10:00 a.m. and 2:00 p.m. Recently there have been some studies that indicate that the blue spectrum is the important part of the spectrum and that full spectrum isn't necessary. I'm not willing to jump on that band wagon.

Tight tissues can also cause fatigue. When I was nineteen, I used to work for a smelter. The first day on the job, an old guy walked by me and told me that I was going to work myself to death. I had been assigned to shovel ore and was really trying hard to get the job done. I expected to be tired. He shocked me when he went on to explain that I was wearing tight Levi's and I would have to fight them all day long doing my job. He said I should get a pair of loose overalls. I tried it and was amazed at the difference in my energy level at the end of the day. If our tissues are tight, we have to use precious energy to fight them. By the end of the day, it takes its toll. The same occurs if you are overweight. It takes energy to carry around the extra pounds. I seldom find an obese patient who is not fatigued.

A social acquaintance of mine, Tommi, gradually became tired, grouchy, and hard to live with. When she came to see me, her husband brought her in. When this happens, I have to wonder who brought whom to the appointment.

On examination, her internal energy was about forty percent of what it should be. Her cranial rhythmic impulse was terrible. She was exercising adequately but she was not eating properly. I administered a short test for depression and she scored at the moderate level. I do not blame her. She had good reason to be depressed.

In the past, depression has gotten a bad reputation. On occasion, the depressed patient was and still is strapped down and electrical shocks are delivered to their head. It was not too many years ago that "One Flew Over the Cuckoo's Nest" won Academy Awards, and we were all exposed to some of the methods of treating mental illness.

Even today, most of the medications used to treat depression are horrible. Fortunately, a lot has been learned about the mind. Several newer medications are available, for those who need them, which have fewer, more tolerable side effects. Often, a person will only require a few months of medication before they can be taken off them. Sometimes, it takes longer. I don't like these medications and think they are over-prescribed and abused.

In Tommi's case, I was blessed. She was one of the few patients that actually listened to me and did everything I told her to do. She also prayed about what I told her to do to get confirmation of my directions. It's great!

She was not difficult to treat. Her tissues loved being treated. I told her to walk twenty to forty minutes a day in the sun. Walking is great when it comes to fighting fatigue and depression, but it must be done in the sun to achieve its maximum benefit. A recent study reported comparable results from walking 45-60 minutes a day to that achieved by taking one of the more popular antidepressants. As for walking, that means as close to noon as possible. Exercise is crucial. I had one patient who couldn't walk thirty seconds without being totally exhausted so I started her out walking 20 seconds at a time. Exercise is very important and though I think walking is an excellent exercise, we also need some resistance training, i.e., weight training. It helps in facilitating weight loss and it also increases bone density.

Most people who are fatigued have breathing problems so during the initial exam I will ask a new patient to breathe for me. Invariably, it is a shallow breath. They have to fight to get a deep breath. When I'm able to facilitate a release of their diaphragm, it's amazing to see how much deeper they breathe. I am surprised at how many people, who should know better, breathe poorly. Many people believe that to breathe properly, they should be breathing into their abdomen. I'm not sure where they get such ideas.

If we take time to examine the anatomy of breathing, we notice that the primary muscle of respiration is the diaphragm. When it is tightened, a negative pressure is created in the chest and the lungs expand to fill the space created and air flows into our lungs. This is what we usually know as belly breathing. If the diaphragm alone were responsible for breathing, we would "belly breathe."

The fact is that we have secondary muscles of respiration in our chest. These are the intercostal muscles. A proper breath should start in the belly and end in the upper thoracic (chest) region. That process brings energies from the lower abdomen up through the first four major chakras and passes them on to the fifth. If you want to be healthy, that process has to function properly.

As for Tommi, another problem I encountered in her was that I was certain her thyroid was not functioning properly. I tried her on Synthroid and she did not get better. I wondered if her body might not be adequately converting T4 (thyroxin) into T3 (triiodothyronine), which is what the body primarily uses.

Your thyroid profile may look great but at the tissue level, you may be deficient. I tried her on Cytomel (T3) and it worked.

The number of physicians that refuse to believe anything unless it is written in a book constantly amazes me. If I put someone on a thyroid medication and then tell them to make sure their family physician is aware of this, too many times the patient will come back to me and say that their physician disagrees with them being on it even though they feel better. I am not even talking about large doses but very small doses. The literature just does not support this approach but it should. This failure to convert T4 into T3 is called "Wilson's Syndrome." Some doctors refuse to believe such a thing exists. Remember: If it walks like a duck and squawks like a duck, it's probably a duck. Physicians should be treating their patients and not their preconceived notions.

Tommi did everything I asked of her and she got better. She says nice things about me but she deserves all the credit. She says she has her life back.

Another case involves Emma. Emma is an intelligent woman with many strange abilities. She used to work with computers and was what could be called a professional hacker. She was paid to try to break into computer systems to see if they were safe from hackers. She can also wave her hand over a light and it will glow brighter. She can change channels on my radio by waving her hand over it as well.

On initial examination, she was pleasant and her mind was nimble. She was overweight, but not markedly obese. When I felt her energies, however, they were scrambled.

Energies in our bodies need to be organized. If there is no organization, there is no force and very little can be accomplished. If the energies are scrambled, I usually look at diet or yeast as the possible culprits but scrambled energies can occur for other reasons.

Usually, fatigue responds readily to bioenergetic treatment, proper nutrition, and moderate exercise. All it did for Emma was make her hurt. I remember seeing her in a stuporous state as she continued to deteriorate and become more fatigued.

Whenever I feel stumped, I go back to the beginning and start all over. I must have taken her history a half dozen times before she told me that when she was a child she had a similar episode of fatigue. At that time, she was treated with B-12 injections.

I am in favor of vitamin therapy but whenever a person is injected with an individual B-vitamin, it is necessary to also treat the person with a B-complex because the individual "B" will deplete the remaining "B's" in their system. Anyway, I tried injecting her with B-12 and placed her on a B-complex and it did not help.

She and her husband were desperate so they found another practitioner in our area who treated her with chelation therapy. It cost her several thousand dollars but that was about all it did. I did not know what to do next.

It occurred to me she might be toxic, but I did not know where it was coming from and why. Then, one day, she told me she had the ability to absorb pain from others. The church she attended had a service on Tuesday evenings where she would embrace people, absorb their pain and illness, and they would get better. The problem was she could not get rid of what she absorbed so she continued to get worse. She was dying because of this. It sounds like something out of "The X-Files" or "The Twilight Zone" but it was happening.

Emma was surrounded with a lot of pain. She was also surrounded by people and animals that were either consciously or unconsciously using her to get rid of their pain.

I remember taking her to the sink in my treatment room and placing her hands firmly against the stainless steel basin while I ran water on her wrists and projected energy down her arms into the sink. As soon as the channel opened up, "bad" energies poured out of her and her knees buckled. I caught her as she started to fall to the floor.

She got better but it did not last. Since then, she has run a roller coaster course of improvement and then getting worse that continues to this day.

As I said earlier, those with whom we associate profoundly influence us. The people we are exposed to, even if we do not speak to them, profoundly influence us. Quantum physics implies that we are influenced to one degree or another by everyone on this planet. We have to be keenly aware of the energy patterns to which we expose ourselves.

As for fibromyalgia, most of the things that cause fatigue also cause muscles to ache. Muscles ache when they don't get enough oxygen, when they are overloaded with toxins, or when they have been overworked and aren't used to it.

A few nights ago, I tossed and turned until about 3:00 a.m. when I'd had enough. I was unwinding. Some time during the night my body started treating itself and it started unwinding. I was also heating up. I tried to go back to sleep but as soon as I relaxed, it started up again so I gave up and got out of bed.

The next three days were terrible. I felt like I had been mugged. I ached all over. I don't know why it happened but it happens from time to time. Yup, I ached! Fortunately, it went away. When it doesn't go away, we call it fibromyalgia.

The cure for fibromyalgia is fairly straight forward. The first thing I do is clean out the patient's bowels.

A patient is supposed to have a bowel movement the first thing in the morning and then after every major meal. It's not once a day or once a week. If the bowels aren't moving on a regular daily basis, the body will start to reabsorb that which it is trying to get rid of and that is nasty stuff. I'm amazed by how many patients balk at the suggestion that they need to have more frequent bowel movements. Colon Activator by Healing America works very nicely to stimulate the bowels but that's not all that is needed.

The next thing is to detoxify the body. It makes no sense to start detoxifying the body until the bowels are moving or you will just reabsorb the toxins released into the bowels. There are several approaches to detoxification but it takes awhile. Generally, I will tell the patient to start a juice fast followed by a restricted diet that eliminates all unnecessary sugars and all artificial sweeteners. If a person smokes or drinks alcohol they will have to quit these before we even start this program or there is no sense in proceeding with a program that may run several years.

I will also check the patient to see if systemic yeast is a problem and if necessary place them on a yeast elimination diet in combination with the drug Diflucan until the yeast is under control. The addition of soluble and insoluble fibers will also help in the restoration of normal bowel function and in the elimination of toxins.

Probiotics will be taken with each meal for at least six months. AlliPRO, a probiotic formulation by Healing America, works very well and is the best probiotic I've come across. In fact, Healing America has a "Perfect Start" 21-day detoxification "kit" that works extremely well to not only help clean out the bowel and restore normal bowel movements but it also helps detoxify the gallbladder, liver, and blood and it helps to get rid of parasites.

Sweating is very helpful and healthful for our bodies. Nowadays, we try to avoid sweating at all costs. It's that "odor thing" and that "sweaty armpit" thing. The problem is that our skin is designed to help us remove toxins. Often I will tell patients who have been treated to soak in a tub full of hot water with either apple cider vinegar (if it's a treatment reaction) or a pound of sea salt (if they are toxic) until they are sweating. It takes about twenty minutes. An even better approach, which I highly recommend, is the regular and judicial use of saunas.

Saunas are wonderful for helping us detoxify. It's important that the wood that the sauna is made of is not treated. Otherwise you would be sitting there breathing in varnish, etc. I was recently at an Anti-Aging Seminar in Las Vegas and learned of saunas that use far-infrared heat. These saunas don't heat up the room they are in so they are ideal for office use and can even be placed in a master bedroom for daily use. As a physician, I fully realize that if the "cure" isn't "convenient," the patient probably won't do it. These are very convenient and they work wonderfully.

At this point the treatment gets more individualized. If a patient makes it this far they are probably committed to getting better. I say that because when I start eliminating foods or tell a patient what they have to eat, some patients will try to bargain with me. Those who are not committed to getting better will tell me what they "can't" do. I have learned that it's not worth arguing with those patients. I let them do what they want and hope that at some point they will understand that if they don't do what I tell them to do, they will probably not fully recover.

The bottom line is that we first have to clean out the gut and then detoxify the system. Once that is done, the patient usually stops aching and starts to recover. It's a long process and we will be married to each other for several years and they will be treated by me once or twice a month during that period of time. I think that the ache of fibromyalgia is the result of the disengagement of the spirit from the tissues so it's vital that these people be treated throughout this period so they can heal at their energetic/spirit level.

Awhile ago, I had one of my patients, who was going through this program, come into my office. She is a very nice lady who says she has her life back and gives me the credit but the truth is that she did most of the work. To illustrate the significance of detoxification, she brought in two of her bras. The first she wore during the first year of treatment. It was stained grey by toxins that had been released from her tissues. The second bra was one she had been wearing during the past year. It was almost new looking.

The bottom line is that we carry a lot of "junk" around in our tissues as the result of the pollution we bathe ourselves in daily. Sooner or later, it takes its toll on the tissues. Some of us are more resilient but it takes its toll nonetheless.

I also recommend that if you are on city water, that you install a whole house dechlorination system. Chlorine is a poison and it has an affinity for fatty tissue. It is a known carcinogen and it is readily absorbed into our bodies through the skin by bathing and through our lungs by showering. Our children and our elderly are especially susceptible to the affects of chlorine. I've seen remarkable recoveries from ill health after installing a whole house dechlorination system. "In 1992, the American Medical Association published information that stated <u>"nearly 28% of all cancer of the intestines and 18% of all cancer of the bladder</u>

were caused by the drinking of chlorinated water." Chlorine may also be a culprit in cancer, although studies undertaken to determine if this is the case remain incomplete." (http://www.triangularwave.com/f9.htm)

Simply put, putting fluoride in our drinking water should be outlawed. It is an industrial waste product and a poison. It makes bones brittle. "Would you intentionally ingest a material that is used as a pesticide and has been suspected of causing cancer, hip fractures, intellectual impairment, fertility problems, deformed fish and dental deformities? Well, two-thirds of the population of the United States, and soon the entire population of the city of Los Angeles and its surrounding communities, take this material into their bodies every day if they use tap water in any way." Additionally, "Fluoride was the top chemical hazard of the U.S. nuclear weapons program, not only for workers, but for those living in nearby communities as well." (**Fluoride—Poison in the Water?** Healing Our World: Weekly Comment By Jackie Alan Giuliano, Ph.D.)

The data to confirm the toxicity of chlorine and fluoride is readily available. I encourage you to learn more about what is so briefly stated here.

23

My Second Basic Course

"Just as your hand, held before the eye, can hide the tallest mountain, so this small earthly life keeps us from seeing the vast radiance that fills the core of the universe."
(Nachman of Bratslav)

Several years ago, I attended my second "basic" course in craniosacral osteopathic medicine. For many years, I had attended the "advanced" course that is held in Biddeford, Maine at the University of New England, College of Osteopathic Medicine, each fall. It is nice to get away for a while each year. I generally consider the course a success if I learn something I did not already know. Even if I do not learn something new, the scenery is beautiful in the fall.

There has been such a demand for the advanced course that the people in charge decided that to be eligible to attend, a physician must have attended two basic courses even if they have been going to the advanced course for years. I've had five basic courses, but the Cranial Academy and the Sutherland Cranial Teaching Foundation sanctioned only two of those courses. Until a few years ago, I only had one such sanctioned course.

My second "sanctioned" course was different from any I have had in cranial. To start, the number of participants was about half that which is normally allowed. The course directors were Jim Jealous, D.O., and Michael Burrano, D.O. I have told you about Jim. Dr. Burrano was the president of the Sutherland Cranial Teaching Foundation at that time. What is most important, Dr. Burrano was taught by Jim. In fact, the faculty was all pretty much of the same mind bent.

What I mean is there are basically two different schools of thought when it comes to cranial. The predominant school of thought is that the bones of the cranium (skull) move in certain patterns and it is important to try to work within those patterns. It is very empirical. The other school of thought is more intuitive.

Empirical reasoning is very neat. It's linear. If a bone moves, it moves only within a certain framework. When things are out of sorts, the patterns are easy to name. The problem with this is that the bones do not always move the way they are supposed to move. Sometimes they move in directions they aren't presumably capable of moving.

The major problem with this school of thought and reasoning, as I see it, is that things happen which cannot be explained by empirical models. If we know and understand half of what is going on in and around the body, I would be surprised. It used to be that hardly a day went by that I didn't learn something new. That had slowed down a bit, but with my acknowledgment of both past life experiences and demons, it's an every day occurrence once again.

This course was divided into two sessions of two and one-half days each, which were separated by three weeks. It was perfect. I wish I could say what made this course special, but I can't other than to say it seemed to have been designed with me in mind. I am almost embarrassed to admit I almost did not go.

I should have known how important this course would be to me when Dr. Burrano called to ask if I would attend. Six months earlier, I had heard of the course and had expressed an interest but I was told I could not attend. It was only being offered to a certain group of physicians in New England. I was a little ticked off but I recovered. Then, unexpectedly, Dr. Burrano called. I told him I thought I was not allowed to attend, but he said I could.

No one before or since has ever called me to ask if I would be attending any course. That should have been my first clue. Somewhere in the back of my mind, I knew something was afoot. The saying "When the student is ready, the teacher will appear" comes to mind.

As time drew closer, I realized I was not going to be able to afford to go to the course so I wrote Dr. Burrano explaining this. He wrote back and encouraged me to attend anyway. At that point, I decided I needed to do whatever was needed to place me there.

It is important to listen to the coincidences in our lives. <u>It is important that we allow ourselves the opportunity to "feel" what's going on in the universe and that we position ourselves so we can be swept along in the "current" that has been created.</u> It's important that we allow things to happen when those things are for our greater good. I'm getting better at this, though I still struggle with it from time to time.

After having said all this, you're probably wondering why this course was so special. Basic stuff was taught, but this was not like any basic course I have ever attended. Everyone at that course had taken another basic course. No one was a novice. The faculty picked all attendees. The first new thing was that we were paired off with another physician for the entire course. Usually we trade off quite frequently. By not trading off, we got to know the mechanism of our partner.

I was paired with Ted. We had never met before the course. It took a little while, but before the end of the first session, his mechanism was in pretty good shape. This meant that when we reconvened for the second half of the course three weeks later, I only had to do a little work before he was in great shape.

Another good thing about this course was there were plenty of table trainers providing a lot of supervision. Because of this, I could relax and not worry about being damaged by Ted. I should say, though, that Ted's skills were quite good already.

The best part of the course for me was that Dr. Jealous watched me constantly. It seemed like every time I turned around, he was observing me. I remember one day I was treating Ted and was riding the crest of the tide. Jim walked up and from about eight feet away said, "Not there. Come off the top." I didn't realize at first that he was talking to me. I didn't think it was possible to stand eight feet away and know where on the tide someone was treating. What he was doing was very much like someone walking up to you and telling you what you were thinking at the time.

When I realized he was talking to me, I came forward off the crest and he said, "Not that way, the other way." I came back up over the crest and down to an area where it "felt" comfortable to me to be. When I hit that point, he said, "There!" I figured he could not possibly know where I was treating so I moved back up the crest a little bit. His response was, "don't go up there. Come back down." It blew me away. I do not know how he does it, but someday I will. As for now, I'm getting better at it.

The best treatment I have ever had was while I was at that course. Ted, with Jim standing a few feet away talking him through a few difficult and tricky areas, treated me. It literally changed me and set into motion things that I am still benefiting from.

What I liked most about the course was that I could treat unfettered. I do not like to tiptoe around the tissues. I treat like I flew jets. I love to feel the power of the mechanism. I am fairly aggressive. It was while "boldly going where…" that I had the most bizarre experience I have ever had while treating someone.

It was during the second session of the course. I had Ted pretty well tuned-up and there wasn't anything specifically worth treating so I was just exploring his tissues. I had gone from the tissue level to the fluid level and then to the membrane level and wasn't doing anything other than watching Ted's mechanism work. Then the tide started coming through. I'm not quite sure what prompted me to do it, but I somehow managed to blend his energy with that of the tide. I wish I could be more specific but it was a fluke. I had never done it before and I haven't been able to do it since. Somehow, I was able to drop him into the tide. At first, it seemed like the edges softened and then it seemed like he dissolved into the tide.

On *Star Trek: The Next Generation*, when a star goes super nova it explodes and expands outward in a shock wave through the universe. This is what it felt like. Something that was part of Ted was rapidly expanding outward. He blasted through the table trainer sitting next to me and then through the two physicians on the next table and was starting to shoot through the walls. It felt like I had all four people in a wave pattern of sorts and I was treating all of them at the same time.

I looked up to see the table trainer and the two physicians staring at me. The table trainer said, "Reel him in, Bob," so I brought him back. I woke Ted up and asked how he felt. He said he was okay. During the break, I asked the two physicians at the next table if they felt anything while I was treating Ted. They both said they did. When I asked what they felt they replied it was as if a breeze had blown through them. I do not know if what happened was therapeutic, but it was certainly awesome.

At the end of each course, each physician is examined and treated by a member of the faculty to insure no one goes home with some sort of physician induced strain pattern. It's great!

I came away feeling I had received the best treatment ever. In addition, not only did I receive a treatment from Ted while Dr. Jealous supervised, but I also received a treatment from Dr. Jealous at the end of the course. Ted's treatment was so thorough that I was dizzy when I sat up after he was done. I could tell things were in motion. It's something my patients have often remarked about, but it is not something that I had felt prior to that course.

In some ways, that course may have marked the end/beginning of many things. At this point, I am not sure where I am going, but I feel it is in the right direction. In some ways, it feels like I have been lifted out of the Grand Canyon and now stand on the rim looking over the vast expanse. The view is different, to say the least. My understanding, awe, and respect for what I am working with have broadened considerably.

24

The Healing Crisis

"Only when we have learned to listen selflessly and to be inwardly receptive, without any personal opinion of feeling stirring in us, can the higher beings described by spiritual science speak to us. The beings of the spiritual world will remain silent as long as we still pit any personal feelings or opinions against what we hear from others".
(Rudolph Steiner)

I don't get sick like I used to get sick. My body has been changing over the past fifteen or so years. Since I've returned from my second basic course, my body has felt like it has undergone one change after another. I actually look younger than I did fifteen years ago.

About two months after that course, the following occurred. It was a Monday. I started working at 7:00 a.m. and felt pretty good but I could feel something was up. My body temperature is normally around 97.4 but by 8:00 a.m. I was starting to feel warm. When I checked my temperature, it was about 98.0. After a few more patients, I felt even warmer so I checked it again. It was up to 99.0.

By the time my temperature got to 102.0, my patients were starting to complain that my hands were so hot they were uncomfortable. When I treat patients, my hands normally heat up. I figure they usually run about three to four degrees hotter than my core temperature.

During lunch, I took some time to get some blood tests done to see if something was wrong. I didn't expect to find anything and I didn't. In fact, I have never had such good test results.

When my temperature reached 103.3 I decided to call it a day. I went home and straight to bed. I was exhausted, but that was the only ill effect I experienced from the whole process. I canceled the next day and spent the day in bed. I guess I needed the rest.

What had happened to me? I think it was a reaction, or to be more specific, a treatment reaction or healing crises, to what happened both at the course and during the ensuing period. I briefly talked about a similar episode earlier in this book. A healing crisis normally occurs almost immediately after a treatment but that isn't carved in stone. It can take quite a bit of time for it to happen.

One of the problems I am constantly faced with is my "upbringing." I too was raised with faulty paradigms. I was trained in the "traditional" medical establishment. When something goes wrong, I try to think of some "ailment" that matches the symptoms. The trouble is that when we start dealing with "energies" there are a whole lot of things that the body does that do not match any syndrome or disease. People who deal with energies have coined the term "healing crisis" to cover the aches, pains, and oddball things the body does as it goes through the healing process.

It is not abnormal to feel worse after being treated. Some patients get very sore. Some patients feel like they have the flu or have been run over by a truck. It doesn't have to happen immediately after a treatment, either. There can be a delay of 72 hours or more.

About two weeks after I got back from the last basic course, I started to feel like I was coming down with a cold. My sinuses were plugged and my nose ran. My eyes watered and I perspired like I was in the tropics. I didn't run a temperature and I didn't feel sick. It was a healing crisis. I'm positive that my hyperthermia (my elevated temperature) was also due to the treatment I received while in Maine. I wish I could say it is over, but even years afterward I am still experiencing changes in my body and how it functions. I think it's fascinating!

It is possible and desirable for us to continue to evolve during our lives. We are after all, spiritual beings having a physical experience.

Of course, medicine in itself is fascinating. I love what I do. Once or twice a year I used to contemplate leaving my solo practice in favor of one of the almost daily offers to join some medical practice in some area at considerably more money that I make now.

These offers usually include vacation time, retirement benefits, and medical benefits. All of these I currently have to supply myself. It's one of the "joys of being self-employed." One of the true joys of being self-employed is that it's so peaceful. I pray I will always be able to do this. I don't plan on ever retiring. That would be terrible. This work is hard work, very hard work. As I've gotten older, I have had to cut back to working the equivalent of three days a week. The best schedule I can come up with that allows me to treat effectively and not spend all of my off time in bed is to work half days Mondays and Fridays, and full days Tuesdays, and Thursdays. That allows me time to recover. I like to get up when my body is ready to wake up. As such and if possible, I arrive at the office about 10:00 a.m. on Mondays and Fridays.

A few years ago, I went to Florida for the weekend. It was the first time I had done such a thing. Living in Indiana, I had grown tired of winter. I longed to walk on a sunny beach and listen to the roar of the surf. My last true vacation was about fifteen years ago. I get away every year or so to a three day seminar but it's not the same and it certainly isn't a vacation. While in Florida, I realized that I live to work rather than work to live. I really enjoy my work. The problem is that I really enjoy living as well.

A lot of my patients don't love their work. They kill themselves slowly for the sake of earning a living. Stress can kill you. What's really strange is that I have some very wealthy patients who work for themselves yet continue to work like their lives depend on it yet they already have enough money to last several lifetimes. When is enough, enough? Few have been able to answer that question when I put it to them. One fellow was actually surprised that I asked him how much enough was.

Too often the "A" type personalities live for the "buzz" versus living for peace. It's a choice. The secret is to find peace in your life and then nurture it and the resultant health that always comes with that change.

A few years ago, a fellow came to me for a treatment. There was something about him that I couldn't put my finger on. When I was done treating him he paid me in cash and said he didn't need a receipt. He then looked me square in the eye and asked "Have you found it yet?" I knew what he was asking though we had not talked about it. In fact, little was said during the encounter because of the overwhelming calmness that prevailed in the room.

I looked him square in the eye and said, "Not yet but I'm close." He said, "I know" and left. I have not seen him since. We were talking about peace. I'm pretty sure he was an angel but the question really is, "Why was he there?"

25

The Mind/Body Connection

"All matter originates and exists only because by <u>virtue of a force</u> which brings the particles of an atom to vibration and hold this most minute solar system of the atom together... We must assume behind this force the existence of a conscious and intelligent <u>mind</u>. This mind is the <u>matrix</u> of all matter."
(Max Planck, Nobel Prize-winning father of quantum theory)

Jesus Christ said as quoted in John 14:12: *"Verily, verily, I say unto you, He that believeth on me, the works that I do shall he do also; and greater [works] than these shall he do..."* How could we do "greater works" unless we are not what we think we are and/or we are greater than we think we are?

I've previously discussed an instance which occurred when I was treating one of my fellow students during one of my lunch breaks at medical school. That day I realized that my thoughts affected the mechanism and the tissues of others. It was an epiphany.

During the past few years I have learned that research has been done to help quantify what I am able to feel. Einstein said $E=MC^2$ and it revolutionized our world and lead to the creation of the atomic bomb but is that it? No. That formula states that energy and matter are interchangeable and are essentially the same. Thought energy can become matter and it can influence our physical world.

I've long maintained that we are spiritual/energetic beings having a physical experience. Additionally, I have said and I believe that our energetic being forms a matrix or mold into which our physical tissues flow. If the matrix is bent, tissues will become bent and if the matrix is repaired the tissues will try to repair themselves. One form of energy follows and flows into the mold laid down by another. It's that simple.

Max Planck took that even further and proposed that everything we perceive is the result of a matrix that has been created by an intelligent mind which is far greater than that which our own spirit can create. That mind is the mind of God. That being the case, we are all linked to everything and everyone.

What I did that day during my lunch break and what I have done daily since then in helping my patients regain their health is to essentially "co-create" with God a new reality. This is not a "Bob" thing. It's something that we were all created with the ability to do. It has been said that when the angles heard the plan to create humans they complained that we'd be more powerful than they but God said "Yes, but they won't remember."

What we feel influences what we are. What we feel influences our very cells and our health. In a May 2001 interview with Stephen Marshall, Gregg Braden said, "When we find ourselves living a life of anger and rage and hate and jealousy and fear—those are the words of the language we use—that translates to a chemistry in our body that actually defeats life in our bodies. There is what we call a 'hate' chemistry and a love chemistry. So when anger and rage and hate and jealousy rule us (and sometimes we don't even know when we are having those emotions) our immune systems are compromised. Our bodies don't heal the way they could have healed—cells, cuts on your hands don't heal the same way. There is an antibody called SIGA in your saliva. It's your first line of defense. When we are angry, that saliva SIGA antibody decreases and makes us susceptible to opportunistic infections. On the other hand, when we find ourselves in the presence of compassion, love, understanding, forgiveness, gratitude, that's the terminology in the English language that translates to a chemistry in our bodies that affirms and supports life, we have tremendously enhanced SIGA antibodies in our saliva. Our immune systems are tremendously enhanced. And I'm just going to tell you how far this is going."

"A study was done in 1998, the first time a global blood study was done to find out how bad the AIDS epidemic really is on a global scale—the first time blood had been taken from people of all the nations for this study. And one of the first things researchers found, and it was just an amazing thing for them to be able to see, was that there is a mutation that is occurring in human genes in this generation that allows us to have a tremendously enhanced immune system against the HIV virus. Now this is an amazing thing to be able to say because, in the 1980s when we discovered AIDS, we said there is no cure. Whenever anybody tests positive it's only a matter of time, and it's terminal. And there were speculations that the entire world could be infected and eliminated through the HIV virus. That simply is not true now because humans have shifted something in their consciousness—their belief systems that translates to emotion and feeling in their bodies. And for some people now, they have actually changed the genetic code in their bodies. The University of Alabama at Birmingham has done studies with this and the Aaron Diamond AIDS Research Center, right here in New York City, was responsible for doing the studies. They might have very different conclusions about what's happening but they are showing conclusively there is what's called a *spontaneous genetic mutation* happening in human populations. To make a long story brief again, the common denominator, what changed these people's genes is their belief systems—we believe. That's the only thing that we found that was in common with all of them. They didn't give in to the possibility of losing their lives and they weren't angry about what happened and they said we are going to choose a new belief system, where we honor life in our everyday world and by doing that they also find that their body responds in the same way." (http://www.greatmystery.org/interviewgb.html)

Think about this. This means that we do not have to accept the "reality" that we see. We can change this "reality" to a different "reality." Both are real. One may be unacceptable while the other is quite acceptable. What is the key? Gregg Braden says the key is "feeling" and I believe he is correct because it matches what I've learned in the course of practicing bioenergetic medicine.

Gregg talks about three experiments that have been done. The first was done by Dr. Vladimir Poponin, a Russian quantum biologist. In this experiment the pattern of photons within a vacuum was measured before, during and after the introduction of DNA into the vacuum. Initially the pattern was random but when the DNA was introduced the pattern changed in alignment with the DNA. This alignment was maintained even after the DNA was removed.

The second experiment was performed by our military. Human leukocytes (white blood cells) were collected from "donors" and placed in one room. In another room those donors were subjected to "emotional stimulation." The response from the donor and the response from their cells in another room were identical and it occurred simultaneously. The donors and the cells were then separated by fifty miles and the experiment repeated and the results were the same.

The third experiment was done by the Institute of Heart Math and was published under the title "Local and Non-local Effects of Coherent Heart Frequencies on Conformational Changes of DNA." This is a fascinating study in which human placental tissue was placed in an environment where trained researchers emoted strong feelings and the conformation of the DNA was examined. When strong feelings of love, compassion, etc. were emoted, the DNA strands elongated and unwound. When the opposite emotions were emoted the strands of DNA shortened and the coiling tightened. This affect was reversed when positive emotions were emoted. Furthermore, they went on to run this experiment on HIV positive patients. "They discovered that feelings of love, gratitude, and appreciation created 300,000 TIMES the immune resistance they had without those feelings." (Gregg Braden "How to Attract Anything", http://www.healthtap.net/generic.html?pid=21)

So what does all this mean? For one it clearly shows that our thoughts, feelings, and emotions affect our cells and the cells of those around us even to great distances. If it can occur instantaneously at distances up to fifty miles, imagine what happens within your body when your thoughts are focused on the feeling of health. Likewise, if you are focused on your disease, you are literally programming your cells contrary to that which is pro-health. Think about it. If you say "I have cancer" or "I have Fibromyalgia", what are you doing to yourself?

It also means that we might be able to control our genetic code even to the point where we unlock our healing potential. It also shows that if our DNA is affected then the energies around us are also affected. Obviously this takes a lot of the healing burden off of our physicians and places it upon ourselves so we can truly heal from within.

It's vitally important to remember that healing is not totally dependent on the skills of the physician. You play an important part. It's also important to understand that diet and nutrition aren't the whole answer either. Your habits, lifestyle, attitudes, fears, self-image, faith, and emotional supports all affect your healing process. What you accept and feel is real is very important because you program your cells with that reality. If these elements are negative, they become part of the disease process. However, if these elements are positive, healing is accelerated.

Too often, people think of themselves as a disease. In medical school, we were cautioned to not refer to a patient by their disease yet too often that is what they do when they think of themselves. It's incredible at a time when positive thinking books abound that tell us that we are what we think, that people, who need to be positive, are so out of touch with the harm they are inflicting upon themselves. These people program themselves with disease. The worst I have seen are those with fibromyalgia or chronic fatigue.

When someone tells me "I have…" that certainly sounds like a negative affirmation to me. Innovative technology is being used to research the effects of neuro polypeptides on the body. These are neurotransmitters generated in the brain then flow through the blood stream to other parts of the body to elicit certain responses. In short, if you think it, your body believes it. What is really fascinating is that the affect is often faster than the blood can travel.

Remember, our thoughts, feelings, and emotions have a profound affect on our DNA. The affect is instantaneous whether we are in the same room with the DNA sample or if our DNA has been moved several hundred miles away. Our bodies literally recognize and mirror our thoughts. If you believe you are ill, your body will try to become the illness.

A friend of mine, a physician and shaman, once told me that there are recorded stories of wounded Indians going to their shaman for care. The shaman would simply wipe his hand across a bad wound and the wound would be erased. It sounds far fetched.

At the National Convocation of the American Osteopathic Association a few years ago, Dr. Valerie V. Hunt presented some of her work and research. Her book "Infinite Mind" is a worthwhile read and her credentials are noteworthy. She discussed similar phenomena and eye witness reports of such.

Gregg Braden, in his book *The Isaiah Effect* discusses an instance where he witnessed a woman stroke a fresh wound on another person until it totally healed within minutes. In that same book, he discussed a video tape he had seen of a "miraculous" healing of bladder cancer in China. In that instance the tumor disappeared within a few minutes as the result of the thoughts, feelings, and emotions not only of the patient but of three Chi Leil Chi Quong practitioners. I have a copy of that video and it is truly amazing.

26

Nutrition and Healing

"You as Osteopathic machinists can go no farther than to adjust the abnormal condition, in which you find the afflicted. Nature will do the rest." (A.T. Still, M.D., the founder of Osteopathic Medicine)

Since A.T. Still penned those words, life and understanding have continued on. Dr. Still was an amazing man but we have moved beyond where he was and not everything that he said has withstood the test of time. Some things that he said are just plain silly. Some things that he said are very accurate. As I have pointed out in this book, we are more powerful than even A.T. Still imagined.

This is not a book about nutrition. That would take the entire book and then some. Our nutritional status, however, is very important. We can't be healthy if we are not adequately nourished. We can't heal properly if we're not adequately nourished. Since many books have been written on the subject of nutrition, I'm going to use this chapter to hit some salient points and tell you about some of my favorite nutritionals. It's not all inclusive.

In addition to the influence that our thoughts have on us, what we eat also has an enormous influence on our bodies. Bill is a friend from one of the churches I've attended. He has lived an active life and has not been too kind to his body. He was in severe pain. X-rays of his lower back revealed that his spine was in terrible shape. I tried everything I could think of to help him, but it did not stick. His lower back pain radiated into his legs. He couldn't lie on his back without being in pain and if I asked him to keep his leg straight and raise it up to where it pointed to the ceiling, he couldn't get past about twenty-five degrees without being in extreme pain. Laughing, coughing, or sneezing made it worse.

Things looked really grim for Bill. I was 98% positive he had a herniated disc that was rubbing against a nerve root. His x-rays indicated that if he did have a herniated disc, he was a poor surgical candidate. The bones in his lower back were in terrible shape. They looked like a gorilla had been stomping on his lower back. There was no easy way to operate on such a mess.

Over the past few years, medical philosophy on herniated discs has changed. There was a time if a patient had a herniated disc the treatment was surgery. Fortunately, that way of looking at things has evolved. I have seen patients with four scars, one right next to the other on their lower back, indicating that they had been to surgery four times, and who still had no relief from the pain.

I went to a symposium a few years ago where a noted surgeon, who works on many of the drivers at the Indianapolis 500, told us if a herniated disc isn't causing symptoms, it's best to leave it alone. The body will absorb it in time. Yes, the body can heal itself if circumstances permit us to use a "tincture of time."

Well, Bill was a mess. I was not the first doctor he had seen and he was hurting. I threw everything at him but the kitchen sink. Generally, I have very good success with this type of problem, but nothing worked and time was running out. Bill had plans to spend the winter in Florida and needed to leave. I was able to help him a little but he still hurt when he left. He shook my hand and thanked me for my help, but I knew we were both disappointed.

A few weeks later, he sent me a postcard. He was one happy camper. His pain was gone and he was enjoying life. I wish I could say that I am the reason for this but that would be very arrogant, even if he had gotten better with the treatments.

Let me state this again—doctors usually do not heal people. Healing comes from within. We help facilitate the healing but generally we don't heal people. We can place the tissues in balance, but normally we cannot make them move. Movement, just like healing, normally comes from inside.

Too often, we look for cures outside of ourselves. I have patients who will continue to seek out physicians for the rest of their lives rather than accept responsibility for their own health. There are many reasons for this. Some people do not want to give up their life style. Some people are afraid.

I had a patient come to me recently that had lupus. This connective tissue disorder can be fatal. She had been to many other physicians. I looked at the list of things that other physicians had told her to do and knew none of them would cure her but rather would only make her more comfortable by treating the symptoms of lupus.

I treated her and wrote out a list of what I thought she should do. I told her she would benefit from taking three tablespoons of BarleyGreen a day and prescribed a natural progesterone cream and would have probably replaced that with pregnenolone in a few months. A few days later, I received a letter from her saying that she had decided not to follow my advice and would not be coming back for treatment.

Did she want me to wave my hand over her and cure her? Probably. Did she take offense because the treatment was too simple? I don't know. Would the BarleyGreen and the progesterone cream cure her? I do not think so, but they would probably have helped, and she would have benefitted from both. Nothing anyone else had done for her was of any help but she had tied herself to "traditional" medicine. Don't get me wrong, I think "traditional medicine" does a lot of good but it's not geared for health. It is geared towards treating the symptoms of disease.

Oddly enough, the fastest growing segment of medicine today is "Longevity Medicine." People want to live longer, healthier lives. It's driven by the "baby-boomers" who now have good jobs and want to live longer and look younger. They control a lot of money. Perhaps it will benefit us all.

Remember Bill's case? What was missing? Why wasn't he getting better? Was it because he was in his seventies and wearing out? Possibly. Was it because I was not proficient enough at what I do? I hope not but it is a possibility, but fortunately, with each passing day, I get better at what I do.

Remember that many things come into play when we are "healed." If any of those factors are out of sync, healing will be delayed, or even halted.

So, what had made him feel better? Nutritionally, he was deficient. He was hobbling down the beach one day when someone mentioned to him that he should try carrot and celery juice. I wish I could claim credit, but I learned this one from Bill. He drank a quart of carrot and celery juice (one pint of each mixed together) and took ten alfalfa tablets a day for two weeks and the pain went away.

I don't know what these do but I do know that it is essential that all three are taken together and that the juices be made "fresh" daily. There is a synergy among the three that is greater than each if taken separately. If one item is left out, it does not work. Occasionally someone drinks a pint of this concoction expecting relief but a pint is not enough. It has to be a quart and the patient also has to take ten alfalfa tablets each day. I can say that because I have recommended this to many patients and have always seen improvement. The bad news is that some people find the taste to be terrible. Some say it tastes like mud.

Personally, I like the taste. Some people gag on it, however. Some patients will add apple, tomato, and/or radish juice to the mix to help the taste. That's okay as long as they get the basics in at the quantities listed. This is not the "Pepsi Challenge" but some patients probably think it's like the "7-Up Challenge." The bottom line is that it's not designed to taste good; it's just good for you.

Having said all that, the "concoction" has to be made fresh daily and it takes about four pounds of carrots to make a pint of juice. The sweeter and more tender the carrots, the more palatable the juice. Words of caution, however, do not juice the greens or it can taste like mud even if the greens may be good for you. I should also say that grinding carrots and celery up in a blender is not the same thing. You need a juicer.

After the pain has subsided, and it may take months, you can decrease the quantity and you may be able to totally withdraw from taking it. One other note, it can make you slightly orange, temporarily.

Another similar experience where nutrition affected the healing process occurred within my own family. My parents live in California. A few years ago my dad developed severe leg pain. It progressed to where he could not walk without a great deal of pain. He saw several doctors and surgery was recommended. After the surgery, he had immediate relief <u>for one day</u> and then the pain returned with greater intensity.

The immediate problem was that my younger brother was getting married in Colorado. Dad was to be his best man but could not stand. I took my portable treatment table to Colorado and treated him once before the wedding but his tissues were in very bad shape and it would have necessitated a miracle for one treatment to do the job. Nevertheless, he was able to stand during the wedding. We left the next day and returned to Indiana and he returned to Southern California.

Nevertheless, severe pain will drive a person to do many things that they normally would not do. It will even get them to drink a quart of carrot and celery juice and take ten alfalfa tablets a day. When I heard from Bill, I called my mom and dad and told them of his experience.

In medicine, the first rule is to do no harm. I knew that it would not hurt dad and it might help him. Dad was reluctant, to say the least, but he was also desperate. He committed to a two-week trial period.

After eight days, I called my brother and asked how dad was doing. He told me that dad did not want to talk to me. I asked why and he said, "Because he's feeling better."

I should stop and explain that my dad wanted me to be a M.D. and he was very disappointed when I applied to osteopathic medical schools. I don't blame him. He was trained as a pharmacist and worked for a pharmaceutical company selling medications. From 1950 through the 1980's, he saw how osteopathic physicians were treated and how they were regarded in the medical community. He even had M.D.s tell him that if he called on osteopathic physicians that he could not call on them. At one time, there were many animosities between the two groups. He wanted the "best" for me, but I've never been sorry for the decision to become an osteopathic physician.

After I got off the phone with my brother, I called my dad. The conversation went something like this:

"Hi dad, how are you doing?"

"Ohhhhh," he groaned. I knew I had him.

I said, "You're getting better, aren't you?"

"Yes," he agreed. "But I hate to admit it." He then asked how long he had to "drink that stuff" and I confessed that I had no idea. I told him that as long as he saw improvement, he should continue taking it and that when it slowed down, he could cut back to a pint a day.

By now you are asking yourself, "Should I be drinking carrot and celery juice and taking ten alfalfa tablets a day?" The answer is probably "No." This is just an illustration of one of the many, many ways that we can help our bodies to do what they were so wonderfully designed to do. Sometimes we have to search for the specific nutrient needed to unlock our inherent ability to heal. Sometimes you need to exercise more. Sometimes you have to see a healer.

My interest in nutrition started in the mid-1970s. I was at a dinner where I met a man who ten years earlier had been diagnosed with multiple myeloma, osteoarthritis, rheumatoid arthritis, and chronic lymphocytic leukemia. He was told he had three months to live. He said that his bone scan lit up like a Christmas tree there were so many areas that were diseased in his bones. He then said he was now totally disease free.

I asked him what his secret was. He told me that he stopped eating anything artificial including sugar. He got hard red winter wheat and soaked it overnight. He then would drink the water and eat the wheat kernels. He also sprouted wheat and ate the sprouts or juiced the sprouts and drank the juice or made bread with the sprouted wheat. That was essentially all he did. For him, it worked miraculously.

What's the moral of all this? What does this have to do with what I do? Simply, you must do your part. If you don't eat properly, get adequate rest, or if you can't deal with your stress, you are impaired. When you are young, you have so much in reserve that you think you are indestructible. When you get older, the cumulative effects get to the point where you have to be proactive in seeking health. It will not come automatically. Obviously, not waiting until you are in pain or on your death bed is a good idea!

Basically, eat sensibly. Exercise daily. Get plenty of rest. Drink lots of water. Think good thoughts and help others. Turn off the television and get involved with your family and your community. Find an osteopathic physician skilled in cranial or better yet, Bio-Dynamic or Bioenergetic medicine and get treated on a regular basis.

Now for another very important matter, I remember being in medical school and being told that when a patient gets older the most important thing that happens to them during the day is to have a bowel movement. They refer to it as their "daily constitutional." Having said that, what is normal? Believe it or not, "normal" is a bowel movement first thing in the morning and then <u>after every major meal</u>. I've seen it written that you should have one bowel movement for every major meal you had yesterday but that's not correct. Eating stimulates the alimentary canal and a bowel movement should ensue immediately thereafter. If your bowels do not function like this, it should be your first major goal to get them to do so if you want to be as healthy as possible.

In medical school, I was taught that "normal" depends on the individual and may mean once a day or once a week. That is wrong. I was taught a lot of "wrong" things in medical school primarily because physicians are hired to come in and teach and as such, myths are perpetuated.

How often does a baby have a bowel movement? It's certainly not once a day or once a week. If you feed a baby, they will have a bowel movement. The same applies to dogs, cats, horses…Do you get the idea?

We destroy our normal intestinal flora by the over use of antibiotics and poisons such as chlorine, which we add to our drinking water. Then, after our normal flora has been destroyed, we train ourselves to avoid having a bowel movement until it is convenient. All that leads to a variety of illnesses and I believe this failure to "take out the trash" is a major cause of fibromyalgia and chronic fatigue. The nastiest stuff in our bodies is housed in our intestines where the longer it sits, the more it ferments and has a chance to damage us from within. Take out the trash!

I am a major proponent of eating a blend of natural fibers, not just psyllium, daily and of drinking enough (2-3 quarts) of <u>water</u> a day. Walking is an excellent exercise when it comes to stimulating gastrointestinal motility and hastening the transit of material through our gastrointestinal tract. Besides that, walking stimulates the cardiovascular and lymphatic systems and helps in "taking out the trash."

For all of us and especially those people who have any major health issue or concerns, cleaning out your bowels and then establishing proper nutrition so that you are fed properly is mandatory. Unfortunately, it can take over half a year to retrain a bowel that has become lazy and over distended from years of abuse.

I recently had a patient come to me for treatment. She said that she had tried eating correctly and it hadn't helped and didn't want to "do that again." It's not a matter of doing this or that. It's a matter of doing everything you can do at the same time FOREVER. That includes being treated bioenergetically on a regular basis.

If your health is terrible, <u>there are no quick fixes</u> and it takes time and dedication. The number of truly sick individuals who want to haggle with me when I tell them what I think they need to do to get better amazes me. If they don't want to hear what I have to say, why do they come to me? Perhaps they expect me to wave my hand over them and make them better. I wish it were that easy.

I've tried to describe enough case histories to give you the flavor of what I do. Years ago, I had to decide what I enjoyed doing most. I used to do general osteopathic medicine along with a lot of manipulative medicine. I even worked out of the hospital from time to time. As my practice grew, I arrived at the point where I needed to decide which direction I wanted my practice to take.

Manipulative/holistic medicine is very time intensive and as such it doesn't pay very well. Traditional medicine pays better but it would require me to do things that I don't like to do.

I now practice osteopathic medicine the way I believe it is supposed to be practiced. I am an osteopathic physician. No special title is needed yet we, the osteopathic profession, have moved so far away from what we are supposed to be that the original meaning no longer means anything special. Nevertheless, I am an osteopathic physician.

Simply put, I like the adventure. I still treat the things most general practitioners treat. I still prescribe medications, if needed, but I prefer to use diet, exercise, rest, homeopathic medicines, and herbs. Occasionally, I even remove a mole or lesion and, occasionally, I even sew someone up.

Awhile ago, one of my patients called to say she was not feeling well and asked whether or not I thought she should still come for her scheduled appointment. I told her to come on in. When she arrived, she looked bad! Once I got her on my treatment table, it didn't take long to figure out she was having a heart attack. I treated her to the point where her color returned and her cardiac status had improved, and then sent her to the hospital.

I like doing things like that. Ninety to ninety-five percent of my practice deals with osteopathic treatment but that is what an "osteopathic physician" is trained to do. In this case, I used it to help my patient's heart to heal. I treated her everyday for the week she was in the hospital. She improved dramatically. Her cardiologist was amazed. She wasn't.

As for your part in the healing process, I've said it before and I'll say it again, healing comes from within you. As a doctor, I sometimes feel like a janitor who comes along to clean up when my patients do not do what they are supposed to do. Smoking is the most obvious example, but there are other things such as physical and emotional abuse, stress, improper diet, poor emotional state, and poor physical fitness that influence our health every bit as dramatically. As you can see, the patient can control many of these.

Obesity

It has been said we are what we eat. This isn't totally correct, but it is important. Our "western" diet is horrendous. We eat a lot of food that has been over processed and laden with chemicals and dyes. Unfortunately, we do not listen to our bodies as we should and we consume large quantities of foods that do us little or no good. We've been taught that big is better when it comes to ordering food. Obesity has reached epidemic proportions. According to the C.D.C. website, "Results of the National Health and Nutrition Examination Survey (NHANES) 1999–2000 indicate that an estimated 65 percent of U.S. adults are either overweight (BMI 25-29.9) or obese (BMI over 30)." That percentage increases every month. To figure our BMI, take your weight in pounds divided by your height in inches squared. Take that number and multiply it by 704.5. The resulting number is your BMI. If you want to quickly "estimate" what you should weigh, men are "allowed" 106 pounds for the first five feet and 6 pounds/inch thereafter. Women are "allowed" 100 pounds for the first five feet and 5 pounds/inch thereafter. BMI is far more accurate. (http://www.cdc.gov/nccdphp/dnpa/bmi/calc-bmi.htm is a quick link to an online BMI calculator)

For those of you who are looking for a way to "hedge" on these numbers, the CDC has the following to say: "According to the weight categories, any person with a BMI over 25 would be classified as overweight. This may not mean they have excess fat. Such categories are based on scientific findings that the risk for disease increases as BMI increases."

Years ago, I was out with my son and decided to stop and get a soft-serve ice cream cone for both of us. It tasted okay but when I was done, I noticed my nose was stuffed and I had a lot of mucous in my throat. I asked my son if he was experiencing the same symptoms and he was. It intrigued me so I started paying attention to how I felt after eating other foods that were prepared in "fast food" outlets. I did not like what I realized my body was telling me.

I decided to eat more fresh fruits and vegetables and ate very little red meat. I tried to eat fish one or more times a week and I thought I was doing okay, but though I felt better, I still did not feel great.

Over the years, I had gradually put on weight and I was about thirty pounds overweight. I felt sluggish. I started exercising and it just about killed me. When I was in the Air Force, I went through some prisoner of war training. As part of this training, I had to crawl on crushed rock and I damaged my knees. Once a year I had to run a mile and a half in a certain amount of time. I jokingly referred to this as my "survival" run. If I survived the run, I was allowed to stay in the Air Force for another year.

Anyway, since I did not like how I was feeling, I got myself a NordicTrack and started working out everyday. I lost weight and started feeling better. It was a drastic but necessary step.

I know none of this is new or earth shattering. It is good old common sense. Eat right and exercise and your body will feel better. It is that simple.

The problem is that many people are morbidly obese and are grossly out of shape. Many patients tell me they cannot lose weight. I do not argue with them, but feel they are only fooling themselves. They commonly tell me that they do not eat but still gain weight. It is a lie. The only way to become overweight or obese is to eat more than you need. I'm not talking about "want" but I am talking about "need."

The simple fact is that if you use more calories than you take in, you will lose weight. That may mean you only get to eat once a day. It may not be comfortable and will require some life style changes, but that is the way it goes. I recently had an obese man come to me for treatment. He was over a hundred pounds overweight. His heart had been operated on. He was fatigued and he ached all over.

I told him what he should weight but his wife, who was sitting in the room with us, spoke up and said that he should actually weigh ten pounds more than I said. I asked if she was a nurse or physician. Her reply was that she was an English teacher. Hello! Even when I had told him that he may only be able to eat two meals a day she asked, "What about snacks? He has to have snacks." It was absurd! She was haggling over his health.

One of my patients competes in body building tournaments. There is very little fat on him. He works out four hours a day! I asked him how many calories he eats a day. The answer surprised me. He eats 1,000 calories a day but every fourth day he eats 1,500 calories.

Starving yourself makes your body feel like it is hibernating and your metabolism will slow down even if you are working out four hours a day. To avoid gaining weight, every fourth day he adds an additional 500 calories so his body will not start hibernating. It works for him. He has figured out what it takes for his body to maintain the weight he wants to be. Each of us is different, however.

Unfortunately, many people are obese because they have become insulin resistant. Their own insulin acts to keep fat in the cells and they will use protein as their energy source. We even have a name for this: Syndrome-X. The next step in that disease process is diabetes, which has become epidemic in proportions.

The "catch 22" is that the more out of shape you are, the harder it is to regain the "proper" shape and to lose weight. There is no magic cure. You just have to make yourself do it. To be very blunt, look at the photos of prisoner of war camps in World War II. People simply cannot stop eating and still maintain or gain weight. It's impossible. Those photos prove that point.

NutraSweet

While I'm on the subject of nutrition, I want to talk briefly about NutraSweet. Go to the web and look up http://www.holisticmed.com/aspartame/. It is an eye opener. That site lists the following list of disorders associated with the consumption of NutraSweet (aspartame):

- seizures and convulsions
- dizziness
- tremors
- migraines and severe headaches (Trigger or Cause From Chronic Intake)
- memory loss (common toxicity effects)
- slurring of speech
- confusion
- numbness or tingling of extremities
- chronic fatigue

- depression
- insomnia
- irritability
- panic attacks (common aspartame toxicity reaction)
- marked personality changes
- phobias
- rapid heart beat, tachycardia (another frequent reaction)
- asthma
- chest pains
- hypertension (high blood pressure)
- nausea or vomiting
- diarrhea
- abdominal pain
- swallowing pain
- itching
- hives/ urticaria
- other allergic reactions
- blood sugar control problems (e.g., hypoglycemia or hyperglycemia)
- menstrual cramps and other menstrual problems or changes
- impotency and sexual problems
- food cravings
- weight gain
- hair loss/ baldness or thinning of hair
- burning urination & other urination problems
- excessive thirst or excessive hunger
- bloating, edema (fluid retention)
- infection susceptibility
- joint pain

- brain cancer (Pre-approval studies in animals)
- death

Aspartame Disease Mimics Symptoms or Worsens the Following Diseases

- fibromyalgia
- arthritis
- multiple sclerosis (MS)
- Parkinson's disease
- lupus
- multiple chemical sensitivities (MCS)
- diabetes and diabetic Complications
- epilepsy
- Alzheimer's disease
- birth defects
- chronic fatigue syndrome
- lymphoma
- Lyme disease
- attention deficit disorder (ADD and ADHD)
- panic disorder
- depression and other psychological disorders

<u>NutraSweet is poison to the body</u>. It is used in many foods and is commonly listed as aspartame. Avoid it like the plague. I would rather you drank sugared drinks than drinks sweetened with NutraSweet. I hope that some day we will be able to purchase drinks sweetened with Stevia, a low calorie natural food supplement available in most health food stores.

What I commonly hear from my patients is, "I only have a little bit every day." Hello!!! That's like saying you only eat a little rat poison every day. They are saying they only poison themselves a little every day. Is a little poison every day okay?

A relatively new sweetener is sucralose (Splenda). At this time, I have serious doubts as to the safety of sucralose as a sweetener. "Pre-approval research showed that sucralose caused shrunken thymus glands (up to 40% shrinkage) and enlarged liver and kidneys." (http://www.holisticmed.com/splenda/) When I ingest Splenda, I get a low grade headache. I don't know why. I have yet to muscle test someone with Splenda and have them perform well. I'm not alone in my concern about Splenda.

I have personally seen many of the above ailments improve when the patient stopped ingesting NutraSweet. Part of the problem is that NutraSweet breaks down into methyl alcohol and formaldehyde in the body. Both are very carcinogenic (cancer causing) and both are poisons. Why would anyone want to ingest this? If it is to lose weight, I have yet to see a study that says it helps in weight loss. In fact, the best diet drink around is water. From time to time, a patient with diabetes will tell me that they cannot stand the taste of water and have to drink diet drinks sweetened with NutraSweet. They are kidding themselves, not me. The bottom line is that they really do not want to get better.

As I was walking out of a movie theatre the other day, ushers were handing out packets of breath mints that were sweetened with NutraSweet. I wondered if they would also be so inclined to hand out breath mints laced with rat poison. Sometimes a patient will say that they have various items at home that have NutraSweet in them and ask what they are supposed to do with those items. I then ask what they'd do if they had some left-over rat poison. Would they eat it rather than throw it away? I hope I've made my point.

Walking

Walking is a terrific exercise. It requires only a good pair of shoes and it can be done anywhere and in any type of weather. You can walk in the rain. It doesn't matter if you get wet—you'll dry off. I recommend walking in the morning but if you are depressed, I would suggest you walk between 10:00 a.m. and 2:00 p.m., when the sun is high in the sky.

Your walking session should last forty-five minutes or longer. You should walk five rather than seven days a week because your tissues need time to rest and heal. The pace should be brisk. Having said this, when you start a walking program, go easy, but increase the pace and the duration consistently. I've had patients who couldn't walk thirty seconds so I started them out with fifteen second walks and built up from there.

When it comes to nutrition, I am often asked what type of food a patient should eat. It's great to say we should eat "organically" but that isn't always practical in today's setting. Most people just do not have the time or inclination to eat that way. I do not believe in being a vegetarian, but I think meat and all the foods we eat should be as fresh as possible and that meat should be eaten sparingly, they should not be injected with hormones or antibiotics. Generally, whole grains such as rice, wheat, barley, and corn are tremendously good for our bodies. Fresh vegetables are also very good for the body.

"Organic" is an interesting label. Chemically it means that there is a carbon atom involved. That means that pencil lead is "organic." In health food stores, it should mean that the fruits and vegetables are grown or produced using feed or fertilizer of plant or animal origin without using chemically formulated fertilizers, growth stimulants, antibiotics, or pesticides.

I think supplements are necessary. I ate very well for a week and then placed the foods I had consumed into a computer program and analyzed my diet for nutritional content. I fell short in a couple of areas in terms of the RDA. I think the RDA is understated so I was probably eating much worse than I thought. If we understood nutrition completely, such a program might be helpful but we don't completely understand nutrition. Research continues and we are constantly learning new information and discarding old ideas. Because of that, I think eating as well as we can and also taking supplements is essential for optimum health.

Some food supplements need to be taken on an empty stomach. Take those when you get up in the morning. Then, after you are dressed and have eaten breakfast, take the rest of your supplements.

BarleyGreen®

BarleyGreen® is an example of one supplement that works best on an empty stomach. This is the most amazing product I have ever come across. It is the juice from young barley grass that has been extracted, dehydrated, and bottled. I could write a book on BarleyGreen® alone. No other barley grass product comes even close to this product though many have similar names and many manufacturers claim they are better. More information can be obtained by going to http://www.barleygreenhi.com on the web. It is sufficient to say, however, that with few exceptions everyone would benefit from this product. An Amish healer I know says it is a "marvelous product" because it "vibrates right." Since it works better on an empty stomach, take it as soon as you get up. If you are fatigued or feel sick, you should be drinking BarleyGreen® 2-3 times a day. It helps.

Some patients say that they don't like the taste. Again, this is not the Pepsi challenge! This is not a taste test. It tastes like grass because that is what it is. I put it in grape juice. Some put it in water. My mom puts the powder in her mouth then takes a sip of water and then swishes and swallows. I like the taste. It's what I eat/drink for breakfast every morning.

Many years ago, I tested markedly positive for thirty of the forty allergins for which I was tested. I used to take two allergy shots a week then it occurred to me that I was injecting stuff into my body that I was highly allergic to and stopped it. At that time, I cleaned up my diet and started taking BarleyGreen®. Allergies do not bother me any more. It's also great for arthritis. It's great for detoxifying your system. Again, you can try something else but you'll never get the same results.

MSM

Another supplement that needs to be highlighted is MSM (methylsulfonal methane). It sounds terrible but that is how organic compounds are named. Is it good for you? You bet! I told you that I hurt my knees while in survival training in the Air Force and suffered for over twenty-six years with pain. My knees hurt going up and down stairs. They hurt if I knelt on the floor. I couldn't run or jog without pain and it occasionally hurt to walk.

Several years ago, I broke the fourth toe on my right foot. I was walking through a door that had an automatic closing mechanism that made it close a lot faster than I thought and I ran my toe directly into the edge of the metal door. I was wearing Birkenstock sandals. A month later, one of my children stepped on that toe and then a few weeks later another did the same. It was not healing and it really hurt to walk. I had it x-rayed and was told it was okay but by the way it hurt, by its color, and by the way it was bent, it obviously was not okay. I was even contemplating having it removed so I could start walking again.

I had been telling patients to try MSM for arthritic conditions for several years and was basing my recommendations on what I had heard and read others say on the subject. The dosage I was taking and recommending was 2,000 milligrams/day. What got my attention was a physician on a tape that I had been listening to on MSM who had been involved in researching MSM. His suggested dosage was twelve grams (12,000 milligrams) a day for two months and if that does not get results he said to double it. I had previously tried two grams (2,000 milligrams) a day and wasn't happy with the result. Listening to that tape made it obvious that I had not been using enough. Since MSM is not toxic, I figured that I had nothing to loose so I bought some more and tried it.

It took a couple of weeks but my toe, which was dark and swollen and had been so for over 1½ years, started to shrink back to it's normal size and returned to a normal pink color. The pain also started going away. What really got my attention was that at about the two week mark, I noticed that I was able to go up stairs two at a time, something I had not done since before I damaged my knees over twenty-six years earlier and, they did not hurt. I could even kneel on the concrete next to my Harley Davidson motorcycle, while cleaning it, and I did not have any pain. I have been taking 12 grams a day for over eight years and my foot has healed. None of my joints hurt. More importantly, I have been recommending it to my patients and have experienced similar results with them. It also works wonderfully for fibromyalgia. Since everyone is different, you may not need 12 grams/day but that's what my body needs.

MSM is an organic compound, a food, which is rich in sulfur. At the biochemical level, sulfur is the fourth most common mineral in the body but unfortunately our diets no longer are rich in organic sulfur so we get depleted. This is not "sulfa," which many people are allergic to. There is no lethal dose. You would drown before you could take enough to hurt you. It can be taken with or without foods but it seems to be better tolerated if taken with food.

The richest natural sources of MSM are fresh, uncooked fruits, vegetables, and meats. I have heard that the body can use up to 750 Mg MSM a day, if it is available. Given enough time and a poor diet, we may be running very low and not know it. What I know from clinical experience is that 750 Mg/day is not enough! For MSM to work effectively, you have to load the system. I have been taking 12,000 milligrams a day for over eight years and if I cut back to 8,000 milligrams a day I notice a difference in my energy level and in how I feel. 750 milligrams/day is simply not enough. Two thousand milligrams a day is not enough!

Its major side effects are that your hair and nails will grow faster than before and if you have wrinkles or scars they will soften. You will also experience in increase in your energy levels so don't take it in the afternoon or evening because you will have trouble sleeping. Some people experience gas or abdominal discomfort with large doses especially if taken first thing in the morning on an empty stomach but that's when and how I take it and it doesn't bother me. If it does bother you, the effect is transient and shouldn't last more than a few days. I have not experienced bad side effects but have heard that taking it with food helps. If 12 grams is too much for you, start at 3 grams a day and build up. The important thing to remember is that the affects are dose related. The more you take, the better it works. I have yet to see a patient need more than 12 grams (12,000 milligrams) a day, however.

The problem is that it comes in powder, capsule, and pill/caplet forms. If you opt for the capsules, you are looking at 8-24 capsules a day, depending on who makes the MSM and the amount of MSM in each capsule. The 1.5-gram caplets/pills are so large that few people can swallow them. MSM powder is bitter. I think capsules are the preferred way to take it. I don't think caplets/pills are as well absorbed.

When I first started researching MSM, I asked one patient if he had heard of MSM. He said that he had chronic constipation but when he takes MSM, his bowels move normally. Another patient told me that she had chronic diarrhea but when she took MSM, her bowels moved normally. The bottom line is that it helps to heal the gastrointestinal tract.

MSM is great for treating aches and pains in the soft tissues <u>and</u> joints. It is great for treating asthma. It is a vital component in the production of collagen so it is good for arthritic conditions and back pain. It is good for your vision. The list goes on and on. Among other things, it has been touted as a cancer cure, but I would not bet the farm on that. At best, it might slow the growth of tumors so that your body has time to mount a response. The bottom line is that the body needs organic sulfur to function normally.

I can't tell you which brand is best. Different manufacturers add different things to it to make it marketable <u>which makes most of them unusable</u>. The brand I'm presently taking is made by Young Living Essential Oils and is called Sulfurzyme. I continue to search for another good brand of MSM but have yet to find one that works as well as Sulfurzyme. *Doctor's Best* brand has an MSM product in 1,000 Mg capsules called *Best MSM* which works almost as well as Sulfurzyme and is the only other brand I currently recommend.

If a patient brings their supplements with them, I will usually muscle test them to see if the patient can tolerate the supplement. I've come across several brands of MSM that have reacted badly with patients and I've run across several brands that don't seem to "work." Unfortunately, Sulfurzyme is the only form that works essentially all the time. I say unfortunately because it is expensive in comparison to what you can obtain in a health food store. Having tried several brands, the extra cost is worth the money. There is no other brand like it. If you decide to try another brand, <u>make sure there is no potassium or magnesium in the product because both affect your heart and at large doses potassium and/or magnesium can cause problems</u>. Likewise, make sure there is no glucosamine in the product because it's expensive and is dosed differently than MSM.

Occasionally a patient who is taking blood thinners such as Coumadin (warfarin) will tell me that their physician has told them not to take MSM because it might also thin their blood. That makes my blood boil! Why tell someone not to take something that is good for them in favor of something that is potentially dangerous to them? I don't get it. If the physician has to adjust the dose of Coumadin does that make MSM bad? No! Physicians are trained to regulate Coumadin dosages based on bleeding times. If a physician tells you not to take MSM because you are taking Coumadin, he/she is just plain lazy!

Twelve grams (12,000 milligrams a day) seems to work best. I don't recommend anyone start at that dosage because it's just asking for stomach problems. Let your body acclimate to it by starting out at 3,000 milligrams a day and building up to 12 grams/day by adding 1,000-3,000 milligrams a day until you are eventually taking 12 grams of MSM a day, either in divided doses or all at once. Think of it as high powered broccoli. If you develop diarrhea, cut back on the dose until you get use to it and when your bowels have stabilized, build back up. Twelve grams is better than six. Dose matters. It supposedly works better with Vitamin C but research has failed to prove that point.

Enzymes

I've learned the biochemistry behind enzymes and theoretically that should have been enough, but it wasn't. I knew they were important but like almost everyone, I figured I didn't need to worry about whether or not I was getting enough because I figured my body was producing what I needed. I was wrong. You see, knowing the biochemistry doesn't mean I understood what I needed to do, i.e., my part in the whole process. If I mention enzymes to my patients, I get the "deer in the headlights" stare or a shrug as they act like I'm just full of hot air.

A few years ago, I attended a seminar where the importance of enzymes was discussed. I was amazed at what I didn't know about enzymes. Essentially every biochemical reaction in our bodies requires an enzyme. Uncooked foods, both from plant and animal sources usually come equipped with their own enzymes but cooking them above 118 degrees essentially kills them off. That's where supplementation comes in.

Enzymes are usually divided into two groups: Digestive enzymes and metabolic enzymes. There are three main categories of digestive enzymes: Amylases, proteases and lipases. Amylases help in the digestion of sugars such as lactose, sucrose, maltose, etc. Proteases help in the digestion of proteins and in tissue repair. Lipases help in the digestion of fats.

"Of the tens of thousands of enzymes needed, the body uses more of its enzyme-producing potential to produce the two dozen enzymes that control the breakdown and utilization of proteins, fats, and carbohydrates than it uses to create the hundreds of metabolic enzymes necessary to maintain the rest of the tissues and organs in their functions." ("Prescription for Nutritional Healing, 3rd ed.," Balch and Balch, Avery books, p. 59)

Obviously, if we can supplement the needs of our bodies for enzymes we can reduce some of the stress our bodies are exposed to.

My initial college degree was in Political Science. I had planned on attending law school and eventually becoming an attorney. It took me five years to obtain that degree and I realized after receiving it that everyone is an "expert" at politics whether or not they have a degree in Political Science.

I'm a "holistic physician." I have studied nutrition since the mid-1970's and I use nutritional supplements in my practice. I've used a lot of different brands of nutritional supplements throughout the years. I've found some that work very well. The problem is that when I tell a patient what "works" more often than not, they want to try to educate me about the brand that they use.

Some supplements are outstanding, some are good, some are mediocre, and some are terrible. Most people really don't know if their supplements are good or bad. They all believe their supplements are good. If a patient is a "distributor" in a network marketing system for their particular nutritional supplement, they, as a rule, believe their brand is the best on the market and they are usually wrong! Additionally, it's a waste of my time to try to convince them otherwise.

Folks, I do this for a living. I can feel what affect a supplement has on the body. If I recommend a particular brand, it's because I know it works. There may be brands that work equally well and if you think you've worked with as many brands as I've worked with, and are more of an expert than me, you should continue to use what you are using.

Supplements are insurance. It's best to get your nutrition the natural way but we have no guarantee we are getting all that we need. Supplements fill the gap. Think of them as food. Everyone should take a daily multivitamin that is based on an authentically natural, organic food-matrix. That eliminates the vast majority of supplements available on the market. I hate to say this but most of the multivitamins are little more than junk food. If you're buying them "cheap" you are getting what you are paying for.

Water is essential to our health. Drinking three quarts of pure water a day is a good goal. I am not talking soda, coffee, or tea. That is additional. Drink water. Many ailments we suffer from are the result of not drinking enough water. Most diseases improve or go away when the body is properly hydrated and fed. Many hunger cravings can be nullified with a glass of water.

I had one obese mother and grandmother bring their son/grandson to me because he suffers from Attention Deficit Hyperactive Disorder (ADHD). I asked what he drank for fluid and was told Diet Mountain Dew. I asked what he drank if that was not available and he said Jolt! No wonder the kid was pinging off the walls. I told his mom the only drink he was allowed to drink was water and she said, "What will I drink if I have to keep those out of the house?" I told her "Water." They never came back.

And, as I've said before, sleep is very important. Think good thoughts and associate with good people. Our thoughts govern what we are and what we accomplish. Our brain is the physical interface between our spiritual/energetic self (mind) and our physical body. Our spirits do not reside passively within our bodies while we sojourn here on earth. Mental/spiritual health is essential to good physical health. The reverse is also true.

Stress can be good and it can be bad. How we deal with it is the problem or the answer. I have found that when I do things aimed at improving my spiritual self, I am happier and healthier. You will discover the same.

Conclusion

Healing comes from within us. We were designed to live long, healthy lives, but our bodies were not designed to be abused. Abuse comes in many forms. It can be inflicted upon us, or we can do it to ourselves. Since we are energetic/spiritual beings having a physical experience, the spiritual aspect of our life is very important. Our thoughts, feelings, and emotions markedly influence our health. Likewise, what others think about themselves and about us can influence our health. It's important to be happy and at peace with ourselves and our surroundings.

I could go on and on but my purpose is to stimulate your imagination on the reality that we are designed to heal ourselves. With that in mind, stay out of the cesspools of life. Eat properly and exercise regularly. Do your part and accept responsibility for your own life and your own health.

I hope you found answers to some of your questions in this book.

My dad told me if I chose to become an "osteopath" I would have to explain what an osteopathic physician is for the rest of my life. I wish he was wrong, but the truth of the matter is, he was right. It is the best-kept secret in medicine and it is hiding in plain sight.

If you decide to seek out an osteopathic physician, I commend you and I caution you. Make sure you know what you are looking for.

If you want to know more about craniosacral osteopathic medicine, you can contact the Cranial Academy (www.cranialacademy.org) in Indianapolis, Indiana. If you want to know more about osteopathic medicine, you can contact either the American Academy of Osteopathic Medicine (www.academyofosteopathy.org), also in Indianapolis, or the American Osteopathic Association (www.aoa-net.org) in Chicago, Illinois.

I hope this book proved helpful. Peace be with you.

APPENDIX

The Death of Osteopathy

"What you do speaks so loudly that I cannot hear what you say"
(Ralph Waldo Emerson)

"To find health should be the object of the doctor." (A.T. Still, M.D., founder of Osteopathic Medicine)

"This above all, to thine ownself be true. And, it must follow, as the night the day, thou canst not then be false to any man." (Shakespeare, *Hamlet, Act I Scene III*)

"*Osteopathy has shamefully hidden its Greatest Mystery and resources.*" As quoted by Dr. Jealous, *"I believe that to acknowledge a higher wisdom at work and to sense rather than palpate is at the Soul of Osteopathy. A soul that will not compromise the beauty and Consciousness that lies beyond our intellect. Integrity demands that we speak undiluted truth. We are always perfect beginners, inspired, awed, apprehensive and self-searching; teaching is an act of love for the truth that is at the cornerstone of Originality.*

"*Within the Dynamic Stillness we are healed without process or time. From the Breath of Life a new living matrix is created in each moment. The Tide brings us the power of Life and "feeds" us. The fluids respond, lawfully balancing the power of life and skillfully "driving" the hydraulic/potency continuum towards perfect proportion. The remainder imitates, dances, and flows but does not make "decisions." Here is the Key. Decisions are made by the Breath of Life, decisions that dictate the priority, proportion, and endpoint of healing; decisions that the physician can perceive and sense using instinct and intuition followed by an intellectual understanding of the format. We begin with sensing Health, Life at work, not structural lesions. In a sense the plat-*

form has been reversed. We are following motion to its Source; the finite and infinite into the Whole."

How eloquent the simple truth can be. Dr. Jealous is indeed a poet and his love for osteopathy is without question. Unfortunately, there is a problem. A problem that is as present as an eight hundred pound gorilla in a china shop. The problem and its adherent question: "Is Osteopathic Medicine dead?"

Once proposed it is not an easy question to answer. People have been posing that question for many years, but the "playing field" has changed enough over the past twenty years that the question may be very, very relevant today.

Indeed there is an American Osteopathic Association and an American Academy of Osteopathy and numerous other "osteopathic" organizations. Undeniably, there are an every increasing number of colleges of osteopathic medicine, and indeed there are "osteopathic physicians" practicing medicine. So does that mean that "osteopathic medicine" is alive? Does growth indicate life? Perhaps. If the number of osteopathic physicians is increasing, does that mean osteopathic medicine is alive? Unfortunately, no, it does not but neither does it mean that it is "dead." It only means that more physicians with the *title* of "osteopath" are being produced.

The problem lies in the definition of osteopathic medicine. If someone practices medicine in harmony with the definition of "osteopathic medicine," and if they have a degree in osteopathic medicine, then they can justifiably claim they are an osteopathic physician. If they do not practice in harmony with that definition, then they really aren't osteopathic physicians regardless of what is printed on their medical school diploma. In my office, I give out cards that I obtained from one of the national osteopathic associations that say:

"What is a D.O.?"

"There are only two kinds of physicians qualified to be licensed for the unlimited practice of medicine in all 50 states: those holding the M.D. degree and those who have earned the D.O.—doctor of osteopathic medicine—degree.

"Osteopathic physicians perform surgery, deliver babies, and prescribe medicine in hospitals and clinics across the nation. Whether they are family doctors or specialists, D.O.s use all the tools of modern medicine…and more.

"They help their patients develop attitudes and lifestyles that don't just fight illness, but prevent it. They give special attention to how the body's nerves, muscles, bones and organs work together to influence health. And, *through osteopathic*

manipulative treatment, they can use their hands to diagnose injury and illness…and encourage the body's natural ability to heal itself.

"These "extra touches" distinguish the D.O.s whole-person philosophy of medicine. It's a century-old tradition of caring for people, *not just treating symptoms.*"

To me, that is the "accepted definition" of what an osteopathic physician is. The question has to be asked, does that describe ninety percent of all osteopathic physicians? The answer is no. It doesn't even describe ten percent of all osteopathic physicians. From my experience, I do not think it describes three percent of all osteopathic physicians. If D.O.s are not practicing medicine in accordance with the definition of osteopathic medicine and are practicing medicine just like any M.D., does that make them a D.O. or an M.D.? A.T. Still, M.D., the founder of Osteopathic Medicine said, "…I want it to be understood that drugs and I are as far apart as the East is from the West…"

"In the 1960s in California, the differences between osteopathy and conventional medicine blurred enough that the California Medical Association and the California Osteopathic Association merged, and D.O.s were granted an M.D. degree in exchange for paying $65 and attending a short seminar. The College of Osteopathic Physicians and Surgeons became the University of California, Irvine College of Medicine." (http://en.wikipedia.org/wiki/Osteopathy)

Does that sound bizarre to you? This was the result of legislation passed in the State of California forbidding the licensure of osteopaths. To get the law through the legislature a provision was made to make D.O.s acceptable by granting them an M.D. degree. Forbidding the licensure of D.O.s was eventually ruled by the California State Supreme Court to be unconstitutional but the result was that in the blink of an eye D.O.s stopped being "unacceptable" in the eyes of M.D.s and became "equal." Indeed a rose by any name…

My point is that the reason that could happen is that most D.O.s are the same as their M.D. counterparts and though D.O.s have more training, they practice the same type of medicine. With the exception of some holdouts, such as myself, there are no differences. Indeed, "Today, except for additional emphasis on musculoskeletal diagnosis and treatment, the scope of osteopathy is identical to that of medicine. The percentage of practitioners who use osteopathic manipulative treatment (OMT) and the extent to which they use it have been falling steadily." (Source: *Dubious Aspects of Osteopathy*, Stephen Barrett, http://en.wikipedia.org/wiki/Osteopathy)

If there is "growth" in the numbers of D.O.s but the D.O.s that are being produced are practicing medicine much the same as M.D.s and there are fewer D.O.s that truly practice "osteopathic" medicine, it seems to me that osteopathic medicine is dying. Sure it can be argued that osteopathic medicine is evolving but the reality is that more and more M.D.s are practicing "holistic medicine." That being the case, when will the lines blur and the two become one? Or, has it already happened and are we just waiting for someone to read the eulogy?

Osteopathic manipulative medicine (the training that we have that eventually gave birth to the chiropractic profession) is the one element that nowadays distinguishes D.O.s from M.D.s though at the beginning "holism" was also very important.

As an osteopathic physician, I treat all manner of disease processes and essentially practice family medicine but I am not certified in any specialty. I am broadly grouped under the classification of General Practitioner. A few years ago, a "residency" process was established whereby osteopathic students, once they have completed their internship, could enter a residency in osteopathic manipulative medicine. The name for that residency has changed and I imagine it will change again since if is woefully inadequate and misleading.

Osteopathic medicine is holistic medicine at its finest but unfortunately, many who practice "manipulative medicine" have no concept of what it takes to be holistic. They too are not osteopathic physicians. Osteopathic medicine has indeed evolved and an understanding of traditional medicine is important. It is also important to not forget about the other aspects of "medicine." We shouldn't "throw the baby out with the bathwater" no matter which approach we take but if we are to be truly "osteopathic," holism has to be at the core of our practice.

I love the quote by Nelson Mandela at the front of this book:

> *"Our deepest fear is not that we are inadequate,*
> **Our deepest fear is that we are powerful beyond measure.**
> *It is our Light, not our darkness, that most frightens us.*
> *We ask ourselves, who am I to be brilliant, gorgeous, talented, and fabulous?*
> *Actually, who are you not to be?*
> *You are a child of God. Your playing small doesn't serve the world.*
> *There's nothing enlightened about shrinking so that other people won't feel insecure around you.*
> *We were born to make manifest the Glory of God that is within us.*
> *It's not just in some of us; it's in everyone.*

And as we let our own Light shine,
We unconsciously give other people permission to do the same.
As we are liberated from our own fear, our presence automatically liberates others."

Nelson Mandela
Inaugural Speech 1994
Taken from:
"A Return to Love" Ch. 7, Sec. 3
Marianne Williamson

As the years have passed, there has been an ever increasing emphasis to force all physicians to become "certified" in some aspect of medicine. Passing the National Osteopathic Medical Boards is not enough. My malpractice insurance would drop by a third if I were board certified in anything even if it is not in what I do!

With that in mind, I decided to start the process of becoming board certified in neuromusculoskeletal medicine. Supposedly, it is the "broad category" for what I do. For some reason, however, when I started the process I started losing sleep and my weight was dropping. It rankled my spirit. The more I studied, the less I liked what I was doing. Eventually I stopped studying and decided to sit for the board "cold turkey" to see first hand what I would be committing myself to.

Prior to that time, I signed up for and went to a preparatory course in Florida. It was an "eye-opener."

In late May 2003, prior to that course, I broke off a relationship with a woman I truly loved but I'd had enough. (Remember, we are spiritual beings having a physical experience.) Anything we do affects our body. Our feelings affect not only us but also everyone and everything around us. The direct result of the breakup was that my left shoulder froze up. I could no longer lift my left arm over my head.

I can do a fairly good job of treating myself energetically but once my physical body locks up, there is little I can do. Unfortunately, I do not know anyone in my town that I trust to work on me. Since I knew the course was coming up, I figured I would just wait until I was surrounded by "the experts" and get one of them to treat my shoulder.

The first day at the course, I approached the physician running the course and asked if she would treat my shoulder. She said that she did not "do shoulders." What? Doesn't do shoulders? How could that be if she is an "expert"? How could that be if she is a D.O.? She did say, however, that there was <u>one</u> physician on the panel (of experts) who specialized in such disorders.

I asked the designated physician if he would look at my shoulder. He had me move my arms as he had me perform a number of "tests" to see what the problem was. Eventually he told me that my shoulder was impinged and that it would take six to eight months of extensive physical therapy to fix the problem. He never touched me! HELLO!

I thought I was in the Twilight Zone! I was in a room full of "experts" in neuromusculoskeletal medicine and the "experts" were telling me that they could not fix my shoulder. I fix shoulders like this several times a week.

The "expert" asked me several times what I had done to my shoulder. I told him I had broken up with my girlfriend. He could not grasp that as a reason. He could not grasp the concept that our feelings affect our bodies. He assumed that I had suffered some physical trauma and he was wrong.

I asked him if he would at least try to manipulate it. He said that even if he "put a knee in my back" it would not help. A light "went on" in my head and I said, "I don't know that technique. Would you mind showing it to me?" He then did what I had been wanting him to do, i.e., actually treat me and it was a half-hearted attempt at that.

After doing so, he then proceeded to try to tell me once again that there was no reason to try to treat me because it would not help. As he was telling me this, I reached my left arm up over my head into the air to show him that I was able to move the arm. A little chagrined, he said a few more words and then walked off.

A few days later, another member of the panel, in response to questions about what we could expect when "sitting for the board" told us that they were not interested in nutrition or energies. They wanted to know that we are aware of the side effects of different medicines "so that other physicians will see us as experts." I was flabbergasted! I am viewed as an "expert" because of the results I achieve and that should be the primary criteria upon which an expert is judged.

I sat for the board and was disgusted with the process. Indeed, it is not what I do. I was asked questions about things that I had not encountered in fifteen years of practice. The "practical" portion of the exam was inadequate. In fact, I was never asked what I do in my practice. I was never asked to demonstrate what I do.

I have since written the board and withdrawn my application. If I struggled hard enough, I could probably do all that they require but then I would be incorrectly labeling myself and as such would be an active participant in deception. I have viewed attempts to "certify" and "standardize" what I do as an effort to do away with the art of osteopathy. It's like making all painters paint by the numbers.

Emerson said, "Do not follow where the path may lead, go instead where there is no path, and leave a trail." That means I will continue to pay more for my malpractice insurance. It also means that I will not be able to teach in osteopathic colleges that require their instructors to be board certified. Ironically, I am still, however, a guest lecturer to M.D. students in the Complementary Medicine Department at Indiana University School of Medicine. Go figure.

Emerson was correct. What we do does speak very loudly. A patient of mine, a pharmaceutical sales representative, told me today that he was surprised that sales representatives didn't call on me because "Osteopaths are known as 'writers' (for medicines) in the business." A change has occurred. The evolutionary process that has taken place not just within the osteopathic community but also in the allopathic community has blurred the distinctive lines between the two. We are no longer separate.

In general, Osteopathic physicians no longer practice a distinctive form of medicine. "Osteopathy" as a philosophy, however, will endure, if not in the community as a whole, in the hearts of those dedicated physicians who seek out the truth and who desire to practice medicine in harmony with divine principles.

About the Author

Dr. Brooksby has seven children and ten grandchildren. After spending twelve years as an Air Force pilot, Dr. Brooksby enrolled at the University Of New England College Of Osteopathic Medicine where he earned a Doctor of Osteopathic Medicine (D.O.) degree. His practice is located in Zionsville, Indiana, a suburb of Indianapolis. Patti, the mother of their children and his wife for eighteen years passed away years ago.

In his spare time, Dr. Brooksby enjoys golfing, playing guitar, reading, writing, riding his motorcycle, and exploring new ideas and concepts. He has a commercial pilot's license and he has black belts in three different forms of karate, the highest being a 5th degree black belt (master ranking).

Robert C Brooksby, D.O.
1500 W Oak Street, Suite 200
Zionsville, IN 46077
Ph. 317.873.3321
http://www.drbrooksby.com
Bob@drbrooksby.com

978-0-595-37693-3
0-595-37693-2

Made in the USA
Lexington, KY
31 January 2014